KIMONO

KIMONO

Fashioning Culture

Liza Crihfield Dalby

Yale University Press
New Haven and London

Design and layout by Liza and Michael Dalby.

Composed in Minion, with Tekton display.
Produced in the United States of America
by Avery Press, Inc., Boulder, Colorado.

Library of Congress Cataloging-in-Publication Data

Dalby, Liza Crihfield.
    Kimono : fashioning culture / Liza Crihfield Dalby.
        p.   cm.
    Includes bibliographical references and index.
    ISBN 0-300-05639-7 (acid-free paper)
    1. Kimonos.   2. Costume—Japan.   I. Title.
GT1560.D35   1993
391´,00952—dc20   93-4079 CIP

A catalogue record for this book is available from
the British Library.

The paper in this book meets the guidelines for permanence and
durability of the Committee on Production Guidelines for Book
Longevity of the Council on Library Resources.

10 9 8 7 6 5 4 3 2 1

For Michael and Owen

CONTENTS

ACKNOWLEDGMENTS

I BEGAN THIS BOOK NINE YEARS AGO while pregnant with my second child, Owen. It has gone through many different versions as our family moved from Berkeley to Hong Kong, to Seoul, and back to Berkeley. The passing of time, the people we met, and the progress of computer technology during the past decade have all had an influence on the ultimate version of *Kimono*.

Many people have helped this book take shape. I would like to thank Linda Butler, Mary Deeming, Mary Dusenbury, Norma Field, Nahoko Fukuhara, Yuki Ishimatsu, Tomie Kondō, Helen and William McCullough, Joshua Mostow, Hiroshi Sakamoto, Hiroaki Sato, the late Edward Schafer, Donald Shiveley, and Sachiko Takeda for their help and suggestions over the years. I thank the geisha of Pontochō, Kyoto, for everything they taught me about kimono, and Peter Ginsberg for his faith in my writing.

I was able to design this book thanks to the software that has given the tools of book layout to the individual. At the same time, I am enormously grateful to Steve Renick, head designer at the University of California Press, who taught me the basics of book design during the production of my earlier book, *Geisha*, and who guided and encouraged the design of *Kimono*. I also thank the artist William Gatewood for his friendship and inspiration. His painting and calligraphy appear on the jacket.

Martha Avery and John Stevenson have been intimately involved in shaping *Kimono*—without them it could not have happened.

Finally, my husband, Michael Dalby, has been a co-producer of this book at every step, from editing to designing and providing support. Our children Marie and Owen helped to clean up illustrations on the computer by pixel-vacuuming, and Chloë helped by being a patient two-year-old.

An earlier version of Chapter 7, "The Cultured Nature of Heian Colors," appeared in the *Transactions of the Asiatic Society of Japan*, fourth series, 3 (1988); an earlier version of Chapter 9, "Geisha and Kimono," was published in the *Threepenny Review* (Fall 1992). My research was supported in 1984 by a grant from the National Endowment for the Humanities.

I

CLOTHING AND CULTURE

ONE   KIMONO THEME AND VARIATIONS

THE KIMONO PROCLAIMS ITSELF the national costume of Japan
and is duly recognized as such throughout the world. Yet today
the kimono is said to be dying, to be utterly too cumbersome for
modern life, to be as elegantly anachronistic as the conservative old
ladies or geisha who wear it. Kimono is the garment men discarded a
century ago in the name of modernity and efficiency but in which
women continue to enfold themselves for formal and official occasions. Kimono is the soft silk robe requiring a corsetlike obi that
modern young ladies are allegedly unable to tolerate. Kimono-obi
ensembles have a price tag nothing less than ruinous, but remain the
sine qua non of a proper middle-class trousseau. Beautiful but imprac-
tical is the modern rational consensus on kimono.

No item in the storehouse of material culture maintains as strong a
hold on the Japanese heart, mind, and purse as kimono. Moribund
during World War II and somewhat unfashionable directly thereafter,
in the 1960s kimono underwent a revival that continues unabated. Yet
some people regard kimono as cut from the fabric of feudal oppression
and revile it for the same reasons that traditionalists revere it—the
cultural (not to mention physical) restraints it places on women.
Love it or loathe it, the kimono evokes strong opinions.

This should not be surprising, for clothing is a serious cultural matter. Innocents may wear their hearts on their sleeves, but everyone displays something of his or her personality there. Indeed, clothing is one of the most pliable aspects of selfhood, most easily changed and manipulated. The essential function of clothing is undeniably to protect our naked hides, but more important, it defines our precious persons. As such, clothing is one of the richest aspects of material culture available to the anthropologist. Culture, history, art, and personality all cling to the material that has been fashioned into clothes.

Western tradition tends to characterize clothing as facade—a wolf in sheep's clothing is anything but sheepish. In Japan, clothing and wearer merge. Even now, 'antique kimono' are cheap for foreigners because there is little market for other people's cast off clothing among Japanese. Something of the original wearer's soul has irrevocably imbued the garment. Once worn, a kimono defines itself as part of the discourse of Japanese life, unquotable out of context.

I have taken up the subject of kimono in this book as a way to explore Japanese culture through one of its most particular and concrete manifestations. Dress can never be analyzed separately from the universe of possibilities that shape its particular historical meaning. The relevance of an item of dress may lie in a single attribute or in a web of intricate detail. The challenge is to reconstruct the social and æsthetic meanings attached to the clothes as and when they were worn. What follows is not a history of kimono, although I examine its past. Nor is this book a catalogue of Japanese traditions of dress, although I depend heavily on the work of Japanese ethnographers of clothing. Rather, it is a collection of essays on the cultural aspects of kimono that interest me both personally and anthropologically.

My original focus was the modern kimono—how it came to define itself in the late nineteenth century and, reflecting changes in society, how it attained its present form. I intended both to trace a history and to analyze kimono as a system of meanings. The results of this early endeavor have become the three chapters making up the core of this book: Part II, Kimono in the Modern World. As I delved into kimono's past, however, my interest expanded to wonder at its minimal change over the course of centuries. I felt it would be useful to sketch the development of the stable elements of the kimono robe from its earliest origins in China to its place as the national dress of Japan. Many books in Japanese and several in English expound the history of Japanese clothing, but by and large they treat each epoch as a discrete closet of detail. While these books were useful as source material, nothing traced the remarkable continuity of the characteristic kimono elements (square sleeves, lapover collar, geometric construction, use of obi, and so on) over time. Thus Part I, Clothing and Culture, includes a chapter on the history of kimono in which I borrow the biological metaphor of evolution as a device to discuss kimono's adaptation to social and æsthetic impulses over the course of its genesis and development.

As I studied past modes of kimono, I was struck by the formidable influence of two eras in particular. These are the Heian period (ninth through late twelfth centuries) and the early part of the Tokugawa period (1603–1867). I am not a specialist in the history or literature of these eras—it is possible to devote a career to learning to read the language of either. I have thus relied heavily on the work of twentieth-century Japanese scholars and their renditions of historical texts into modern Japanese. Part III, Kimono Contexts, contains two essays on premodern kimono from these periods. While my main subject and experiences concern contemporary kimono, the three excursions we shall take into history—Heian, early Tokugawa, and Meiji—highlight the eras most responsible for the image of kimono today.

My interest in Japanese clothing in general, and the kimono in particular, developed during the years 1975–76, when I joined the geisha community of Pontochō in Kyoto while researching geisha for my doctoral dissertation in anthropology. Geisha are professional kimono wearers. Not only does the kimono not interfere with their work, it is a prerequisite to it. During my life as Ichigiku, I wore kimono every day. It was the hardest thing I had to learn as a geisha. It was also the skill that, once mastered, won the respect of those reserved older geisha who had raised their eyebrows at my debut.

Inevitably anthropologists become interested in the things that interest the people they work with. Geisha are interested in kimono. Their wardrobe is their biggest professional expense, but geisha don't add to their brimming cedar chests just because they have to—they long to. With a feeling akin to the satisfaction Gatsby presumably took from his neatly closeted shirts, geisha revel in the luxury implied by the Kyoto-dialect term *bebe-mochi*, 'to have lots of kimono.' Geisha have good reason to aspire to be bebe-mochi, since dedication to their profession demands that, besides practicing the arts of music and dance, they must present themselves as works of art.

Geisha are professional kimono wearers, but they are among a select few who wear a version of kimono different from that which has crystallized into the official style worn across the vast spread of Japan's middle class, the version claiming the title National Costume of Japan. Had I not first learned the intricacies of kimono from the geisha, I would probably never have realized that the bourgeois version of kimono is just one style among what was once a rich variety of local and social clothing traditions.

Geisha have a finely developed sense of the realm of kimono, and judge others by their critical standards. By immersing myself in the concerns of the geisha, de facto I became immersed in the concerns of kimono. My challenge, not only as an anthropologist but also as a social being trying to catch my bearings in unfamiliar territory, was to make sense of the torrent of information that came pouring in. This was the time when I began to think systematically about Japanese clothing.

Learning to judge kimono with a geisha's eye led me to write a chapter on kimono in my earlier book, *Geisha*. Writing that chapter pushed me further to consider how the modern kimono assumed its present form. Likewise, in reflecting on the arbiters of kimono fashion through the past three hundred years, I have written a concluding chapter on geisha in this book, *Kimono*. Eventually, in following one or another aspect of kimono, I explored such diverse topics as political hierarchy, the æsthetics of color, the sociology of gender, and the logic of formal systems. Kimono has been both starting point and common thread binding the chapters that make up this book.

Clothing carries messages that reflect its society and era. Like language, clothing reacts to changed social conditions by incorporating new elements, shifting forms, or sloughing off old styles into obsolescence. The capacity of clothing to convey information is enormous. Its messages are silently and efficiently broadcast to other members of society, who are all equipped by cultural knowledge to read its codes at a glance. Through the uniform, clothing announces profession. A person's clothing sends less specific but nonetheless clear messages about wealth. Still other subtle details indicate taste. This interpretability is especially pervasive and consistent for Japanese traditional clothing. Without exaggerating we can say that kimono are coded for messages regarding age, gender, season, formality, and occasion—not to mention wealth and taste.

While Americans acknowledge the social necessity of the uniform or the business suit, many swear that they dress mainly for comfort and function. Without argument, Americans hold comfort and function to

CLOTHING AS A
CULTURAL SYSTEM

be the legitimate objectives of clothing. The functionality stick has also been used to beat kimono for a century. The issue of what is or is not functional, however, conceals profoundly cultural questions, involving many aspects of social life. The current manifestation of kimono tradition can be accused of incorporating nonfunctionality into its very being—yet clearly, the kimono did function perfectly well for more than a millennium before the present century. I explore the question of how the modern kimono distanced itself from the utilitarian concerns of everyday life in chapter 4, "Women Who Cross Their Legs."

Clothing is generally a prime indicator of class, rank, and status in any culture. Delineation of rank was probably the most important social function of clothing in premodern Japan. Ironically, the modern kimono has almost completely lost the ability to express distinctions of rank. This is because the old class system was broadly clear-cut, whereas social rank in modern Japan has become a more subtle and complicated affair. Just as Americans like to de-emphasize overt markers of class in dress, making them more subtle in the process, in modern Japan sartorial commentary on class and status has moved to the realm of company pins, Bally shoes, and Gucci bags. By contrast, kimono has come to express a unified Japaneseness rather than social divisions.

Often clothing is overtly political, as when the ruling elite regulates the colors, designs, and styles permitted to the lower classes. In Japan the dictates of such sumptuary laws have strongly influenced the kimono— the stuff of which it was made and how it was worn—since the origin of the garment. Forbidden colors were important guidelines in Heian palace fashions. In the nineteenth century the understated chic of plain stripes in the mode known as *iki* was a direct outgrowth of taboos on opulence for commoners.

Yet another quality we attribute to clothing is psychological: dress as an expression of state of mind. The idea that a person dresses primarily to express individuality is the most tenuous clothing proposition to analyze but perhaps the most exquisite when achieved. In the case of kimono, at any rate, one must know all the rules governing required distinctions to discern how and where individual taste is being expressed. The goal of chapter 6, "The Structure of Kimono," is to lay out these precise rules of kimono dressing.

People generally wear more or less what is expected of them. The edges of this safety zone snap into focus when trespassed. At that point clothing becomes political statement (blue stockings), social comment (punk), or a mark of madness (bag ladies). Fashion is the ultimate clothing game, played tantalizingly at the threshold of the unexpected. At the same time, fashion has an amoeba-like ability to expand and ingest certain tidbits, like punk, and in the process to stretch the borders of what is socially acceptable.

Whether the categories of dress are straightforward and culturally prescribed—as they have been in most societies in the world throughout history—or multifold, shifting, and subject to fashion, as in our own society, the categories themselves are not usually noticed until they are overstepped, nor questioned unless society itself is undergoing rapid change. As a result, certain historical periods throw the categories of dress, usually taken for granted, into high relief.

Meiji Japan (1868–1912) was one such era. With a brashness nothing short of amazing in retrospect, Japan plunged into the Western-dominated international arena after three cozy centuries of virtual seclusion. Within the country as well as abroad, clothing was one of the most important ways a person could identify with civilization and enlightenment. Frock coats and bowler hats for men, corseted waists and bustles for women were more than mere fashion—they proclaimed their wearers a new breed of Japanese, personæ fully the equal of Europeans and Americans. Conversely, one could display scorn for the West by remaining in kimono. The soldiers of the Satsuma Rebellion (1877) marched kimono-clad to their doomed battle against the new order. We shall examine kimono's first confrontation with shirts, pants, and dresses in chapter 3, "The Kimono Discovers Itself."

In clothing as in life, self-definition requires an 'other' to provide a vantage point of understanding. Until the seamless web is torn, the question of identity never arises. Only when Western clothing, or *yōfuku*, first became widely available to Japanese in the 1880s did native dress become objectified through the parallel term *wafuku* (*wa*, Japanese; *fuku*, clothing). Until the Meiji period, wafuku had been the only thing there was to wear. Japanese didn't realize they were wearing ethnic clothing until the appearance of an apprehensible *yō* set up a contrast to the normal, invisible *wa*. But since Meiji, whatever people have put on their backs in Japan has come in one of these two irreducible categories—Western clothes or kimono.

Even the term *kimono* itself gained broad currency in Japan through this process of self-discovery. It spread in Japanese at about the same time it was adopted into English—the late nineteenth century. Along with the neologism *wafuku*, kimono was used generically to denote one side of the previously unnecessary distinction between native Japanese clothing and Western dress. Interestingly, wafuku in its broadest sense includes numerous traditional types of Japanese work clothes, jackets, aprons, pants, and skirtlike garments. During a century of use, however, wafuku has forgotten its folk components and has come to be largely coterminous with the one style of robe now known generically as kimono. Chapter 5, "The Other Kimono," takes up the neglected side of native dress.

Western clothing has almost completely taken over most domains of Japanese life, crowding kimono into ever more limited circumstances.

Yet even as this domain shrinks, the Japaneseness of kimono becomes more concentrated. How kimono came to define a certain mode of clothing culture in the modern world is an important aspect of the saga of defining Japaneseness that continues today. As a result, kimono is not a passively preserved relic from the past. During the process of transmission, particular modes of Japanese dress were elaborated and others ignored in a far from random pattern that illuminates political, social, and æsthetic developments in modern Japanese culture.

When kimono was just clothing, there were many ways to wear it. Kimono fashions and fads blazed through different social groups like chicken-pox in summer camp. As kimono became the preeminent form of wafuku, though, the particular style of the erstwhile samurai class became dominant. Samurai were serious people who did not wear their kimono frivolously. This ultimately accounts for the overweeningly stiff and proper aspect that typically characterizes kimono today.

When confronted with a significant 'other' culture, especially one deemed superior, the Japanese have historically bent great effort to adopt, then adapt, things from it. In the nineteenth century, Western Europe and the United States comprised the other of greatest significance; in the eighth and ninth centuries, China had played this role. At each period of cultural borrowing on the grand scale, and probably in no small part because of them, Japanese have become greatly concerned with their cultural identity. Indigenous Japanese clothing was as different from the kimonoesque robes adopted from seventh-century China as kimono were different from trousers a millennium later. Much as some Japanese cultural chauvinists resist admitting the fact, the prototype of their national costume is undeniably Chinese. The adoption of Sui and Tang courtly styles and their eventual evolution into kimono is the subject of chapter 2, "The Natural History of Kimono."

The forms and æsthetics of clothing had become distinctively Japanese by the ninth century. Chapter 7, "The Cultured Nature of

Heian Colors," focuses on this fascinating period. In the flowering of Heian culture, an authentic Japanese sensibility (at first highly influenced by, but then departing from, Chinese models) came to be expressed exquisitely in literature, in painting—and in clothing. The first truly Japanese version of the garment we now call kimono appeared at this time in the intimate layers of women's costume. Kimono's native ancestor was a plain white undergarment hidden beneath the multiple strata of colored silk robes worn by ladies of the court.

The cut and shape of these robes were the same for all. The type of silk material and number of layers was decided by season. Certain colors, accoutrements, and weaves were assigned by rank. Yet within the confines of these givens, the women of the court created individual æsthetic expressions in the way they combined the colors of their gowns. Like poetry, dress was a vehicle for the expression of artistic sensibilities. Outfits and poems alike were composed within the dictates of structured systems. In poetry, a tightly self-referential literary corpus formed a common pool of images and expression for all educated people of the time. In dress, an analogous structure existed in the system of seasonally defined and named color combinations.

The Heian courtly elite created a culture of nature in which plants, insects and other animals, weather, colors, and especially the seasons became the terms of a poetic idiom defining cultured existence and sensibility. In the process, the language of nature attained a life of its own in a coherent system of meanings, metaphors, and nuances informing the discourse of palace life in Heian-Kyō. In this context, I examine the composition of colors occurring over a yearly cycle of robes—a wonderful example of how nature was once fashioned into culture.

Another crucial development in kimono's history is the appearance and popular rise of the *kosode* in the seventeenth century. The kosode (small sleeve) garment took its name in contradistinction to gowns with great, billowing, fingertip-covering sleeves. The kosode crept out from under all the layers of Heian costume to become standard clothing for men and women in the Edo period (seventeenth through mid-nineteenth centuries) as Japan developed an ingrown yet prosperous and vigorous cultural style. The kosode is recognizably linked to both the tenth- and twentieth-century versions of Japanese dress as foundation of the former and forbear to the latter. On its own terms, kosode represented kimono's golden age of exuberant design and dramatic display. Chapter 8, "Moronobu's Fashion Magazine," reproduces and translates a kimono pattern book (*hinagata*) as a way of exemplifying the tastes and mores of the seventeenth century.

Even now in Japanese, the word *kimono* rides but loosely atop a hierarchy of terms that people use when referring to an item of native dress. One says *kimono o kiru* (I'm going to wear kimono) only when the implied choice is between Japanese clothing and Western. Otherwise, garments will be identified according to various criteria that map out the domain of kimono from within. This process of operating within levels of semantic categories takes place for us when a businessman looks into his closet and chooses his 'gray pin-stripe' (operating in the realm of business suits) or a woman decides to wear 'basic black' (the cultural understanding being the realm of cocktail dresses). The difference is that the Japanese classification system for kimono is much more pristine. Categories map precisely onto socially or æsthetically articulated interpretations—which is to say that a glance at a person wearing a kimono ensemble reveals categorically a number of things about his or her age, sex, class, the season, and the occasion, not to mention personal taste or the lack thereof.

The 'meaning' of kimono lies just below the surface. The code is not buried, and it does not require an analyst to see deep connections of which the natives are ostensibly unaware. For all the complicated possibilities of dressing in wafuku, the kimono sends its code in bell-like tones provided the receiver is properly attuned. Structuralist theory, with its insistence on system, binary oppositions, and hierarchy, has found the perfect subject to elucidate in the kimono. A number of studies of clothing use a semantic analysis or linguistic analogy to probe their subject. Most notable among them is Roland Barthes' work *Système de la mode*, which gallantly attempts to find a logic connecting speech and dress in the world of French couture as described in fashion magazines. In spite of his analytical tour de force, however, Barthes is ultimately defeated by French Fashion, the very *mode* he tries to skewer with the analytical pins of structuralism.

The winds of fashion blow much more gently in the domain of kimono. Those distortions making the structural analysis of Western clothing like an attempt to catch butterflies in a hurricane are largely absent from the world of wafuku. This is partly because the system is now a closed one. After the coming of yōfuku, wafuku began to be sewn up into certain categories that will be altered no more. It is unlikely that a designer will invent a sleeveless kimono, for example, as an option in the realm of Japanese dress. Ironically, if such a style were to appear, it would more likely be considered a kind of weird Western fashion, a 'kimona.'

Certain parts of the kimono, such as sleeves and collars, are saturated with significance and have developed webs of metaphor connecting literature, aphorism, and daily life. When we take seriously the proposition that clothing is woven of meanings as much as it is of fiber, its structure can provide a dimension of understanding that greatly illuminates a purely historical chronology of changing modes of dress.

Costume histories almost inevitably seem to focus more on women's dress than men's, and this book is no exception. Although admittedly I am idiosyncratic in my choice of topics, the fact that these chapters concentrate more on women's clothing than on men's is not arbitrary. In the case of kimono, this gender bias has less to do with some notion of women being the more flamboyant of the species than it does with kimono's evolution. Throughout its history kimono has, with few exceptions, received its major stylistic hallmarks from women's dress rather than men's. The characteristic kimonoid collar was worn by women in the eighth century at a time when men wore high, round, side-fastened collars. In the seventeenth century, the emergence of kosode as kimono's immediate predecessor on the clothing family tree was also traceable to its matrilineal inheritance. In our own century, the kimono is seen primarily in its feminine form.

Over the years I have become able to appreciate an artistically coordinated ensemble of kimono, obi, and attendant accessories in modern Japan, as well as the masterpieces of textile design from kimono's past. I have worn kimono intensively during a period of my life and have even come to understand the requisite body language that must be developed to wear it gracefully. Yet at the same time, as a non-Japanese and as an anthropologist, I can criticize kimono's bourgeois tendencies and chauvinistic proclivities. Unlike a Japanese, I need not decide whether I love or loathe kimono. My goal is to interpret kimono in the cultural terms it so richly exemplifies.

TWO

THE NATURAL HISTORY OF KIMONO

IT MAY SEEM STRANGE TO SPEAK of the natural history of something as egregiously cultural as clothing. Living organisms are inescapably linked to their predecessors by the genes that make up their being, whereas the whole point of clothes is that they can be put on and taken off. Inheritors of a tradition of fashion as radical change, we of Western mode are also likely to think of fashion history as a rapid succession of discontinuities—the antithesis of the gradual evolution of a group of genetically related organisms.

Yet the biological metaphor of phylogeny seems oddly appropriate for the history of kimono. The shape of the modern national costume of Japan is clearly derived from a seventh-century Chinese robe, and although the kimono has evolved and adapted throughout the eras, it has at the same time maintained a strong resemblance to its earliest progenitor.

In contrast, historical changes in Western fashions have produced infinitely greater variety and variation, and, one could even say, bizarre mutations and numerous extinctions. Modern French couture is as different from medieval dress as poodle from wolf. In comparison, the kimono is like *Felis catus*, whose resemblance to its feline forbears is immediate and obvious.

Being modish in kimono has seldom involved radical changes to its basic shape. Compared to Western fashion, the difference is acute. The language of fashion in the West primarily describes shapes, and we think of fashion history as a parade of dramatically changing female silhouettes. In our own century we have witnessed the hourglass, the S-curve, the A-line, and the inverted pyramid effect of padded shoulders. The perennial interest in skirt length crystallizes this concern, because skirts set the general configuration of the season's fashionable body. The contours of kimono, in contrast, are highly conservative. They shift the issue of fashion away from shape to the areas of color, pattern, and decorative detail. The flat, unbroken sections of kimono have provided an excellent, consistent canvas for display of the dyer's art, painter's imagination, and embroiderer's skill. Pattern and color date a kimono more surely than its shape.

What defines kimono? All garments of kimonoid genealogy have in common four elements of costume construction: geometric use of standard fabric widths sewn with minimal cutting; an open, overlapping front; an attached neckband sewn around the front opening; and sleeves consisting of a width of fabric attached to the selvages.

The various parts of the kimono garment may have narrowed and widened, shrunk or lengthened, and received different fashion emphases throughout the ages. Yet these changes have operated on the same basic parts, which remain recognizable in form and construction. Along the path of its history, the kimono sleeve has covered fingertips, pulled back to the wrist, closed up, hung free, grown long, and been cut short again, but the basic construction of the kimono sleeve remains constant.

A kimono is made from a bolt of cloth of a standard width of approximately fourteen inches. A bolt contains approximately twelve and a half yards, enough to make one adult-size garment. Kimono wearers have always chosen their kimono in bolt form, which they then order sewn up to their measurements. Traditional kimono shops display

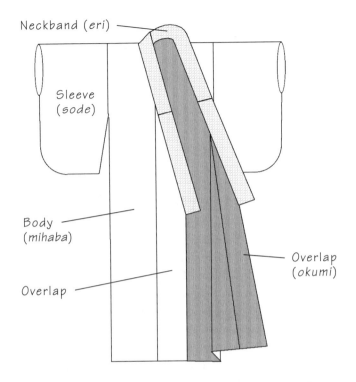

Neckband (eri)

Sleeve
(sode)

Body
(mihaba)

Overlap

Overlap
(okumi)

2.1   The basic elements of kimono

their wares as a row of fabric rolls. The prêt-à-porter kimono phenomenon is just a decade old, confined largely to polyester. Silk kimono are
still acquired in their ancient, pre-sewn form as a bolt of cloth.

Two straight lengths of fabric make up the kimono body. They are
joined up the middle of the back and left open over the shoulders down
the front. Two half-width sections (*okumi*) are sewed on to each side. The
okumi provides an amplitude of fabric where the gown is lapped, left
over right side, and held together by a sash at waist or hip. The neckband
or collar (*eri*) is a folded strip of cloth attached to the front opening
around the neckline reaching about a third of the way down the okumi
on each side. Sleeves (*sode*) consist of another width of the bolt attached
to the sides of the body.

			12 feet 6 inches	
Sleeve	Sleeve	Body		14 inches

Such a geometrical pattern using loomed widths of cloth is economical. There is little wastage of the sort that results when a piece of flat, two-dimensional cloth is cut, sewn, and pieced to fit the curves and bulges of a three-dimensional human body. It is not true, however, that kimono are free size. Japanese are fat and thin, tall and short, like everyone. To sew a kimono to individual fit, the body is measured to determine the kimono's length, the volume required for comfortable front lapover, and sleeve length. A heavy person will have kimono made with full use of fabric width, while a thin person will tuck in wide seam allowances. The excess will never be cut, but simply folded into the seams. A kimono is fundamentally adjustable because the original bolt-width is retained in its seams. In the past, when kimono were always taken apart for washing, each cleaning could also be a refitting.

Japanese parse the human body linguistically into discrete regions that clothe themselves using different verbs. Things worn on the head use the verb *kaburu*. Pants or skirts, socks, shoes, and other items worn from the waist down receive the verb *haku*. Anything hung from the shoulders is described with *kiru*. When Japanese were introduced to gloves, yet another verb (*hameru*) was used to pull them on. *Haki-mono*, 'things worn below the waist,' are different for men and women, while 'things that hang from the shoulders' (*ki-mono*) have always been quite similar. The unisex quality of kimono design was inherent even in the ancestral ki-mono of the seventh century.

Body		Neckband	Over-collar
		Overlap	Overlap

2.2 Cutting layout for modern kimono

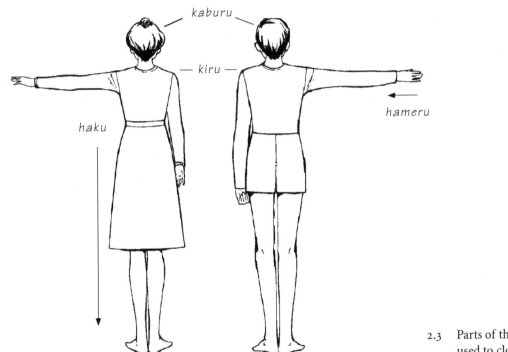

2.3 Parts of the body and verbs used to clothe them

Is there a proto-kimono that can be considered the original dress of the Japanese? It appears not. The prototype of kimono, like so much else in Japan, was Chinese. The history of Japanese garments in the kimono genealogy does not begin until the seventh century, when the nascent Japanese imperial court adopted styles of robes and court clothing from the Chinese. Before that time, Japanese clothing followed two different modes, distinct both from each other and from the kimonoid style.

The first mode was a roughly crafted poncho-style garment presumed to hark back to at least the first century A.D. and to represent the earliest purely indigenous dress of the Japanese. The other mode is represented by the pleated skirts, tailored pants and side-fastened jackets of Japan's Tomb-period aristocrats (fourth to sixth centuries). This style clearly originated outside Japan somewhere on the plains of north China.

The early inhabitants of the Japanese islands wore the simplest of tunics, and expressed social facts such as tribal identity and hierarchy by means of cosmetic paints and tattoos. This custom was noticed in the third century by Chinese explorers of a Japanese society calling itself Wa, which the Chinese found on the southernmost of the Japanese islands.[1]

2.4　Pottery fragment showing incised figure wearing a belted poncho-style garment

> The men of Wa tattoo their faces and paint their bodies with designs. They are fond of diving for fish and shells. Long ago they decorated their bodies in order to protect themselves from large fish. Later these designs became ornamental. Body painting differs among the various tribes. The position and size of the design vary according to the rank of the individual.... They smear their bodies with pink and scarlet just as we Chinese use powder.
>
> Men wear a cloth band about their exposed heads. Their garment is an unsewn width of cloth. Women bind their hair in loops and wear ponchos.

It is human nature to remark on those things which appear remarkable to one's own eyes. Thus the blandly powdered Chinese were

2.5 Figures from a bronze bell-plaque, interpreted to be wearing ponchos as they hunt, spin, and pound grain

impressed by the lavish use of body decoration by the barbaric Wa, and by the men's habit of going about hatless—since any proper Chinese would not dream of going out without a cap. There is much scholarly controversy regarding what the Chinese text meant by "unsewn widths of cloth." Was it a sarong tied at the hip? A cape or a toga? The phrase may have referred to a version of the simple poncho-style garment mentioned for women, 'unsewn' in the sense of being untailored.

Archæological remains from the Yayoi period (200 B.C.–A.D. 250), which encompasses the time of the Chinese visit to Wa, show that Japanese cloth was woven on a kind of backstrap loom. Warp threads were attached by one end to a fixed point, the other end held around the weaver's waist, and the weft threads shuttled into this taut horizontal warp by her hand. This method of weaving produces a piece of cloth the width of which is naturally constrained to approximately that of the human body.[2] Yayoi-period textiles were thus probably about twelve inches wide. Joined at the selvages, with openings left for the head and

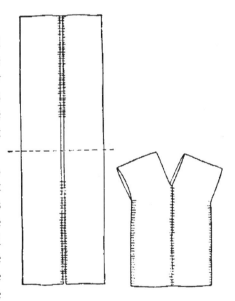

2.6 Poncho-style garments

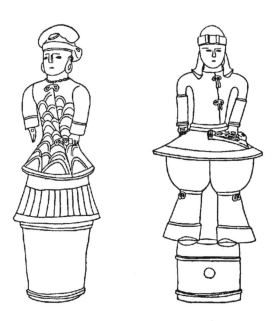

2.7 Sixth-century female and male *haniwa* figurines

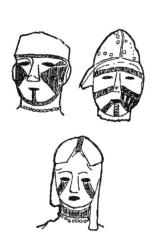

2.8 Haniwa heads with tattoos or cosmetic facial designs

the arms, this otherwise untailored poncho would certainly have appeared crude to the Chinese.

The other pre-kimono style of note in protohistoric Japan was much more elaborate. We see fitted jackets, pants, and skirts on the pottery tomb figurines called *haniwa*, which date from the fifth and sixth centuries. The haniwa represent men, women, animals, and buildings and are a fascinating indication of the culture and society of the Late Tomb period. Aristocratic men and women are portrayed wearing fitted jackets. Women wear long flared or pleated skirts; men wear pants. Both may wear necklaces and earrings, often of comma-shaped *magatama* stones. Many haniwa, regardless of class or gender, have simple designs painted on face and neck that may be either tattoos or more temporary cosmetic adornment.

The gap between crude ponchos and tailored jackets has social and political ramifications too profound to explore here.[3] In terms of the history of kimono as we are tracing it, however, both the haniwa mode and the earlier ponchos were unrelated to the later courtly styles that developed into kimono. Their survival only as objects of scholarly controversy is a sign of their sartorial extinction.

The thread leading back to the prototype of kimono ultimately must be traced to China. A front-wrapping robe with attached collar and rectangular sleeves was a basic shape of Chinese clothing from the time of the Han dynasty (approximately 200 B.C.–A.D. 200). When did this garment shape come to Japan? As early as the fourth century a Han-style kimonoid garment might have been worn by male Japanese tribal chiefs and priestess-queens. Relatively frequent contact between the tribes of Japan and the advanced civilization of the continent is certain by the fourth century, but whether this included the adoption of Han robes is not known. In any case, Chinese styles made a massive impact on Japan in general only several centuries later.

During the seventh through tenth centuries, the glorious reigns of the Sui and Tang dynasties, Chinese culture provided the model of civilization for all the Far East. Any culture aspiring to be a proper realm and be recognized as such would have been powerfully drawn to adopt the rituals, writing, and technology of Chinese culture. It would have been surprising if aristocratic clothing styles had not been among the first things the rulers of China's neighbors borrowed.

Japan's first incarnation as a state with imperial aspirations occurred in the seventh century. This regime controlled a social order that differed qualitatively from the collection of clans that had preceded it. Although peasants presumably continued to farm in their ponchos, powerful clan

2.9   Ancient form of the Chinese character *yi*, 'robe' (*above*); a classic Chinese robe

leaders were gradually persuaded to declare loyalty to a central imperial figure, partly in exchange for the colored caps and gowns of royal rank. Clothing, shoes, hairstyles, and paintings of this time all reflect Sui and Tang courtly styles. It is to Chinese models that we must look for kimono's early embodiments.

In the year A.D. 600 an envoy of the Sui court recorded the appearance of people in the now-developing country of Wa as follows:[4]

> As for dress and adornment, the gentlemen wear a jacket with narrow sleeves and a skirt [Chinese *chun ju*]. They wear shoes with lacquered uppers fastened by thongs. In the past, the men of Wa did not wear caps, and their hair hung over their ears. Since the Sui era, the Wa king has instituted a system of caps to indicate rank. They are made of brocade and colored silk and adorned with gold and silver flowers.

2.10 Female and male courtiers wearing similar clothing styles in the early seventh century

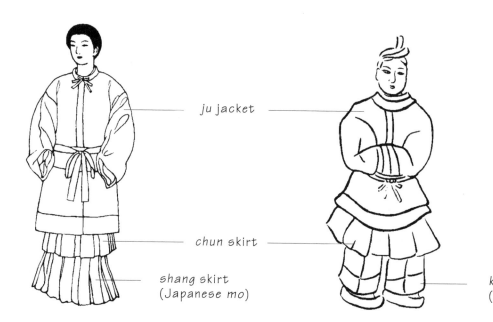

ju jacket

chun skirt

shang skirt
(Japanese mo)

ku pants
(Japanese hakama)

The women wear their hair in ponytails down their backs. Their garments consist of a *chun ju* jacket and skirt, and they wear a *shang* skirt underneath. They wear bamboo combs....

Both men and women paint marks on their arms and spots on their faces and have their bodies tattooed.

The Japanese evidently continued to tattoo and paint their bodies even as they adopted haute-couture continental clothing. From the Chinese point of view the people of Wa were still remarkably barbaric, but they were making progress—at least they now wore caps.

Seventh-century styles did not differ dramatically between the sexes. Men and women wore a similar upper body garment and ceremonial skirt. Beneath this skirt, men wore pants, while women wore another long skirt that Japanese call a *mo*. But skirts soon reached an evolutionary dead end in Japan. Within a hundred years the mo was reduced to a vestigial decorative remnant in the formal court costume of aristocratic women—where it remains, frozen in the amber of contemporary Empress Michiko's coronation costume. Pants, in contrast, held their own for some time. Court women adopted pants into their ensembles during the ninth century and continued to wear trousers under their robes for five hundred years. Not until the late 1300s did kimono eventually outgrow pants.

During the eighth century, though, to be civilized was increasingly to be Chinese. Japanese tomb murals of the late seventh century depict women in garb that would have been at home in any Chinese palace. In the year 710 the Japanese court moved its location to Nara, where in a further great wave of Sinitic reforms it adopted rules for court dress explicitly based on those of the official Tang clothing codes. The Yōrō Clothing Code of 718 marked a high point of Chinese-influenced policies for the early Japanese state.

The code specified that all robes should be crossed left side over right in Chinese fashion. Such 'sidedness' of clothing is important in many

2.11 Tang period Chinese lady (*above*) and Japanese follower of her fashions

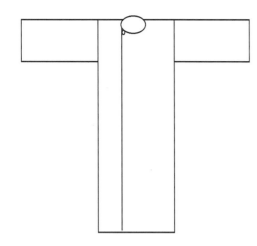

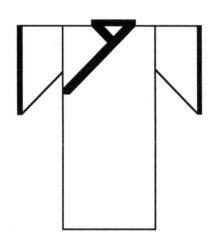

2.12 *Agekubi* high-necked robe (*top*); *tarikubi* kimono-style robe

cultures. Precisely because of the natural arbitrariness of left and right, sides can be used to express cultural differences of great import. A garment's sidedness is not something to be reversed lightly. The Chinese considered right-over-left a mark of barbarism. This explains the Japanese decision to abandon their traditional mode. All Japanese robes, including kimono, have wrapped left over right since the Yōrō Clothing Code demanded it.

We see kimono's earliest ancestor in Japan at the time of the Yōrō clothing reforms. The first great divergence in the style of men's and women's upper-body garment also occurred at this period. Although the palace uniform for men upheld the traditional round-necked, narrow-sleeved style inspired by the Sui dynasty, women adopted the crossover neckline worn by Tang ladies. They also began to wear their skirts tied in Tang fashion, over, rather than under, their upper robe.

The two distinct types of robe are referred to in later ages as *agekubi* (high neck) and *tarikubi* (lapover neck). Distinguished by their different collars and sleeves, the two styles had a long history in China of expressing different modes of being. Japan took the inspiration for round collars and narrow sleeves from the Sui, with its northern continental influences. Pants and narrow sleeves on close-fitting tailored jackets (the agekubi style) are thought to have originated among horse riders in the north China plains. In contrast, the wide sleeves and bathrobe-style robes requiring sashes (the kimonoid tarikubi style) are considered by the Chinese to be a southern mode, arising from basically agricultural peoples typified by the Han.

Just as the northern versus southern dimensions of Chinese culture were expressed in these collars and sleeves, so, too, was the classic Chinese division between soldier and scholar. The military man wore a narrow-sleeved tunic over pants, whereas the gentleman-scholar wore a flowing kimonoesque robe. The emperor's best clothes (*raifuku*) in

China, hence in Japan as well, took the classic Han lapover neck style. Yet outside of those occasions of supreme ceremony, even the emperor wore round-necked collars.

In Japan, tarikubi kimonoid robes made their biggest impression during the eighth century as a fashion for women. For the next several hundred years the gender distinction held. Agekubi was worn by men. Tarikubi, kimono's ancestor, was for women. The Japanese imperial family treasure house, the Shōsōin, preserves many costumes of this era. Most of the upper-body garments are men's palace-uniform agekubi robes. This style, called *uenoginu*, looks clearly different from the early kimonoesque tarikubi. It is also clear that lapping collars did not develop from round collars. Rather, we might say they existed on separate branches of the Chinese-rooted kimono evolutionary tree. As we shall see throughout the history of kimono, the important features

2.13 Chinese imperial high ceremonial dress in tarikubi style (*left*); Japanese palace garb in the agekubi style

retained by kimono come mostly from its matrilineal inheritance. This tendency was inherent in kimono development from the beginning.

Given the eventual dominance of tarikubi in Japanese culture as kimono proper, what became of the agekubi style? In the eleventh century, the round-necked robe was promoted from the status of ordinary palace dress to imperial high ceremonial wear for men. The agekubi subsequently became lodged in this highly ceremonial context, where it has continued, little changed, as male court clothing up to the present. Emperor Akihito was invested wearing precisely such robes. Thus while the tarikubi kimonoid line of clothing continued to branch and evolve, adapting to changing circumstance, the agekubi style found a tiny niche where, like a coelacanth, it persists nearly unaltered in form.

2.14 Emperor Akihito on his succession to the chrysanthemum throne

Japan closed its doors to direct Chinese influence in the tenth century. A truly Japanese sensibility in many areas of culture then began to develop. Naturally, clothing was greatly affected. Although the more official aspects of culture—literature, painting, and the garb of high ceremony—conserved Chinese form, native modes evolved in parallel. The differences between Chinese and native expressions were again reflected in gender. Men upheld Chinese styles, while women developed what we look back on as the truly creative, natively Japanese aspects of Heian culture. Men composed Chinese-style couplets in stiffly brushed characters. Women wrote novels in the fluid native syllabary. Official male Heian dress preserved the round-necked uenoginu style, while women wore layers of kimonoform tarikubi robes that looked increasingly different from anything Chinese. Even at this stage, the kimono ancestor was not yet independent, however. Women still wore trousers called *hakama* underneath their robes and tied the ceremonial mo skirt over all the layers.

During the Heian period (ninth to twelfth centuries), as other costume elements were reduced to vestigial remnants, the kimonoform robe gradually became more important. Besides gender, clothing began to reflect distinctions of age, ceremony, class, and place. For example, married women's trousers were different in color from those worn by girls. Formal occasions required overskirts. Rank or imperial permission granted the right to wear otherwise forbidden colors. Private attire differed from public.

The official costume for public occasions for an adult lady of rank in the Heian age required that, in addition to the basic costume of trousers and layered kimonoid robes, she wear a *karaginu* jacket harking back to Nara court apparel, as well as a mo—by this time only half a skirt, more like an apron really, worn behind. Draped over her shoulders like a stole was an even more venerable stylistic relic called a *hire*. This long

2.15 Aristocratic Heian couple

narrow scarf of cloth traced its origins back to the earliest priestess-shamans of Japanese prehistory.

Ceremonial dress is by nature conservative, though not immune to the fashions of its day. There is a time lag. Elements of earlier ritual importance maintain themselves in the garb of ceremony long after they have disappeared from everyday dress. Eventually, though, even ceremonial wear tends to absorb styles from beneath its ranks, provided it does not completely freeze up into a 'costume.' During the Heian period, round collars displaced the Han-style tarikubi robe as the royal suit of highest ceremony. Likewise, late in the Heian age, women discarded karaginu and mo, treating a previously private-wear cloak called *ko-uchigi* as public formal wear. This process of simplification continued into the subsequent warrior age and even beyond. At each stage, some element of dress formerly considered underwear, or at least informal wear, crept up to respectability.

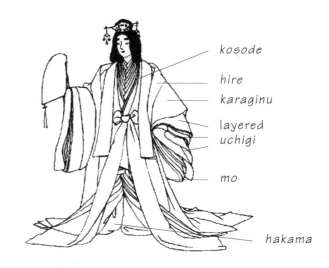

kosode

hire

karaginu

layered
uchigi

mo

hakama

2.16 Heian noble lady
in formal attire

The embryonic kimono was gestated as underwear during the Heian age. Kimono developed from the plain white, small-sleeved (*ko-sode*) undergarment worn next to a lady's skin—under all the gorgeously colored layers of silk uchigi that were the focus of Heian fashion.[5] Female commoners also wore small sleeves as their standard clothing. Kosode differed from uchigi robes most importantly in the sleeve, as its name suggests. The Heian layers and overjackets all had great wide sleeves (*hirosode*) that were unsewn down the front edge. In contrast, the puny kosode sleeve was sewn up like a bag, leaving an opening just large enough for the wrist to pass through. This definitive feature, the bag sleeve (*tamoto sode*), was to remain with kosode permanently.

During Japan's middle ages, the little kosode would come into its own. First white, but later embellished with every color and pattern artists could devise, the seventeenth-century kosode was but a step or two from modern kimono on the family tree.

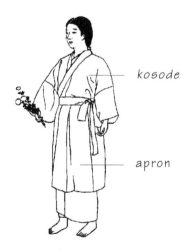

kosode

apron

2.17   Female commoner in
         peasant version of *kosode*

The Heian period was followed by an era of warfare dominated by provincial strongmen. The Kamakura period (1185–1333) is known as an age of military efficiency rather than courtly luxury. During this time the kimonoid neckline became standard even for men. Public wear for men of the warrior class consisted of a two-piece set, with kimonoid top and short trousers, together called *hitatare*. In battle, fighting men donned an intricate suit of armor over the hitatare. High round-necked collars and great wide sleeves were reserved for exalted ceremony, and finally went out of fashion even in that context, except among the now powerless court nobility.

The hitatare ensemble was usually composed in small repeat-pattern brocades. In the succeeding Muromachi age (1392–1573), hitatare came to be created in more flamboyant large-scale decorative patterns called *daimon*. Once again, following what appears to be a law of cultural selection that elevates the informal wear of the preceding generation to become the formal wear of the next, practical Kamakura hitatare warrior suits eventually wound up as ceremonial garb for daimyō regional lords in the Edo period.

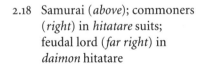

2.18 Samurai (*above*); commoners (*right*) in *hitatare* suits; feudal lord (*far right*) in *daimon* hitatare

2.19 Simplified style of white kosode and red *hakama*, adopted by noble ladies during the Kamakura period

What did the women of the newly dominant warrior class wear during Kamakura times? No longer umpteen layers of open-sleeved trailing robes—yet echoes of Heian courtly styles did not immediately disappear. The court had established a high level of cultural sophistication. Wives and daughters of regional lords would have been ashamed to be utterly unfamiliar with the culture of the capital. So court dress, even if dramatically simplified, remained the foundation for warrior-class women's dress.

The new mode left women wearing their scarlet hakama trousers over the plain white kosode—the embryonic kimono—now for the first time appearing in public on its own. Instead of Heian-style multilayered colored silk, Kamakura ladies might wear a single brocaded gown called an *uchigi*, descendant of the informal ko-uchigi jacket of Heian times, over their kosode.

2.20 *Katsugu*—the mode of draping a kosode over one's head

Beginning in the late fourteenth century, there appeared a fundamentally new cultural order. The power of the Kyoto court had long since crumbled, and the Ashikaga dynasty of shoguns dominated the Muromachi period. Now Kamakura military lords were challenged from below, and defeated—largely because of the strength of the lower ranks of samurai. Not surprisingly, the practical two-piece hitatare costume of the lowly soldier became standard male dress. The small-sleeved kosode replaced wide-sleeved uchigi for women. It is difficult to say whether the kosode, which took center stage at this point in history, developed directly from the aristocratic undergarment of that name or whether it was more closely related to the single garment worn by commoner women, which it also resembled. Probably its connection to both made kosode the natural basis for Muromachi women's dress.

The most important historical change in kimono form occurred during Muromachi when women ceased wearing hakama altogether, stimulating the kosode to grow to ankle length. When kosode was underwear, and visible only above the waist, it was but a skimpy chemise reaching to the calf. Now launched as the major item of dress, kosode needed to reach a respectable length. And once it attained the status of outerwear, kosode began to absorb color and design.

Dropping hakama did create a problem, however. The strings at the waist of hakama held a woman's robes together. Without hakama, women had to find a means to keep their kosode closed in front. An *obi*, or sash, was the solution. The early obi was quite narrow, never suggesting the great wide swath of brocade that developed centuries later.

Women also discovered novel ways to wear kosode—for example, to drape it over the head. Naturally, a different verb described this custom: *katsugu*. A woman of the warrior class would invariably katsugu a kosode on her head when she went out. Soon fashionable townswomen did the same, even capping this headdress kosode with a large straw hat.

For formal dress, ruling class women came to wear a second kosode unbelted, coatlike, over their ordinary kosode. Again, the verb used to describe this usage, *uchikake-ru*, 'to drape upon,' provided the name of the garment. Like outermost garments of the past, the uchikake was most colorfully decorated. It is enjoying a modern revival as bridal dress in the so-called traditional wedding ceremony of today.

Women's formal summer attire permitted overheated ladies to strip uchikake from their shoulders, tying it around their waists like a lumpish wraparound skirt. This odd style, called *koshimaki* (hip-wrapping), continued to be worn by ladies of the shogun's palace straight through the Edo period (1603–1867). Perhaps the effect of a tranquil white kosode rising from a great bundle of brocade created an illusion of coolness.

In the sixteenth century, the nobility ceased to be the sole source of fashion inspiration. Playgirls (*asobime*)—multitalented, trendy ladies who led rather public lives (sometimes glossed as 'courtesans')—wore their kosode belted with long tasseled silk cords. The cords, called Nagoya obi, were woven according to a style then popular in China, roped about the hips six or seven times, and tied in a looping bow. Playgirls also did their hair into Chinese chignons, initiating a fashion for women to put up their hair. In previous ages, men had been the ones to oil and arrange their tresses. Women had favored long straight locks, or perhaps a simple ponytail. This was also the period when *tabi* (split-toed socks) came into general use.

2.21 *Uchikake*—an unbelted kosode worn as a cloak

2.22 *Koshimaki* style of stripping the outer kosode off the shoulders

Creeping out from under aristocrats' layered robes into public view by the mid-fifteenth century, the kosode extended its niche to men and women of all classes during the Edo period. Compared to modern kimono, early Edo kosode appear rather short and skimpy sleeved. Fabric two inches wider than the modern standard of fourteen made the body of the kosode appear broader than kimono and placed the sleeve seam further down the arm. The sleeve section below the wrist opening was sewed and rounded, and hand opening was small. Unlike modern kimono, the back of the sleeve was often sewed directly to the body instead of hanging free.

Japanese on the eve of the seventeenth century were as hungry for styles of the Chinese Ming dynasty as they are today for Louis Vuitton. The corded obi and hairstyles *à la chinoise* were very Ming. The kosode took advantage of new softer weaves of material fabricated by the Chinese, as Japanese weavers learned how to create the figured damasks, satins, and crepe silks they had been importing. The softer draped look for kosode was not limited to new silks. Cotton came to be cultivated extensively in Japan at this time. Commoners started weaving and wearing it in place of traditional resilient but stiff bast fibers like hemp, flax, and ramie. The more supple new fabrics lent themselves to new techniques of dyeing and decoration. Stiff heavy brocades were outmoded by dapple-dyed, hand-painted, foil-stamped, and embroidered pliable robes in an extraordinary artistic outburst of textile design the likes of which the world has seldom seen.

The efflorescence of creativity expressed through the kosode occurred during the early seventeenth century. Its vitality arose from the energy of city people, primarily the merchant class, who increasingly had the money, time, and interest to patronize the arts. These people flaunted their wealth and taste on their backs, commissioning ever more exquisite kosode. Until then kosode fashion had been dominated by the taste and station of women of the elite, who favored fancy overdraping garments richly decorated in detailed surface embroidery and gold leaf. The elite taste of this era is preserved today in the robes of the Noh theater. It is characterized by the use of large horizontal planes of color and randomly scattered patterns that project a busy, two-dimensional gorgeousness.

The social shift from the era of the warrior to the era of the merchant-artisan was reflected in clothing both by the appearance of a stunning design æsthetic and the growth of a consumerist mentality toward clothing as fashion. A new look, characterized by dynamic asymmetry, irregular forms, and sweeping curves, appears in the kosode of the Keichō period (1596–1615). Suddenly the kosode became a means for defining a new artistic concept of space. A riveting coherence of design, incorporating large abstract areas of color, dapple tie-dye, embroidery, and metallic leaf into its vision, sets early Edo kosode apart from the densely diffuse designs that pleased blue-blood samurai ladies.

Stylistic clarity of design reached fulfillment in kosode of the Kanbun period (1661–1673). Now the robe was treated as a canvas for a single bold subject, writ large and asymmetrically placed, sweeping diagonally from shoulder across sleeve and down to hem. Design subjects focused on themes from classical literature—a cavalier way to wear cultural pretensions on one's sleeve. Townsmen and women became the keenest devotees of such highbrow cultural pursuits.

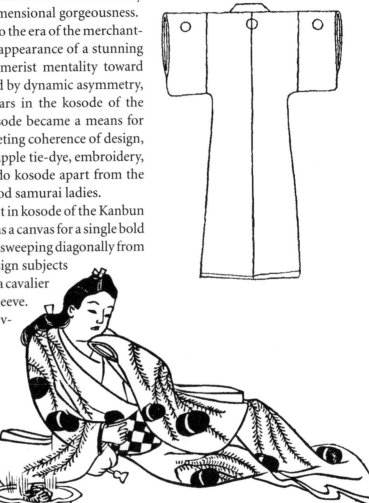

2.23 Kosode proportions in the seventeenth century

2.24 The look of early Edo kosode was made possible by more supple fabrics

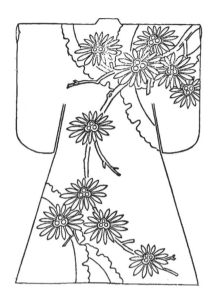

2.25 A Genroku kosode design
from a contemporary
pattern book

The dramatic early Edo kosode style culminated in Genroku (1688–1704). A new technique of silk dying called *yūzen* allowed freeform drawing of fine white lines in resist that when dyed created crisp outlines between sharply defined small areas of color. Yūzen was a more painterly technique than earlier methods of dyeing, and it provided the technical means to create wonderfully detailed pictorial themes. With yūzen came unabridged freedom of expression in kosode design and execution. The Genroku kosode stands out as the peacock's pride of all kimono.[6]

Ironically, one stimulus to the development of yūzen was that Edo authorities were setting limits on the degree of luxury allowed to kosode. When the labor-consuming process (hence ostentatious effect) of tying individual minuscule knots in silk to create a dappled effect was banned, yūzen offered a means of obtaining a similar look by mere painting. The result may not have been the equal of the designer original, but it had the look—and, more important, it was legal.

In addition to the inherent appeal of Genroku color combinations and designs per se, Genroku kosode marked another major step in kimono's evolution. At the end of the seventeenth century, the fashionable mind made its first appearance in Japanese society, and with it the notion of change for the sake of change. In fashion's fierce competition to be au courant, the corollary notion of obsolescence arose, stimulating the development of a commercial establishment that catered to these values. Genroku sensibilities seem positively modern. At the pinnacle of popular attention were the nouveaux riches, who vied for the newest and the best of everything consumable.

Kosode proportions also changed slightly during Genroku times. The width of the back narrowed, and that of sleeves widened to more or less modern size. About this time the sleeves of women's kosode began to grow longer. Kosode's little sleeves grew in another direction. In the 1660s an eighteen-inch-long sleeve was called *furisode*, swinging sleeve.

2.26 From left, the small *marusode* of early Edo, fluttering *furisode* that followed, and squared-off *kakusode* of late Edo

A decade later, a sleeve had to be at least two feet long to be considered swinging. By Genroku, sleeves had grown another six inches. Sleeve lengthening was kosode's first major stylistic ramification. Along with the widening obi, sleeve length came to characterize the luxurious aspects of Edo life.

2.27 *Date otoko* with sideburns,
stiffened sleeves, and
padded linings

Kimono sleeve trends are nearly always stated in terms of length, but during the Edo period the sleeve opening also experienced fads and changes. During the 1650s kosode wrist openings became wider. This fashion was started by men known as *date otoko*, disreputable yet dandified commoners who swaggered about in flamboyant padded kosode. Their exaggeratedly round sleeves were held in shape by wire or whalebone. Kabuki theater preserves some of the more outrageous aspects of the dress and mannerisms of these stylish hooligans.

The vogue for wider sleeve openings, perceived as daring and fashionable, also influenced the lengthening of the sleeve. There was a physical limit on display of the opening as long as the original kosode sleeve remained short and tubish. Longer sleeves would provide more area to embellish. Two types of ornamental border emerged at the sleeve opening: *buki*, or fabric of the kosode's lining turned back, and *fukurin*, an accent of different fabric. Black satin or cotton was favored at sleeve edges and at necklines. Whereas Western dandies at this time were accenting wrist and throat with spills of white lace, their Japanese counterparts were doing the same, in black. Young girls spent their allowances on exotic velvet and strips of patterned cloth, puffing them with light padding for greater effect.

Sleeve corners changed from the rounded *marusode* style to a sleeve with a corner edge (*sumiiri sode*) like the modern sleeve. The only garments with unsewn sleeve openings were cotton *yukata*, unlined summer robes in other fabrics, and short padded jackets called *tanzen*. Meanwhile, the originally aristocratic open-sleeve hirosode ended up as an informal or lower-class style—not extinction, but not an evolutionary success, either.

2.28 Working wear: the ultimate
fate of open sleeves

Lengthening the kosode sleeve had an unexpected side effect on the obi. In modern times it is fashionable to say that the widening of the obi somehow correlates with the degree to which women were socially oppressed in feudal Japan. Although it is easy to construe the wide obi as symbolic of oppression, such a political interpretation can only be anachronistic. The original stimulus for the growth of the obi was a by-product of the vogue for fluttering sleeves and the æsthetic urge to maintain congruent proportions in dress.

In the early decades of the Edo period, young people wore longer sleeves than adults. The side seams of their kosode were left unsewn under the arms. Maturity, among other things, meant shortening one's sleeves and sewing up the sides of the kosode. By the late 1770s, however, an adult woman's sleeve had become as long as a maiden's sleeves of yore. If these sleeves had been sewn to the sides of the kosode, free movement of the arms would have been severely inhibited. Thus from this time, women's kosode were constructed with the side seams under the arms left open and the sleeve hanging free—the form maintained in women's kimono today. Once the sleeves were detached from the sides of the kosode, the obi had both the room and the æsthetic impulse to expand.

Like kosode, the obi was originally hidden when worn. From serving as a functional and unobtrusive fastener, the obi grew in size and importance during the Edo period. Finally it claimed parallel status with the kimono as a fundamental element of Japanese costume. The early obi was either a ropelike cord (the Nagoya obi) or a narrow sash about three inches wide. And like the kosode, the early obi differed little between the sexes. The man's obi widened from three inches to a limit of six in the 1730s. Rampant growth of the obi occurred in women's dress alone.

During the early 1600s men and women alike wore a three-inch obi. By 1680, women wore an obi twice that width. Fifty years later the woman's obi was ten inches wide, and by 1800 a foot-wide obi covered a woman's torso from pubic bone to sternum. At this point, obi scarves and cords were required to hold the obi itself together.

In the beginning, the obi was usually tied in front, a 'natural' thing to do with a functional cord. Soon fashion stepped in, however, allowing leeway to tie the obi at side or back. As the obi became wider, front-tied versions became a nuisance for everyday wear. By the late seventeenth century, the obi knot had generally moved to the back. By far the most popular style of tying it was the Kichiya style (originated by a Kabuki actor of that name), described thus: "A four-inch-wide obi tied in back in a bow so as to resemble the droopy ears of a Chinese doggie." Yet even as the back-tied obi became standard, there was still room for variation. Complete standardization of tying the obi in the back was not attained until the early twentieth century.

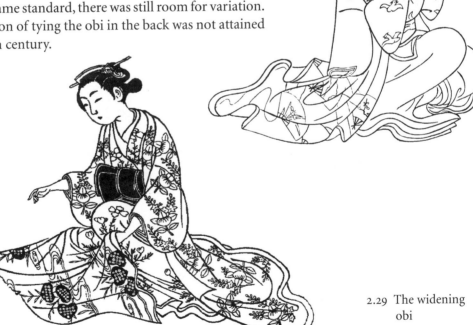

2.29 The widening obi

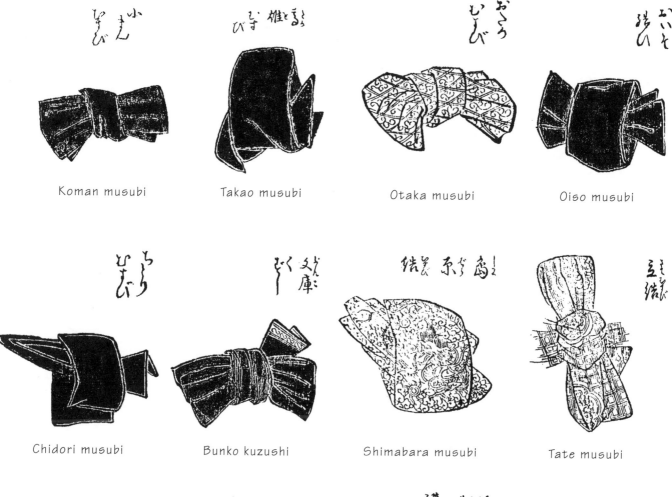

Koman musubi

Takao musubi

Otaka musubi

Oiso musubi

Chidori musubi

Bunko kuzushi

Shimabara musubi

Tate musubi

2.30 Variations on ways to tie the
obi in the seventeenth century

Rokō musubi

Darari musubi   Hitotsu musubi   Kichiya musubi   Bunko musubi

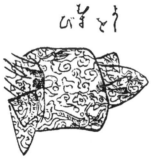

Koryū musubi   Yoshio musubi   Hikiage musubi

Shinko musubi   Hiki musubi

Any organ that has overgrown its original function seems slightly ludicrous. Like bubble-eyed goldfish, the hypertrophy of the obi has a certain charm, but is fundamentally off-putting. Even in the early stages of its growth, obi fashions were criticized thus:[7]

2.31 Dealing with excess length by hitching up kosode with the *shigoki obi*

> It used to be that the obi was narrow and tied high, so a woman's hips would then appear small. Obi were not tied in great standing bows either, so that the overall shape of the body was slim and rounded. You never saw a woman with a big derriere. But now the obi is too wide, the bow looks like a kitchen chopping board, and the general effect makes women look like targets for archery practice. This is particularly unflattering for short women.

The rise of the obi also affected kosode design composition. With its middle section progressively hidden by a wider obi tied in more elaborate bows, the kosode lost some of its dramatic unity of design. Instead of sweeping boldly down from shoulder to hem, patterns were interrupted at the waist. Taking this into account, kosode designers focused the balance of the design on the lower portion. Hems and shoulders now carried completely separate motifs. The area above the obi was much less embellished than that below.

In Western fashion, longer skirts seem to demand higher heels to maintain a sense of proportion. Likewise, longer kimono sleeves invited the obi to widen, and this in turn enjoined the skirts of kosode to lengthen. By the later eighteenth century women's kosode puddled about their feet indoors. When going out they had to hitch up the robes with an auxiliary belt called a *shigoki obi*. The mode of constructing kosode several inches longer than a person's height persists in women's kimono today. Now, however, the excess fabric is never permitted to trail. Rather, it is bloused over a hidden cord at the hips and held firmly by the obi.

2.32 An early Edo couple (*below*) wearing narrow obi—the woman's is tied in the Kichiya style; a late Edo couple (*left*) shows the disparity in the growth of the obi for women and men

2.33 The epitome of restrictive feudal dress for women: the outfit of the courtesan

Late Edo fashion for women was undeniably restrictive. The longer length of kosode meant that even the activity of walking would throw the skirts into disarray. The wider the obi and more fanciful its knot, the more it prohibited movement. Hairstyles for women had developed into the elaborate comb-studded coiffures familiar from woodblock prints. With such a coiled oiled structure on her head, a woman couldn't even sleep freely. Finally, the practice of applying lead- and mercury-based whitening cosmetics, originally a custom limited to the nobility, had now spread into common popularity. By the nineteenth century, being fashionable was truly hazardous to a Japanese woman's health.

Stylistic extremes were not limited to women in the late Edo period. One of the most striking exaggerations of human form ever seen anywhere in clothing styles is found in the formal outfit of the samurai: the *kamishimo* (upper-lower), a two-item set worn over kosode. The lower part consisted of a hakama tied at the waist. The upper section, *kataginu*, was a vestlike affair with whalebone stays stretching the material at the shoulder into stiff wings of fabric. Anything that has ever been said about the use of shoulder pads to project an image of authority in the West must apply in triplicate to the kataginu.

This set of wings developed from a formal crested court robe from which the wide sleeves had been removed, perhaps by an impatient general in the field. The sleeveless crested garment then grew across the width of the shoulders, incorporating the whalebone stiffener in the 1750s. This outfit was deemed official dress for males of the samurai class, with variations allowed to commoners on rare special occasions. So it came about that even a commoner could enhance his image of authority by sprouting wide shoulders on his wedding day, while his bride symbolically promised to forego jealousy with a special wedding headdress called a 'horn hider' (*tsuno kakushi*).

2.34 The two-piece *kamishimo*
worn over kosode by men of
the samurai class

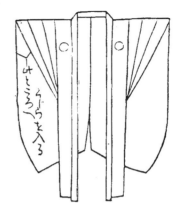

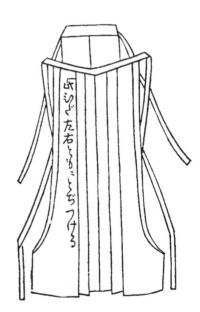

One reason Genroku gleams so brightly in retrospect is that it didn't last. Æsthetic and economic overindulgence led to sumptuary crackdowns. Stunning oversize patterns and exuberantly colored kosode disappeared by the 1720s, when the innocently lavish and radiant Genroku mode began to be replaced by the darker, sophisticated æsthetic called *iki*.

The development of iki reflects two aspects of later Edo society, one political, one stylistic. First, a pervasive aura of governmental and social repression, exemplified in sumptuary edicts, limited ostentatious display by people richer than, but socially inferior to, the samurai class. To see a merchant's wife strutting under the cherry blossoms in gold-stamped, dapple-dyed satins seemed an unbearable affront to the proper Confucian-inspired social order embraced by the ruling class. The other aspect of iki was more purely æsthetic—a reaction in terms of fashion's pendulum, swinging away from the obvious to the subtle, from bright colors to dark, and from jumbo freeform patterns to petite repeats.

Iki implies, above all, high connoisseurship. Eighteenth-century urban Japan was home to the *tsū*, the slightly jaded bon vivant who frequented the pleasure palaces in the licensed quarters—a man unstinting in his quest for a pose of casual virtuoso chic. Think of a merchant living in the city of Edo. Grown wealthy in an environment of peace by dint of careful buying and selling, he was precluded by his social class from using that wealth to attain real social or political power—all of which was reserved to the sphere of latent samurai violence. Moreover, fine clothing lavished with the gold thread, painstaking dapple dye, and sumptuous embroidery favored by the fashion-conscious Genroku city dweller had now been slashed away by governmental edicts linking consumption with social status. What was a fashion-minded person to do?

The edicts drove luxury underground—not burying it, but making it subtler and, in the process, slightly twisted. Iki was just as expensive as opulence, but it was not overt. How better to sidestep the stiff samurai who forbids you to wear gold-embroidered figured silk than to wear a

2.35 The cool nonchalance characteristic of the late Edo mode of *iki*

dark-blue striped kosode of homely wild silk—but line it in gorgeous yellow patterned crepe? Or commission the lining of your plain jacket to be painted by one of the foremost artists of the city? One got the satisfaction not only of complying with the law but also of one-upping its snobbish perpetrators. Relentless arbiters of style, the townspeople turned the fashion tables back in their favor by disdaining the gorgeous ostentation now denied them. Let the samurai and prostitutes cling to colorful brocades. Anyone with taste would turn to the subtle details marking a person as iki. To be iki, less was more.

The particularly stringent spate of sumptuary laws promulgated in the 1720s locked colorful attention-getting patterns out of reach for commoners. In their place small-scale repeat patterns (*komon*) and stripes done in dark shibui colors, such as subdued browns and off-greens, came into favor. Even ceremonial wear, usually conservative of tradition, was affected by this curious, quiet mode.

A woman's best kosode had always been extravagantly patterned. In the early eighteenth century, however, plain kosode with crests on top and pattern limited to the hem became de rigueur for women's formal dress. Formal kimono today preserve this patterning. The brightest color in the generally drab mid-Edo palette was a pale blue called *asagi-iro*, and for a period in the 1770s this pale blue dominated women's clothing.[8] Men also might have chosen it for their under-kimono—yet the favored attire for a tsū making his way to the licensed quarters remained a simple black kosode.

In late Edo Japan people dared not express their opinions for fear of reprisal. They had to keep their personal feelings under cover of social convention. By the 1820s, the passion for hidden luxury created a fad for underwear made of expensive silks and imported Indian calicoes. A kosode demurely patterned on the lower edge of its hem hinted, by the movement of a footstep, that its true beauty was hidden on the reverse. Iki denies the obverse and obvious. And the notion that what is truly valuable is hidden has political reverberations. As a mode of expression, iki flaunted the rebellious heart even while concealing it.

Iki has had far-reaching impact on Japanese æsthetics. It is still deemed better in Japan not to be too direct. The habit of veiling one's meaning in a swath of social platitudes is hard to break. Derivative iki, as social convention, works within Japan, where everyone understands the principle of facade and true feeling, but it hampers Japan mightily in its dealings with the international community. As with iki, the notion of concealing beauty and truth in places the eye cannot reach will work only when all are attuned. To non-cognoscenti, iki must appear somewhat shabby.

Growing out of the necessity to be discreet, iki made discretion its virtue. Yet it was a cool discretion, shunning the propriety of the established social order. The energy of iki lay in its streak of perversity.

In fashion, geisha were the most iki of women, and they came into their golden age at this time. A shy maiden was too innocent to be iki, a proper wife too correct. But a high-class courtesan in the licensed quarters was not iki, either—she was overdone and hemmed in by her conservative traditions. Geisha were the fashion avant-garde. Their taste in stripes, dark colors, and subdued patterns propelled the mode of iki into the consciousness of an age.

The other side of late Edo taste was a certain garishness in those places where flamboyance was allowed. An embroidered uchikake for a wedding ceremony or a prostitute's robe from this period often sported a frantic snarl of pattern and color, or a heavy paint-by-number literalness in embroidery. When the best of taste reached only for subtlety, the worst seemed to rush toward crude luxury.

Iki is fundamentally an ironic mode—if it must be explained, it has failed. What can be said of an æsthetic that prefers the oblique to the straight, the slightly off to the fresh, a whiff of the possibility of sex to the certainty of it? Iki is rebellious, never straightforward, and it shrivels under direct gaze. As the essence of the sensibilities of the politically stifled, socially jaded, yet highly creative populace of early nineteenth-century Edo, iki was ultimate cool.

KIMONO MEETS ITS MATCH   The social structure of nineteenth-century Japan was a highly differentiated stable order in which minute grades of rank, occupation, and station in life were clearly confirmed in the variety of kosode people wore. Originally transplanted from China, the kimono had evolved over the centuries without real competition, adapting ever more perfectly to the Japanese environment—like an orchid producing increasingly spectacular varieties of itself. But as kimono faced its first competitor, Western clothing, in mid-century, it was as though a frost had descended

to kill off every species except the most hardy. From the fixed and frozen version of kimono worn by Japanese women today, it is scarcely possible to imagine the rich variations of style, fabric, and accessories that made kosode the all-embracing stuff of dress and basis for fashion in Tokugawa Japan. At the turn of the twentieth century Japanese men were transfigured in starched shirts and business suits, and kimono was on its way to becoming women's wear.

2.36 The rich variety of Japanese native dress in the nineteenth century

THREE	THE KIMONO DISCOVERS ITSELF

THIS IS THE STORY of how Japanese native clothing created its own ethnicity and of how, once found, the sense of Japaneseness gradually became attached to a single form of dress—kimono. We think of kimono as Japanese clothing par excellence, but it was not always so. It took most of the momentous half century of the Meiji emperor's reign (1868–1912) for Japanese clothing to focus on the kimono and to define itself as such. The force behind this focus and definition was also new. In spite of a millennium of intense dialogue within Japan about the finest nuances of clothing, only the shock of contrast occasioned by seeing the dress of the outlandish West forced Japanese to identify what they themselves really wore. Pressed to describe something so familiar and never before in need of articulation, Japanese brought into service the word *kimono*, 'object of wear,' and meant by it what used to be called *kosode*—the basic garment of the elite urban dweller.

From the perspective of contemporary Tokyo, the flood tide has risen in favor of Western clothing in Japan. Today kimono, not to mention other now exotic forms of native dress, has but a circumscribed, specialized function. Yet however inexorable this long-term change may appear in hindsight, its course has been marked by advances and retreats, sartorial last stands and stylistic routs, carried out in the all-embracing turmoil of politics.

Unaccustomed as we are to associate clothing and politics, we are ill equipped to appreciate how complex the social fabric became in late nineteenth-century Japan. Thrust into confrontation with Western invaders at the close of the Tokugawa shogunate in the 1860s, the Meiji regime faced the challenge of entering and adapting to an international world after nearly three hundred years of self-imposed exclusion. Mirroring the precise regulation of social status the shogunal authorities had imposed on its subjects, clothing demonstrated who one was and what one could become. Thus early Meiji commoners continued to wear familiar conservative styles and dark colors. The Meiji heroes who pushed Japan out of feudalism, however, consolidated modern Japanese society in Western frock coats and high collars, investing their dominance in foreign garb.

A profound irony marks the modern emergence, flourishing, and retirement of kimono. Japanese clothing, passing from unself-conscious hegemony over its domain at mid-century, was compelled to acknowledge itself as merely ethnic clothing in a world ruled by pants and jackets. Its strongest representative, the eponymous kimono, held sway for a brief time before falling back as the bearer of social power. Only in feminine, guarded form did it live on, signifying Japaneseness in a foreign-infiltrated environment.

KIMONO
SELF-CONSCIOUSNESS

The kimono is as classic a garment as one can imagine. The drastic changes of shape, fabric, and cut found in Western fashion have few parallels throughout the centuries that the kimono-shaped robe has been worn in Japan.

How then, amid all this continuity, can kimono be said to have discovered itself? Simply put, before yōfuku there could be no wafuku. Although the garment was everywhere, there was no kimono. The kimono became recognized as such only when presented with a categorical alternative. Clothing was called by many names, each defined in terms of the others by such characteristics as length, material, occasion when worn, and so on. The Japanese had little social or linguistic need for a single term that would conceptually gather its instances into one category of clothing—such a category had no meaning, because before Meiji it had no opposite.

From Meiji on, however, the nuances that distinguished the various forms of native dress paled in comparison with the greater difference between Japanese and Western clothing. In this shift of perspective, and no doubt in answer to the Western query as to what those long-sleeved front-wrapping garments were called, Japanese said *kimono*, 'things to wear.' For themselves, in beginning to wrestle with the admixture of native and foreign that would so profoundly affect the shape of modern Japanese culture, they used the term *wafuku*, Japanese clothing, as the logical counterpart to *yōfuku*, the word coined for Western dress. Many aspects of Meiji Japan came to be distinguished as yō- or wa- in people's minds, as the arrival of a powerful, alluring, and threatening Other threw traditional culture into high relief.[1]

How Japanese clothing was named, classified, and described gives us insight into what is culturally important. Modern Japanese are used to the idea of their cultural closet having two compartments. They find it hard to imagine that kimono was not always a term of general use, or that not so long ago, when everything people wore was wafuku, the wa-ness of clothing was redundant. When a tsunami of Western culture crashed on Meiji Japan's shores, not only did new terms need to be invented for the new things of the West, but also for some Japanese things, like kimono, which were radically redefined. The former language of clothing contained few terms broad enough to be used as a generic. Most were too context-bound to convey the new meaning attached to native clothing when it suddenly found itself sharing closet space with yōfuku, the clothing of the West.

The interior language of kimono was and is a great sea of specific terms. Yōfuku provided a horizon. Once in the sea, however, the important distinction is not between birds and fish but among dozens of kinds of fish. The terms for items of native Japanese clothing implicate each other in nets of mutual reference. We are not unfamiliar with this phenomenon in English—pants, blouse, and skirt imply nothing other than themselves, whereas 'underwear' defines itself in terms of something worn over it. Most kimono terms are of this second type. Often a garment is known by a synecdoche, a significant part-for-the-whole, which gives its name meaning.

For example, the kimono called *furisode*, 'swinging sleeve,' takes its name from the part (in this case the long sleeve) that defines it as a garment for an unmarried girl. The implied point of contrast is the *tomesode*, 'truncated sleeve,' of an adult woman. The kimono called *kuro montsuki* (black crested), implies the existence of colored, non-crested kimono, whose social meaning lies in opposition to them. A kimono called *awase* (lined) says, by the same token, that there are unlined kimono and that being lined or not is significant.

Sleeves have always been a main focus of kimono—age and gender differences are expressed in their length and form, human passions are wept into their folds. Knowing this, we can understand why the most striking thing about Western clothing to Meiji Japanese was its arm-hugging tube sleeves. Kosode sleeves may have been small in comparison to the aristocratic, wide-sleeved *hirosode* of the tenth century, when the term originated, but since those faraway times kosode had outgrown its name. As Meiji Japanese searched for a word to denote their clothing, *kosode*, 'small sleeve,' was unsuitable. Kosode no longer described Japanese dress once the relevant point of contrast was with Western clothing rather than with the sleeves of other kimono.

Other terms for clothing categories were even more context-bound. Contexts included a robe's level of formality, its character as work or leisure wear, and its position in a set when worn. For example, a pre-Meiji farmer would have described what we call kimono as *nagagi*, 'long wear,' the one-piece, below-the-knee-length robe farmers put on at leisure, as opposed to the two-piece short top and leggings worn while working. Townspeople also wore nagagi, especially if their work did not involve physical labor—this, and the finer materials of their nagagi, set them apart from farmers.

Meanwhile, an urban lady might have suggested that what we call kimono was in effect her *uwagi*, 'outermost wear.' Robes were usually worn in two or three layers. Uwagi was the robe worn on top, as opposed to the *shitagi*, the 'under-wear' (not drawers or panties, but other kimono-shaped robes). Since the term *kakusode* (square sleeve) could mean the kimono gown as opposed to the *tsutsusode* (tube sleeve) of some forms of traditional work clothing, *kakusode* sometimes did duty to distinguish kimono from the cylindrically sleeved shirts and suits of the West. But as sartorial differences finally far outstripped sleeves, kakusode couldn't measure up, either.

Kimono volunteered to fill the linguistic gap. Although the term (a combination of the morphs *ki*, 'wear,' and *mono*, 'thing') was rarely used before the Meiji era, *kimono* was completely comprehensible.[2] Many clothing terms use the suffix -*gi* (the voiced suffix form of *ki*): naga-gi, uwa-gi, and shita-gi as mentioned, but also *hare*-gi, 'fancy wear,' and *fudan*-gi, 'everyday wear.' All these ki/gi things (*mono*) can be thought of as *ki-mono*. Ultimately, however, given the intense pull of the specific within the language of Japanese clothing, even the general term *kimono* quickly narrowed its reference. Now the word means a specific type of thing-to-wear—the originally urban upper-class garment become the national dress of Japan—the robe we all think of simply as kimono.

3.1 An early Meiji bureaucrat ready to face the world in modern Western attire while his wife remains at home in kimono

Changes in Meiji clothing culture were both expressions and determinants of a new national culture. Western clothing was adopted piecemeal at different times and by different groups in society. Each sector had its own reasons to wear what it wore. For men, yōfuku was promoted as more functional and more civilized than kimono. For women, Western dresses became fashion, pure and simple—it was hard to argue that bustles were more functional or comfortable than the wide obi. Ultimately, men made a more complete transition to yōfuku than did women. The upper classes and bureaucrats donned yōfuku before craftsmen and farmers did.

The radical silhouette of Western dress was not the only stimulus for clothing 'improvements.' At the same time that yōfuku was laid on the clothing corpus with dramatic results, the world of traditional clothing underwent significant changes, and many of the first instances of clothing reform occurred within the native domain. Women, for example, adopted the skirtlike masculine lower garment called a *hakama* to correspond to their new roles as students, workers, and teachers. The *haori* jacket, once reserved by law to upper-class males, enjoyed a sudden and widespread popularity among men and women in all walks of life.

As Japanese began to create an identity for themselves qua Japanese, as opposed to the regional, class, or occupational loyalties that for a thousand years had been uppermost in their self-consciousness, one tradition within the wafuku world seized preeminent status as Japanese native dress. This was, of course, kimono. The newly self-aware native dress took its cue from the rising urban middle class, the group that expanded mightily as the cities sucked people out of the villages, transforming them into the labor force of modern Japan.

Over the forty-three-year span of the Meiji emperor's reign, we can discern three phases of clothing history as the kimono adjusted to changes in society. The first decade and a half of the new era (1868–1883) was characterized by the ubiquitous phrase *bunmei kaika*, 'civilization and enlightenment.' This cultural-political mantra referred to the technological and material superiority of Western things, which Japan felt compelled to adopt as quickly as possible. Items of European apparel were handy symbols of civilization and enlightenment. They were tried on and indiscriminately mixed with the wafuku wardrobe. High button shoes, red flannel shirts, hats, and capes—all worn with kimono—were thrown together into eclectic and exuberant outfits. They were early signs of kimono's last stand as the dominant clothing of Japan.

The year 1883 marked the beginning of a brief interlude of high Westernization in the middle of the Meiji period. Kimono, along with other aspects of traditional culture, were thrust aside in favor of foreign things. Cultural historians call this the Rokumeikan period, after the name of an elegant building that had been erected to host Western-style soirées. Infatuation with Western modes was so strong that Empress Haruko proclaimed the kimono a deformity and aberration arising out of Japan's sinified imperial past. If Japanese originally wore two-piece outfits akin to Western blouses and skirts, wrote the empress (referring to the *mo* skirt of antiquity), was that not an authentic and noble precedent for modern Japanese women?

Rokumeikan fashion was followed by a sharp nativist reaction. As Japanese politicians became disillusioned with European and American civilization in the 1890s, kimono staged a triumphant comeback as an expression of Japaneseness. In the end, however, the rehabilitation of kimono was only half a victory—its revival was primarily for women, and an expression of tradition rather than fashion. An official, national version of tradition, transcending regional variation, began to radiate from the Meiji regime, centered in Tokyo. Japan became obsessed with its 'national essence' and, in looking for essence, in effect created it. Language and education were becoming standardized. So was clothing. During late Meiji, the kimono could still assert itself, yet in taking up the banner of tradition, kimono pointed the way to its future fate.

Zubon nagagutsu idedokoro ni he mo komari

"In pants and boots, what escape for a fart?"

—Anonymous *senryū* epigram, 1880

Political Haberdashery

The dawn of the Meiji era awakened a giddy sense of possibilities.[3] Entranced by civilization and enlightenment, Japan looked to Western inspiration for both. The restoration of the emperor in 1868 was in fact a momentous revolution. Displacing the shogun, Japan set in motion a bureaucracy keen to abolish feudalistic practices, eager to Westernize, and committed to promoting economic development. The ultimate success of these policies did not become clear until the turn of the century, but the novelty of Meiji state goals as reflected by society can be traced vividly in the clothes people wore.

Men were the first to be affected. The dramatic, immediate impact of Western clothing was seen at the highest social level. In the second year of the new regime, the duke of Edinburgh visited Japan. Imperial court gentlemen received him in starched shirts, pants, and swallowtail coats. Two years later, the courtiers abandoned Japan's millennium-old tradition of lacquered caps and wide-sleeved robes in favor of formal Western clothing for official government ceremonies. The emperor's proclamation of clothing reform disavowed the traditional courtly robes as, surprisingly, essentially un-Japanese:[4]

3.2 Empress Haruko attired in traditional court dress

> The national polity [*kokutai*] is firm, but manners and customs should be adaptable. We greatly regret that the uniform of our court has been established following the Chinese custom, and it has become exceedingly effeminate in style and character.... The Emperor Jimmu, who founded Japan, and the Empress Jingu, who conquered Korea, were not attired in the present

style. We should no longer appear before the people in these effeminate styles. We have therefore decided to reform dress regulations entirely.

In effect the foreign clothing was as powerful as the Western cultures it came from. Sinified court robes reflected the contemporary weakness of China itself. The adoption of Western styles of dress was a far cry from the copying process usually imputed to the Japanese. The motivation was not to mimic—it was to absorb and master the new source of power. Official approval had to be granted before potentially threatening foreign styles could be assimilated, and in order to naturalize pants and skirts, Japanese had to denounce the contemporary version of their own traditional styles as aberrant.

The imperial edict also abolished the venerable arbiters who had defined proper clothing and color combinations since the fifteenth century. Their expertise became obsolete by definition after high ceremonial costume was imported from European haberdashers. By contrast to these outmoded schools of ceremony, Japanese producers of the new, mixed genre flourished. Not every official could afford to be outfitted in France or in England. Foreign suitmakers and their Japanese apprentices in Yokohama were kept busy sewing the new silhouette of the era.

Occasionally the brave tailors were constricted by their customers' sartorial misgivings. A white linen frock coat from the early Meiji years is preserved in the Bunka Gakkuen Museum of Fashion in Tokyo. From the front, it appears to be a faithful copy of a dapper Western style for men, circa 1870. Yet embroidered at the center back seam is a family crest of sparrows and bamboo, just as one would expect on a formal kimono. Apparently it was not enough that the novel frock coat was proper attire with official recognition. The wearer felt the need to borrow a crest to reinforce due level of dignity.

3.3   The young Emperor Meiji at the beginning of his reign

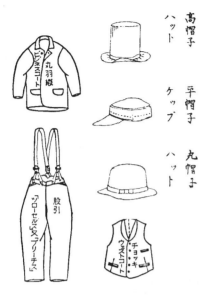

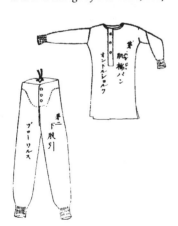

3.4 Illustrations from Fukuzawa Yukichi, *The Clothing, Food, and Dwellings of the West*, 1867

The military also donned Western-style uniforms in early Meiji. These were not imported but produced domestically—another consequence of the urge to absorb. Wool was an exotic fabric to the sheepless Japanese. The government sent students to France and Germany to learn the technique of making worsted wool and sponsored the building of woolen mills with public money. Once the means of processing wool became available, it came into great vogue not only for uniforms but also for kimono, obi, and a new hybrid style of overcoat.

The sudden demand for wool fabric for uniforms, and even more for kimono fashions, stimulated the development of Japan's textile industry. Just as the Industrial Revolution in England had begun a generation earlier on mechanized looms, Japan turned to textiles as the enterprise to launch its program of industrialization. It would not be exaggerating to say that, prefiguring the era of steel, cars, and high technology, the demand for new apparel fabricated the rise of the modern Japanese economy.

During early Meiji, Japan was a discriminating student of the Western world. After careful comparison, Japanese political leaders and bureaucrats chose to set up their educational system on the model of Germany, their army on the French system, and their postal service on the American model. In 1870 naval cadets were all put into British-style uniforms. Army cadets marched *à la mode française*. The following year police and mailmen were issued uniforms with tubular sleeves and pants. The increasing official presence of yōfuku inspired eclecticism in the dress of the general population:[5]

> The yōfuku of the world is strange and wonderful. A man can wear a Prussian cap on his head, French shoes on his feet, the jacket of an English sailor, and American military dress trousers. A woman will wrap her *juban* [underkimono] closely about her, wearing a man's long wool overcoat on top. The ordinary Japanese citizen drapes himself in clothing stripped from the world.

All this amazement stemmed not from lack of primers about the elements of Western clothing but rather from unfamiliarity with the ensemble. Social reformer Fukuzawa Yukichi (1835–1901) had visited the United States and Europe as a member of Japan's first shogunal delegation abroad in 1860. At that point Japan's future political course and method of dealing with the West were far from clear. Members of the delegation all wore kimono, with the addition of hakama and haori for official occasions. Fukuzawa recognized that Japanese were perceived as freakish and exotic by most Westerners in part because of their clothing. When he returned to Japan, he wrote a pamphlet called *The Clothing, Food, and Dwellings of the West*, to familiarize the Japanese population with the mode of the future.[6]

How strange his haberdashery phrasebook must have appeared to the Japanese reader. (Try pronouncing the Japanese quickly):

Ondoru shorutsu	A juban worn next to the skin
Zurōwarusu	A kind of momohiki worn under the *buriichisu*
Howaito shatsu	A juban worn over the *ondorshatsu*
Franeru shatsu	A wool juban worn above the others
Sospendoru	Buriichisu hangers
Sutokkingu	Tabi
Tsurōserusu (or *buriichisu*)	Momohiki
Koraru	The part that goes around the neck
Nekkitai	Holds the *kara* closed
Bijinesu kōto	A curved haori
Furokku kōto	A divided haori

For the upper-class, stylish, or bureaucratic Japanese male, strangeness gave way to charm and then familiarity. The trend-setting kabuki actor Onoue Kikugoro wore pants and boots in his dressing room.

He was said to study Western books while sitting in an exotic device called a chair.[7]

In the early Meiji years woolens were imported and tailors were rare. Traditional dress had not required tailoring. Drygoods merchants sold bolts of cloth in a standard kimono width, and women of the household made it into the required article of clothing. Sewing formed a major part of women's work, for although it was not difficult—straight seams and minimal piecing—it was constant. Wafuku was taken apart and re-sewn at each washing. The home seamstress would have fainted at the idea of the complicated fitting required for Western dress. Since the making of clothing was not a professional activity, there was no pre-existing group that might logically have made the switch to sewing yōfuku. The profession of tailor had to be created from whole cloth.

3.5   Women starching kimono cloth and sewing clothing at home

Because of the expense of wool and the difficulty of finding a tailor, an entire yōfuku ensemble was prohibitively expensive for most people. But because wearing yōfuku was itself a political message, even a few pieces could convey the desired effect. A *shappō*, as a hat (*chapeau*) came to be called in Japanese, or a Western-style umbrella that when unfolded reminded Japanese of bat wings, were easy additions to a wardrobe. They proclaimed their owners aware of the new mode of enlightenment. A Western-style buttoned-up flannel shirt peeking out at the neckline of a kimono was likewise relatively easy to manage. With a bit more money, a man could buy a pair of leather shoes, or perhaps a watch.

The look of enlightenment also affected traditions of personal grooming. How a man wore his hair in early Meiji proclaimed his political passions. In place of the shaven pate and oiled topknot, a *zangiri atama*, or cropped head, signified a modern attitude. As if people's heads were gongs reverberating politics, a popular ditty claimed that if you tapped a head bearing a topknot, it would ring with the sound of the old order, whereas a cropped head would sing out civilization and enlightenment.

3.6 Kimono and hakama worn with shoes and hat, c. 1875

3.7 Dandy in kimono plus overcoat carrying a Western-style bat-wing umbrella, c. 1871

3.8 Hairstyles for men: the traditional teawhisk and topknot (*left*), chestnut burr and *zangiri* of Meiji (*right*)

In 1877, after a decade under the new regime, the Meiji government weathered its last serious internal challenge. The Satsuma Rebellion was a doomed reactionary protest against the influx of Western customs and ideas, which the rebels believed were destroying Japan's traditional samurai spirit. Rebel forces led by ultra-patriot Saigō Takamori from the southern domain of Satsuma, dressed in traditional silk *patchi* leggings and wielding swords, were no match for the uniformed, firearm-bearing national army. The uprising was crushed within a few months. Yet Saigō's obvious sincerity and spirit struck a chord of sympathy in the Japanese people. Though technically a traitor, he was a most noble and loyal one. People expressed their admiration for Saigō the man, if not his ideas, by wearing an ikat-woven indigo-and-white pattern called *Satsuma kasuri*. The stuff of peasant dress became the rage all over Tokyo. A voguish olive-brown color known as *uguisu-cha* was renamed Saigō-brown in his honor. The sons of Edo were not about to join Saigō in his noble lost cause, but as radical chic they were keen to incorporate his spirit into kimono fashion.

The Unraveling Thread

Some women daringly attempted to adopt the spirit of Western clothes in the early Meiji years, but they were few. Outside of a small coterie of unruly students, trendy geisha, and foreigners' mistresses, most women regarded yōfuku as ancillary—something to accessorize their kimono. But popular clothing fads in early Meiji almost all derived from Western sources. An *erimaki*, or collar-winder, was a scarf or shawl worn over kimono. The use of a white *toweru* as a scarf was an early craze that disappeared leaving a trace of embarrassment when people realized that a towel was in fact a utilitarian article for drying the body rather than a piece of Western vogue. (Rumor then resurrected the toweru as a marvelous Western invention: a washcloth that required no soap.)[8] Men favored muffler-length white silk crepe erimaki that were looped about the neck several times. Square-cut plaid shawls came into fashion in the 1880s. Men wore shawls, too, draping them with equanimity over kimono or business suit.

By and large, changes in women's clothing during the early Meiji years were confined to rummaging about within the wafuku closet. The most notable example was the use of men's hakama over kimono to create a public form of dress for women. When female textile workers were first issued uniforms in the sixth year of Meiji, they were given hakama. Female students and teachers also wore hakama and sometimes shoes.

3.9 Throughout the last two decades of the nineteenth century, shawls were popular with men as well as women

3.10 White neckwinders pulled up over the mouth

3.11 Second-class train passengers displaying a typical Meiji mixture of native and Western styles

At the time of the Meiji Restoration, Western women were wearing crinolines—wide, flounced skirts spread over a supporting hoop. Except for a few flamboyant prostitutes in Nagasaki who donned them for exotic impact, crinolines had little impact on Japanese women. Geisha were among the first women to adopt exotic foreign outfits as something more than accessories. According to one newspaper report from 1872: "Some people will try anything. There's a young geisha-in-training in Sakamoto-cho who has become the talk of the town by pouring sake for customers with her hair all done up in Nanking pigtails and wearing a Western dress."[9]

Japanese women, usually from the licensed quarters, who became mistresses to Western men were called *rashamen*, a hybrid term meaning roughly 'wool women' (Dutch *rassen* and English 'women') because they always appeared in public in foreign dress. Contemporary Japanese were astonished at how these ladies walked arm in arm with their men. The Westerners opened doors for them, behaving with a diffused gallantry toward women that Japanese found incomprehensible.

3.12 The crinoline fashion of the 1860s

The intractable coeds of Meiji adopted a different semi-Western, reformed mode. Period cartoons portray them in pompadours and hakama striding through the streets, putting on airs of Western learning, dreaming of boys, and gathering to munch sweet potatoes with their dorm mates. These high-spirited girls helped popularize a full-length, unisex, padded student overcoat (*shosei haori*). It projected overtones of Bohemian nonchalance for several decades.

A few women cropped their hair, but these courageous souls were simply regarded as weird. A newspaper editorial written in the fifth year of Meiji (1872) complained:[10]

3.13 The stereotype of the brash Meiji coed, tucking a roasted sweet potato in her sleeve

> A woman with cropped hair is practically indecent. Although we see such creatures in the cities now, such a practice did not exist of old, nor do we see it among women of the cultured countries of the West. This reprehensible custom is unbearably ugly. In any country, a gentle and temperate lady has long hair which she dresses. Do they think they are the images of enlightenment, these self-satisfied faces who have thrown away their long black hair? They go about in men's hakama over their wide obi, geta on their feet, sleeves rolled up, and carrying books of Western learning. They are absurd.

If cutting the hair short was too radical, as public reaction attests, women's hair did gain a new option in the *sokugami* style, a pompadour resembling the chignons worn by Charles Dana Gibson's popular Gibson girls. The further the front section, or 'eaves,' of the hair protruded, the more daring the style. The sokugami style bunched the hair, coiling it in a bun at the crown of the head. Unlike traditional coiffures, sokugami did not require the heavy use of pomade, pins, bars, strings, and false hair to hold its shape. Its appeal was promoted as healthier and more rational—hence, more enlightened—than the old ways. Before women appeared in Western dress in any numbers, the new sokugami hairstyle worn with kimono marked a progressive

3.14 A stylish young man wearing a student overcoat, neckwinder, and rakish hat

3.15 Common traditional hairstyles: the *shimada*, *icho-gaeshi*, and *marumage*

attitude. It also swept the hair up from the nape, altering the way Meiji women wore the collars of their kimono.

The most startling cosmetic change affecting Meiji women was their abandonment of the custom of *ohaguro*, 'teeth-blackening.' Modern sensibilities are hard put even to imagine how black teeth could have been thought attractive, but they were—for centuries. The practice of mixing ferrous metal filings with an acidic liquid, letting it sit for months, and then painting the vile-smelling fluid on one's teeth seems a cosmetic atrocity akin to neck-stretching, lip plugs, or beehive hairdos. The muss and fuss involved was considerable, since ohaguro had to be reapplied every few days.[11]

During the Edo period, teeth blackening and shaving the eyebrows had been marks of adult or married status for women. Letting both

3.16 A Gibson girl, and Meiji women wearing variations on the new *sokugami* hairstyle

return to their natural state must have made Japanese wives and mothers suddenly feel young again. The empress appeared publicly with unblackened teeth in the sixth year of Meiji. The women of Japan followed her example. When a man cut off his stiffly waxed plug of a ponytail in favor of a short zangiri-cut, or a woman let her eyebrows grow in and her black teeth fade to white, they experienced most intimately and personally the liberation from feudalism proclaimed by the new Meiji era.

Early Meiji mixes consisted of slapdash combinations of geta with pants, kimono with shoes. By the 1880s a more stable stylistic blending occurred. Wool, the popular new fabric, was styled into new kinds of overcoats, such as the Inverness, or *tonbi*, a sleeveless cloak with attached cape, adapted to wearing over the baggy sleeves of kimono. Women embraced a hybrid style called the Azuma coat, which became a standard addition to the wardrobe of every urbanite.[12]

3.17 Tying one's kimono with a soft *shigoki* obi and combining the outfit with Western shoes created a new casual look for men, c. 1872

By this time domestic spinning and dyeing factories had improved in both quality and production of goods. Wool muslin began to be used as material for women's haori, obi, and kimono lining. One thing that did not change much was color preference. Even though new garments and new materials were adopted, æsthetic acceptability still tended toward the darker colors of the old regime: blues, grays, and browns for everyone, and perhaps a dusky purple for women. Garments were usually monochrome and unpatterned. What patterns there were tended to be simple woven ones: stripes, plaids, lattice, or ikat.

3.18 The French military-inspired overcoat called *tonbi* (hawk) overtook the native *kappa* (river sprite) raincoat in early Meiji

3.19 Women (*opposite*) adopted the new hybrid Azuma coat

Hōreta okata wa minna tsutsusode de, sugaru tamoto no nai tsurasa

All the girls are wearing tube sleeves—
Nothing to tug on, thus
No way to flirt

—Anonymous *senryū* epigram, 1880

Although early Meiji leaders of the New Japan had made great strides in uniting the country internally for the task of modernization, Japan still chafed in its foreign relations. Unequal treaties forbade Japan to raise tariffs to slow the great influx of foreign goods. Legal extraterritoriality was still in force. These two points were particularly sore for the Meiji government. Believing that such treatment was due to foreign perceptions of Japan as backward and uncivilized, Meiji leaders thought somewhat naively that if they could recreate the forms and trappings of European high society in Tokyo, they would demonstrate to the world that Japan was a cultured nation on anyone's terms, and as such would merit the lifting of the unequal treaties. To this end, an elegant building, the Hall of the Baying Stag, or Rokumeikan, was erected as a showpiece of high civilization. There Japanese hosted soirées including Western music, knife-and-fork dining, and ballroom dancing.

Meiji leaders Inoue Kaoru and Itō Hirobumi were the strongest proponents of this program of social simulation. They instructed their women to study English, learn to knit, abandon traditional hairstyles, eat meat, wear Western clothes, and learn to dance. Thus accomplished in the arts of the West, the women could appear in corseted gowns and dance with foreign dignitaries at the Rokumeikan. The prospect must have terrified them, but as obedient Japanese wives and daughters, they gave it a good try. Still, to achieve all aspects of Westernization at once

Progressive Representations

was a daunting task. Even the patriarchs of the policy had to allow for some backsliding. Iwakura Sakurako, who as a young girl had taken part in this grand etiquette experiment, wrote, "In order to coax us to eat meat, father agreed to buy us all new kimono."[13]

The bustle, which had briefly dropped out of fashion in the West between 1876 and 1880, returned with a vengeance just when Japanese elite women took their first true plunge into ladies' yōfuku. Suddenly the waist, ignored in kimono, was highlighted by a laced corset, a bosom above, and curvaceous hips below. Feet accustomed to soft cloth tabi and thonged geta were enclosed in leather shoes. Corseted and shod, Japanese ladies occasionally fainted on the dance floor of the Rokumeikan.

Unused to exposing limbs, backs, and bosom as prescribed by the fashion of Western evening wear, Japanese women made some modifications to cover themselves. Empress Haruko herself favored high-necked gowns and had insets made for overly décolleté French dresses.

3.20 Bustled geisha sneaking a smoke between dances at the Rokumeikan in 1888

One catty rumor attributed much of contemporary modesty to the fact that many of the rulers' wives were ex-geisha whose backs bore the scars of moxa cautery, a folk remedy popular among women of that class. True or not, geisha were frequently pressed into service to fill the ladies' ranks at Rokumeikan events. In any case, coquettish dress, dancing, mixing with men—behavior now enjoined for women of the elite—was not the sort of thing that samurai wives and daughters had been brought up to feel comfortable doing. Rokumeikan duty must have been painful for some of them. Undoubtedly some refused. Geisha, however, were right in their element.

During the first year of Rokumeikan parties, many royal ladies still appeared in the scarlet hakama and *hakki* (kimono-shaped over-robe) they were used to wearing for courtly functions. Even in its third year, Rokumeikan kibitzers estimated that the mix of wa- and yō- styles worn by the ladies was about half and half. Dresses received their biggest boost from the empress herself in 1886. In August Empress Haruko and her attendants, all attired in Western dress, attended opening ceremonies at a new hospital. The public impact was tremendous, resulting in the first strong current of yōfuku fashions for women. In January 1887, newspapers published the following "opinion on Western clothing" from the Meiji empress to her female subjects:[14]

> Imperial regulations have applied to women's clothing since ancient times. In the time of Emperor Shōmu an ordinance prescribed a new form of costume for women. At that time, women's clothing consisted of an upper garment and a skirt. Some women were extravagant in the numbers of layers they wore, so henceforth they were prohibited from doing so. From that time, most women wore a single red divided skirt. During the age of civil wars [fourteenth century] the skirt was abandoned and the upper garment lengthened to the point where it covered both legs. In the mid-seventeenth century the obi was

widened. These tendencies foreshadow the deformed shape our dress has taken today, namely the exclusive use of a long upper garment to the total atrophy of the lower....

Now when we regard women's Western clothing we note that it consists of an upper garment and a skirt, and thus accords with our ancient system of dress. Not only is it suitable for the due performance of ceremony, it also allows for freedom of movement. It is thus entirely appropriate that we adopt Western-style tailoring.

As we bend our efforts to this reform, however, we must take care to use only domestically produced materials. If we do so, we will aid manufacturing techniques, advance art, and assist business. In this way the benefits will extend beyond the manufacture of clothing to society at large....This is my sincere aspiration for the reform of women's dress.

During the earlier clothing reform, the men of the court denounced traditional styles as Chinese and effete, hence contrary to true Japanese spirit. Here, the empress declared the kimono with obi to be a deformed version of the original dress of the ancient Japanese. Unlikely as it might seem, she endorsed Western-style two-piece dressing as closer in spirit to true Japaneseness.

With imperial blessing, the wearing of Western dresses spread from the ladies of the upper classes to the growing group of educated middle-class women. Western dress became the uniform of the 'new woman.' During the late 1880s and 1890s, the wives of officials and female teachers and students appeared regularly in dresses rather than kimono. As one newspaper noted, "In Osaka, Western dresses and pompadours have been all the rage since the publication of the imperial opinion. Fifty or sixty dress shops are now open, and the wages of dressmakers have soared. Also, recently we have seen a great vogue for Women's Improvement Clubs, Women's Education Associations, and all sorts of things aimed at improving the state of women."[15]

Geisha, too, proud of their reputation of being in the vanguard of fashion, were not left behind during the heyday of yōfuku stylistic innovation. Geisha appeared in public wearing black silk taffeta gowns with gold earrings and bracelets. They constructed their hair in 'eaves' and even wore leather shoes right onto the tatami mats of teahouses. The Shimbashi geisha performed a group dance number all in dresses. Even the conservative ladies of pleasure in Kyoto's venerable Shimabara district for a time enticed their customers with exotic Western ruffles, flounces, and pompadours.

Two decades into the Meiji reign, one would have had to search deep into the countryside to find a man with uncropped hair or a woman who still blackened her teeth. Western clothing was no longer a novelty. In the cities, the wafuku version of men's lower body wear disappeared. Western-style *zubon*, pants, completely displaced traditional momohiki and patchi from their sartorial niche. The daily *Yomiuri shimbun* reported in 1888 that "the convenience of crisply worn Western clothing goes without saying. Now that Japan is a military nation, we think it particularly commendable that the wearing of Western clothes has increased."[16]

3.21 A geisha gussied up in the latest Western costume is designated a "singer in the movement for progress," 1887

Rationalization
and Restrictions

During the eighties the Japanese became more sophisticated about what it meant to wear yōfuku. Gone was the crazyquilt mix of West and East seen in the early years of Meiji, when a single piece of yōfuku could be a potent talisman of modernity, even when worn atop kimono. As the policies of the Meiji government made themselves felt throughout the realm, the image of its Western-suited leaders was emulated by all those males who felt themselves to be men of Meiji. Men usually changed to kimono once in the privacy of their homes, but the male clothing standard for the bureaucratic workplace and school was fast turning to Western suits. Farmers continued to wear their traditional, regionally diverse work clothing, but even they were likely to put on a suit (*sebiro*, from 'Savile') for formal occasions. The notion of different wardrobes for different aspects of life now began to push men's kimono ever deeper into the private sphere.

Clothing change coincided not only with separation of place—workplace and home—but also with separation of activity, one that corresponded closely to work versus leisure. This came to seem quite natural to men, who began to consider their 'double life' of old and new,

3.22 Under their kimono men wore leggings called *momohiki*, tucking the kimono up at the waist as shown by the two figures at right; by the 1890s momohiki had become a rarity as men switched to pants, like the bureaucrat above

Eastern mode and Western mode, as a purely functional adaptation to social change. Yōfuku was deemed functional for a workplace furnished with chairs and desks. Wafuku was said to be more functional for the tatami mats of the home. As late as the first decade of the twentieth century a Japanese could write:[17]

> There appears to be little ground for the prediction often made by European writers that Japanese national dress is doomed. So long as Japanese houses remain radically unchanged and we are forced to squat on the mat, Japanese clothes cannot be dispensed with. European clothes are not comfortable to squat in, as the body cannot be kept quite straight, the collar presses on the throat, the waistcoat gets creasy, the trousers soon become baggy about the knees, and the socks are but poor protection against the cold since they cannot be hidden under the skirt of Japanese dress.

Of course, the important assumption here was "so long as Japanese houses remain unchanged." If kimono was made for the floor, Western dress was made with the chair in mind. To wear kimono in a chair is as

3.23 Couple relaxing at home in kimono

3.24 *Tokyo Puck* in 1911 depicting typical Meiji figures: housewife, child, and bureaucrat, c. 1895 (*above*); maiden and dandy, 1903

excruciating as the above description of wearing yōfuku on the floor. In any case, to the extent that men continued to wear kimono, they wore it chiefly at home. Men's wafuku became leisure wear rather than work or ceremonial clothing. If a man wears native dress at all today, he wears the casual cotton yukata, the most relaxed of wafuku informal wear.

More broadly speaking, as the somewhat artificial glow of Rokumeikan ideals faded, the clothing philosophies of men and women began to diverge. As Western suits were becoming standard for men, women's wear was beginning to revert to native styles.

Yōfuku had never made inroads as deep into women's wear as it had into men's. Nevertheless the reaction to the extreme forms of Westernization characterizing high society of the Rokumeikan years stung female yōfuku fashions. The word was out that wearing a corset could be hazardous to a woman's health. The ordinary Japanese woman went back to kimono. In 1890, the magazine *Fūzoku gahō* (Customs pictorial) noted: "If we look at what women are wearing these days, the breeze called 'restore antiquity' is definitely blowing in the cities. Except for a few ladies of the nobility, hardly any women are wearing Western clothes this year."[18]

The only women who still aspired to European fashion were the high nobility and wives of officials in the foreign office. They inherited the new hourglass figure and leg-of-mutton sleeves of the 1890s.

To some foreign eyes, reversion was a welcome trend. In 1906, an anonymous foreigner living in Tokyo was interviewed by a reporter for *Jogaku sekai* (Coed world) about Japanese women in Western dress:[19]

> Japanese women wearing Western clothing is something, forgive me, that simply doesn't suit them. The first reason is that the Japanese are always bending over and their bodies have developed a tendency to stoop. Western dresses require a figure that emphasizes the chest thrust forward and full hips, yet in Japan both are denigrated. Another problem is that Japanese women

turn their feet inward instead of outward as they walk, which does not enhance the look of a Western skirt. I must mention one more thing. Fashion in the West changes at an unbelievably rapid rate from season to season, yet Japanese women, unaware, continue to wear the same styles on and on. From the point of view of a Westerner's eyes, it is very strange to see our clothing worn by the Japanese.

Tsuneko Gantlett, writing for the magazine *Fujin gahō* (Women's illustrated), reminisced about her return from Europe to Japan at the turn of the century: "[At that time] a Japanese woman in Western dress was a rarity among rarities. If one ventured out wearing such an outfit, people in the street would stare and ricksha pullers would snicker within one's hearing. I was utterly astounded when I experienced this."[20] No wonder Tsuneko was confused. At the time she had left Japan some years before, it had not been at all unusual for women of means to wear Western dresses in public.

3.26 A Gibson girl wearing the puffed sleeve of the 1890s

3.27 A *kaisha-in*, or what would today be called a *sarariman*, wearing a fashionably high collar

The kimono ensemble for women was also becoming standardized. By mid-Meiji, all women, young and old, noble and commoner, were tying the obi in back. A front-tied obi formerly was an indication that a girl had passed into adulthood, and it distinguished the dress of married and unmarried women. By the 1880s, however, only prostitutes in the licensed quarters, crones over age sixty, and widows tied the obi in front.

The reasons for reaction in clothing were again rooted in politics and thought. The late 1880s were a time of unprecedented ideological ferment in Meiji Japan. A new constitution twenty years in the making was about to be set in place—an event that highlighted the question of the nature of Japan's nationhood. Notions of the state (*kokka*) and the people (*kokumin*) dominated intellectual debate. Everyone became concerned that the citizenry should have a clear sense of nation in order to proceed safely, as a united front, along the path toward modernity.

Reassertions of indigenous culture were an important part of this ideological upheaval. Although progressive and forward-looking men of the rising middle class debated such issues in their high collars and suits, their wives quietly returned to wearing national dress. The tensions between East and West, old and new, were partly relieved by this division of cultural labor, as it were, according to which women took on the role of conservators of tradition.

A feeling grew that Japan had gone too far in aping everything Western. This feeling was expressed in the term *hai kara* (high collar), a clothing metaphor that described people who facilely adopted Western trappings and attitudes. The original 'high collars' were the Japanese foreign ministers who went abroad and came back having accomplished nothing, as far as some satirists could see, except to learn how to wear their Western high collars and fancy suits.

During the nineties, the previous era of high Westernization came to be seen as something of an embarrassment. National pride was much assuaged by Japan's victory in the Sino-Japanese War in 1895. Kimono fashion reflected the ebullient sense of a nation victorious. Women's haori linings, collars, and children's kimono sported patterns of cherry blossoms to reflect the samurai spirit. Chrysanthemum, the imperial flower, crossed with rising sun flags, demonstrated patriotism. Grade-school girls in Tokyo, who had been put into Western-style dresses for school uniforms a decade before, were rewrapped in kimono. Western uniforms for schoolgirls were not seen again until the 1920s.

3.28 Georges Bigot satirizes "Monsieur et madame stepping out," 1887

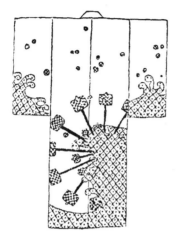

3.29 Meiji versions of the Genroku revival of exuberant pattern

Two clothing distinctions are characteristic of late Meiji—from the late nineties to the emperor's death in 1912. The first was the divergence of clothing of the workplace from that of the home for urban men. The second was a concomitant division of yōfuku for men, kimono for women. Wafuku had already conceded its authority in menswear. Although men continued to relax in kimono for another thirty years, they carried out the important business of life in Western clothes. Meanwhile, on the feminine side, there was a great proliferation of types of kimono, each with its appropriate social and seasonal level. Pattern and color exploded and multiplied, stimulating a renascence of exuberant design recalling the Genroku era in the early seventeenth century.

From roughly the turn of the century to the start of World War I, kimono made its last stand as the primary clothing for women. Women's wafuku reflected class divisions in how it was worn, lines that can still be discerned faintly even today, but one trend gained ascendancy. The future of kimono lay in the style worn by women of the growing urban middle class. These women had been most affected by the rational hairdo movement, reformed dress in school, and perhaps even briefly, corsets. They all wore kimono during the last years of Meiji. Furthermore, the kimono they chose reflected their striving to appear proper by classic Japanese standards—that is, according to a reinterpreted version of the clothing style of the old samurai class.

Although the aristocracy did not discard Western dress during late Meiji, the persistent bourgeois ambition to be high class was a powerful tool in refashioning the forms of the old order. At the same time, forty years' experience of Western clothing, its æsthetic proportions and social meanings, could not help but subtly influence the way middle-class women's kimono came to be worn. Because women's wafuku was not yet frozen into a 'traditional' statement (as it has become today), its renascent reflection of fashion early in this century unconsciously showed Western elements even while proclaiming its Japaneseness.

How does the Meiji kimono differ from what we see in the late twentieth century? In terms of construction, Meiji sleeves were a bit longer than modern, but the main difference lay in the way kimono was worn. Today, interest focuses on the standard set of kimono plus obi. In Meiji times, peripheral furnishings provided just as much scope for æsthetic display. This was an age of padded hems, contrasting linings, layered sets, and colored collars. The modern kimono seems rather flat in comparison to the multidimensional ensembles worn by Meiji women.

One of the most striking characteristics of Meiji women's wafuku, for example, was its presentation in layered sets (*o-tsui*) of two or three garments. The outermost, the uwagi, corresponded to today's kimono. Underneath the uwagi were one, two, or three shitagi (underlayers), showing slightly at bosom, sleeve, and hem. A formal kimono consisted of a coordinated set of uwagi and shitagi in which the patterns might reflect associated trios of subjects. Even informal kimono were usually layered at least in pairs. Modern Japanese take it for granted that a kimono is one robe unless otherwise described. The reverse was true in Meiji—kimono were assumed to be layered unless specifically referred to as single garments.

Meiji kimono also differ from those of today in the prominence of detail. An example is the section of padded lining showing at the hem and sleeve openings. Often in a contrasting color, the fashionable appeal of the *fuki*, as these protrusions were called, ultimately harks back to the aristocratic eleventh-century æsthetic of layered colors. The fuki was more or less heavily padded at the hem depending on the wearer's age and level of ceremony. A silk kimono on a young girl might show as much as two inches of padded lining. A cotton kimono would have less, as would a garment worn by an older woman. A woman trying to disguise her age might show her linings more than was appropriate, although she risked being ridiculous if the discrepancy were too great. By late Meiji such fine distinctions were on the wane.

3.30 Unmarried girl in triple-layered formal kimono

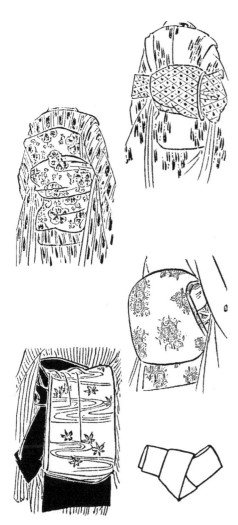

3.31 Styles of obi popular in late Meiji, for girls (*above*) and women, as compared to the simple knot of a man's obi

The immediate forebear of the fashion of the fuki was the trailing, thickly padded hem (*hikisuso*) worn by aristocratic ladies and high prostitutes of the Edo period. These women, who spent most of their lives indoors in elegant attire, knew that a trailing hem held a more pleasing shape and was easier to walk in if weighted with a thick roll of cotton. Trailing kimono were still seen as formal dress for women of good family throughout the Meiji era, but they gradually fell out of favor for anything but the highest ceremony.

We can gain perspective on the Meiji kimono by looking backwards from the present, but the Meiji kimono was also distinctive compared to late Edo period robes. In this context, the greatest change was the abolition of old rigid class distinctions. Anyone having the means could wear styles previously reserved to the elite. Upper-class women's robes, swirling and trailing about their feet, were invariably longer than their bodies were tall. Only those who labored wore closer-fitting kosode. Ironically, the snob appeal of excess fabric coincided with the beginning of more mobility for women. What to do with this redundant length? Blouse it over a narrow sash tied at the hip into a fold called *ohashori*.

Today, even though kimono are never allowed to trail, it would be unthinkable to make one actually short enough to fit. Once expedient, the ohashori has become a useless but æsthetically required part of kimono's gestalt. Trailing hems are preserved today in only two cases: geishas' top-drawer kimono for entertaining, and the formerly aristocratic over-robe known as uchikake, which has been adopted into the modern version of the traditional wedding kimono ensemble.

More kinds of obi existed in everyday use during Meiji years than exist now, but the basic forms and placement of the folds remain the same. During the Edo period, however, the obi was tied in a range of idiosyncratic variations. Meiji wafuku convention standardized a few styles and dictated that the the folds invariably be placed in back. The most common form of obi-tying in Meiji, and still standard today, is the *taiko* style—a boxy pouf. The Meiji woman wore a slightly wider obi than is used nowadays, and she tied her taiko somewhat larger and rounder than the skimpy squares we see today. Then, as now, a taiko tied relatively high imports a sense of propriety, and one tied low (as the geisha do) is more voluptuous.

Kimono underwear is another area of interesting, if unseen, difference. The modern white or pastel underwear æsthetic determines the appearance of the *nagajuban*, the kimono under-robe. In Meiji, by contrast, even older women wore scarlet crepe or colorfully patterned under-robes. Still earlier, during the feudal age, when bright colors and silks were forbidden to commoners, people who wore them did so secretly, under their plain browns and blues. This led to the development of an æsthetic of high understatement in which a tiny flash of red seen as a woman flicked her skirts was deemed much more interesting than a blatantly red garment, exposed to all eyes in its entirety.

The under-robe has a detachable collar called the *han-eri*. This attached collar is the only part of kimono underwear that is visible when a woman is dressed. Today the han-eri is by convention white, peeking out as a sliver of a V-shape under the kimono crossover neckline. In the Meiji period, however, the han-eri appeared in any number of colors and was often embroidered. Since the kimono was not crossed so tightly over it, the undercollar was more prominently displayed. All in all, the effect was less tightly prim than today. But whether one wore one's kimono primly or with panache during the Meiji era was less a mark of personality than one of class.

3.32 Meiji girl wearing sokugami and wide decorated collars

A Mark of Class

Class differences in urban women's kimono continued their influence from the Edo period into early Meiji. In Tokyo, the most evident split was that between the garment as worn by the merchant-class 'low city' heirs to the spirit of old Edo versus that worn by the bourgeois of the 'high city,' high-collar, and highfalutin new elite. The intensely urban *shitamachi* (Edward Seidensticker's 'low city') had its own style, which it considered the height of sophistication. The *yamanote*, or high city district, was more heavily flavored by samurai culture. Its inhabitants tended either to show off or to stand stiffly on their dignity—such, at least, thought the low city. Nevertheless, the fashion future of the kimono lay in the high city, from where it gradually influenced, then rooted out, the more plebeian sexy styles of the shitamachi.

In early Meiji, for example, the outfit that epitomized the taste of a young woman from the low city was a kimono of yellow plaid *kihachijō* in taffeta or a similar stiff silk, with an attached black satin collar (*kake-eri*). This strip of black satin sewed over the kimono collar was never affected by the genteel high-city ladies. Its origin may have been utilitarian, perhaps to hide the soil from oiled hair or grime from daily chores, but its wearers fancied the black overcollar a downtown fashion accessory—a dramatic, nape-enhancing accent.

Low-city ladies lavished much care choosing the color and pattern of the detachable silk collars of their underkimono. But high-city ladies favored plain white or pale unpatterned collars, the almost universal style of today. An elderly geisha I know suggested that the appearance and popularity of white undercollars in the Meiji era was directly due to influence of the look of a white blouse worn under a dark suit jacket. She may be right. Meiji-era photographs show women wearing brooches at the closure of their white kimono undercollars, just as foreign English teachers wore them at the throats of their high-necked white blouses.

How was it that the bourgeois fashion began to gain the ascendancy? Playwright Hasegawa Shigure describes the ambiance in a work titled *Zuihitsu kimono* (Essays on kimono):[22]

> The girls from the low city thought the high city mode [of wearing kimono] was not chic at all. Yet at the same time, they could not avoid being impressed by the image of the 'new

3.33 A Meiji schoolmarm wearing a brooch at the throat of her kimono neckline, 1908

3.34 The pensive 'new woman' of
Meiji, Western-style ruffled
blouse visible at her sleeve

intellectual woman' projected by such a style. As a result, they took the black satin collars off their kimono and began wearing white unpatterned collars for their under-robes.... And there was a hair ornament they all wanted to have in those days—a silver rose with a little button on it. When you pushed it, the rose became a bud; when you pulled, it flowered. Whenever you saw a low-city girl wearing her yellow plaid kimono minus its strip of black satin, you would notice that her undercollar was white, and that she wore a floppy lavender muslin obi. Was her hair in a Gibson girl bun and decorated with a silver rose? Then you knew that you were looking at a girl who, whether consciously or not, was displaying her desire to pick up some of the new learning, to liberate herself from her family.

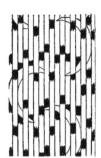

3.35 Some fashionable kimono
designs from 1899,
including art nouveau (*bottom*)

By mid-Meiji, such distinct kimono styles as these, which explicitly marked class background, had been eclipsed. Black satin kake-eri were on their way to extinction. Newfangled department stores hired geisha to model the latest kimono fashions, printing their pictures on the covers of women's magazines for all to admire and aspire to reproduce for themselves. Without fear of censure, a proper wife could copy a new obi devised by a geisha. A student could dress up in the same fashions as a great lady. In society, the traditional markers of class were fading; it is no wonder they began to do the same in clothing. People probably first noticed the former by means of the latter.

At the same time, kimono began to express other nuances and distinctions. New categories of wafuku came into being to take account of the new social situations women found themselves in. Kimono became more specialized in their level of formality.

In early Meiji, classes of kimono were organized straightforwardly and hierarchically according to when they were worn. Times were simpler then, requiring just two major divisions: everyday and special. *Ryakugi* was ordinary everyday clothing. It was made largely from the sturdy 'woven silks,'[23] cotton, wool, or hemp, in dark colors or one of hundreds of popular striped patterns. *Reisō* was ceremonial wear— a three-layered set of fine silk, dye-patterned, family-crested kimono to be worn on New Year's Day and for wedding ceremonies. By the end of the Meiji era an intermediate category of kimono grew up to bridge the social gap between the everyday and the extraordinary. This was *hōmongi*, a class of patterned silk kimono to be used, literally, as 'visiting wear.' Kimono of this category could cover any situation where an urban or upper-class woman had to make a social or public appearance.

By the 1910s fashion had stepped in with the concept of *sharegi*, 'stylish wear.' A woman still wore her plain blue stripes at home when doing housework. But she now had more occasions to be out of the house, to be seen, and to display her own taste. There was a big gap on the formality scale between humdrum striped cotton and silk visiting wear. Sometimes a woman wanted a kimono to express other nuances of self and place. She usually changed to something a little more presentable, perhaps indicative of her status, when she left the house on errands. She wore something a step up from that when she went on outings with friends or family, or to flower arranging or music lessons. This was the role filled by sharegi—an expansion of the category of everyday wear right up to the edge of formal visiting-wear silks. In addition, the kimono wardrobe's traditional reflection of seasonality was given even finer divisions with the introduction of wool.

"In the old days, kimono followed the season from the three-layered set to the double layer, then the single lined robe, unlined robe, thin linen robe, and back around again. Now we have the season of serge and the season of flannel in the interstices."
— *Jogaku sekai* (Coed world) , 1909

3.36 High coquetry, Meiji style

Permitted Colors

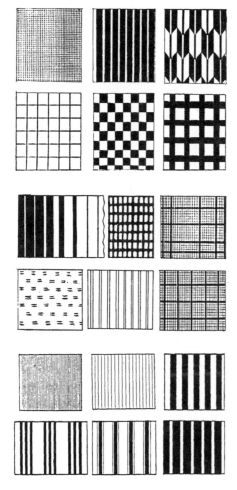

3.38 A sampler of Meiji stripes, plaids, and lattices

The modern eye looks back on the everyday clothing of early Meiji as unutterably drab. There was blue, blue, more blue, black, brown, indigo, grape, slate, seaweed, beige, gray, and blue again. There were narrow stripes, narrower stripes, narrowest stripes, fat stripes, fat and narrow stripes, arrow stripes, narrow arrow stripes, waterfall stripes, bonito stripes, and dozens more variations on straight and perpendicular lines. The fancier dyed silks for formal wear, especially the silks known as yūzen (after the early Edo period dye master Miyazaki Yūzen), were more colorful, but they paled in retrospect next to the yūzen silks of late Meiji, which used new powerful chemical dyes.

Early Meiji yūzen dyed silk had come in one of two styles, carrying on the schizophrenic late Edo tradition of subtlety on the one hand and unrestrained flamboyance on the other. The first, *Edo doki*, consisted of small-scale patterning of flowers and grasses, accented in gold embroidery on a plain monochrome background. In contrast to these iki renditions, the *goshō doki*, or 'palace-style' designs, were florid in the extreme, depicting birds and butterflies, paulownias and waterfalls. Goshō doki did reflect the taste of noblewomen in early Meiji—people who had been completely untouched by iki. Before they exchanged their kimono for bustled skirts, ladies of the nobility wore an extravagantly colored and patterned overkimono called a *hakki* atop their scarlet hakama and white kosode.[24] This was their public dress, and it was often depicted in contemporary woodblock prints commemorating the deeds and proclamations of the much-admired Meiji emperor and his empress. When sumptuary restrictions on colors and patterns suitable for commoners were lifted in early Meiji, the palace style not surprisingly became a model for popular emulation.

Brighter, pastel colors first came into vogue in the 1890s. The most fashionable shade at the turn of the century was *azuki-iro*, a purpled red, the color of the auspicious azuki bean. This was followed by a plethora of bright grays: colors ranging from purple, red, and orange to pink but all filtered through *nezumi*, 'mouse' gray. Compared to the very dark grays, indigo, deep green-browns, and black of early Meiji, these moused colors appeared pale and bright. Compared to the garish colors made possible by aniline dyes, moused colors were iki and sophisticated.

At the same time that colors were lightening, intricate and bold patterns pushed aside the old stripes and lattice-plaids. Crepe silks with a stenciled repeat pattern became the favored choice for dressing up. A small-scale repeat pattern covering an entire garment is called *komon*— referring both to the pattern, and by extension to the kimono decorated this way. Geisha revived the vogue for komon kimono in the early 1880s, and the popularity spread throughout society in a few years.

Because the shape of kimono has changed so little, background color and the size and placement of pattern have always been critical in determining fashionability. By the late 1890s, women who moved in society's upper circles had more occasion to be seen at fashionable gatherings in restaurants and public places. Intricate komon patterns did not show off well in a crowd under the gas lamps of late Meiji evenings. A kimono patterned only at the hem barely saw the light at all if its wearer sat at a table in a Western-style establishment. These women began to look for brighter color and bolder pattern, and called for design to be moved up from the hem onto shoulder and bosom for a new look in wafuku fashion.

The trend toward bold design flourished. In a flurry of inspiration, huge ruffled peonies were dyed on top of stripes, snow-laden bamboo was superimposed on an overall repeat ground. Art Nouveau, called *dessins de Paris*, made a great splash in the world of Japanese graphic design in 1901, and its dramatic sinuous lines were immediately popular for kimono, obi, and under-robes. Never mind that the original inspiration for Art Nouveau had been the European avant-garde's discovery of Japanese woodblock prints.

3.39 Delicate *yūzen* patterns, c. 1894

The tide of exuberant kimono design was stemmed only temporarily by a year of economic depression for the silk industry during the Russo-Japanese War in 1904. A dark shade of blue called 'victory color' (*kachi-iro*) became popular, and classic Japanese motifs began to reassert themselves in fashion. In 1905, Japan's victory over Russia stunned the world. A small exotic country in the Far East had overcome a Western military power. Japan suddenly gained Western respect, and japonisme flourished in Europe.

On the domestic front, nativism re-emerged in a euphoric public sense of national pride. This was expressed in the fashion world by the appearance of dramatic large-scale kimono designs based on the early seventeenth-century kosode patterns of the Genroku period. Such traditional elements as an oversized checkerboard background accented with flowers and birds or scattered chrysanthemums done in a minute dapple tie-dye were stylized and dyed in an array of colors to suit the contemporary taste for brilliance. The late Meiji love of bright color and pattern blossomed fully in this style.

3.4   Obi patterns, c. 1910

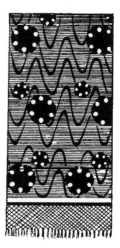

Western fashion influenced women's kimono in two ways. One is obvious—the adoption of physical items of dress, such as coats, shawls, veils, and jewelry. The other is more subtle, having to do with the cultivation of clothing sensibilities, notions of feminine beauty, and ideological aspirations concerning women in society. Eyes that have adjusted to view the female form in corset shape will then regard even a kimono-clad body as invisibly corseted.

As women began to take more active social roles, they proclaimed this fact in part through what they wore. Reformed dress announced women's intention to be taken seriously. Wafuku could be made to appear similar to a Western two-piece dress if one donned a long-sleeved blouse under the kimono and a skirtlike hakama over it. Yōfuku-derived sensibility pushed the ascendency of 'Western' white collars over decorated ones. Yōfuku influenced women's use of the haori jacket as a formalizing accessory, analogous to the way a Western jacket formalizes a woman's suit.

In the ceremonial realm, too, the sensibility spread. Brides began to appear in outfits of solid white. The purity of white was traditional in bridal wear, but so was felicitous scarlet, gold, and silver. The late Meiji appearance of completely achromic layers of kimono topped by a white uchikake robe was due to the influence of Western wedding fashion. On the dark side, funeral wear showed an awareness of Western custom. The use of black for mourning was, again, traditional in Japan, but in many regions, the close kin of the deceased dressed in white. This custom of funereal white gradually died out beginning in late Meiji, probably because of the infiltration of Western notions of crepuscular mourning.

With the exception of jewelry, the new Western-influenced developments in kimono built on native prototypes. These prototypes were influential in determining the ultimate acceptance of new items. They foretold the prospects of assimilation and whether a garment could be

Western Influence on Meiji Kimono

3.41 Meiji reformed dress for girls: blouse, hakama, and shoes

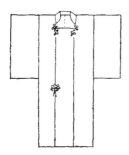

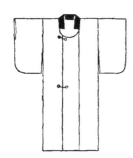

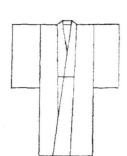

seen as properly belonging to the category of wafuku. A good example is the proliferation of new types of coats to be worn with kimono. Although inspired by yōfuku, a coat-ish thing was not new to Japanese. On a straight-falling, kimono-sleeved garment, round collars, square collars, and tasseled fastenings bespoke a Western sense of design. Veils were a fad similar in spirit to the *okoso zukin*, a traditional, scarflike, partially face-concealing headwrap. Western-style handbags were also eagerly picked up.

Shoes, in contrast, were deemed so different in form and material from Japanese native footwear that, in spite of their acceptance as student dress in the early Meiji years, they were ultimately rejected from women's wafuku wardrobe. Shoes had an irreducible odor of masculinity about them as well. This was part of their charm when women were adopting items of masculine dress in early Meiji and entering previously male social domains. But when nativism re-emerged, women's shoes were banished to the realm of Western clothes. Men, however, incorporated both shoes and hats into their version of native dress.

3.43 Early Meiji cartoon lampooning footwear

The form of the body in Western culture has migrated through many fashion changes. Clothing has been the primary means of reshaping the vision of the body. The ideal feminine form of the 1890s was an S-shaped curve. The corset, by compressing the waist, created the contrast of bosom thrust forward, hips back. The bustle, of course, accentuated the shape behind, and the mono-bosom balanced it in front. This was the 'look' of Western feminine beauty confronted by kimono during late Meiji. The curvaceous form would seem to be antithetical to the straight-falling kimono line. Yet, almost imperceptibly, that idealized figure began to infiltrate the shape of ladies' wafuku even as Japanese women turned their backs on wearing Western dresses.

3.44 The S-curve profile illustrated by a Gibson girl

One of the most striking differences between Meiji and Edo kimono was the appearance of the bosom. In earlier depictions, the lines of the upper part of the kimono are fluid and loose, often dipping over the top of the wide obi. The anatomical bosom is de-emphasized by this treatment, and the eye focuses on the long torso highlighted by the obi. By the 1890s, however, the kimono bosom had changed. The late-Meiji face is framed by layers of wide collars topped by the collar of the kimono itself, tucked neatly behind the top of the obi. The line created is rounded, a solid 'pouter pigeon' effect that suddenly makes fashion sense when we think of the Western mono-bosom in style at the time.

On the other end, consider the Meiji development of the taiko obi. Obi styles were curtailed and standardized during these years, and one particular style—the boxy taiko—gained overwhelming prominence. When the taiko fold was exaggerated and worn low, it resembled nothing so much as a great attached bustle. The overall effect on the kimono line, top to bottom, was to bring it closer to the idealized feminine form of the West.

3.46 The elongated kimono ideal of Edo (*left*) compared to the wider, padded Meiji look

3.46 The odd resemblance between the 1890s bustle and the Meiji obi

Cultural Cross-dressing

This form was to change utterly in a decade. Female voluptuousness gave way to a slenderized ideal of the 'natural' body. The year the Meiji emperor died, 1912, was, by coincidence, a time of fashion revolution in the West. A new woman was taking shape—a woman who shed her corset and cut her long hair. Ironically, one place the French or English new woman looked for fashion inspiration was Japan.

The discovery of Japanese art by Europe's avant-garde in the 1860s had, by the fin de siècle, become a widespread craze for *des choses japonaises* in the decorative arts and fashion. The resulting mode was in turn re-imported by Japan as an appealingly modern 'foreign' style.

Clothing fashion followed a similar circular route, revealed in a 1908 article from the *Osaka mainichi shimbun*, English loan-words occurring throughout:[25]

Femininity in the Urban Centers—Women of Tokyo

It is safe to say that the dress of society women at fashionable gatherings or parties is now entirely Western. And the fashion that parades before one's eyes is limited to the new *kimono sreebu* style. What everyone is calling *kimono sreebu* means simply the sleeve of our kimono. The dress takes the form of an uwagi with the shoulders widened. It is pinned at the front, and the lower part is gathered closely about the hips, from whence it falls, to open at the ankles. The materials used may be crepe, satin, or French voile. Young ladies wear pastel peach, their mothers wear light gray, and older women pale ice blue or black. All are embroidered and painted with chrysanthemum and cherry sorts of japanoiserie on shoulder and sleeve. A very fancy specimen will have jewels glinting among the embroidered flowers, or tassels. The *kimono sreebu* style calls the uwagi the *bodie* and requires a *koat* to be worn over it. Blue satin is a popular material for the *koat*, and it is usually embellished with a fur collar.

To give a finished look, a lady also wears a small cap with a feather (completely unlike the bonnets of old), a scarf, muff, shoes, necklace, and bracelets. The shoes should be of the same material as the dress. The jewelry should be gold, in narrow bands, with large stones.

3.47 Shape of the body in western fashion in 1902 (*above*) and ten years later

The tone of this piece contains the precision of wonderment used when describing something exotic. This amazing hybrid kimono-sleeved evening gown, regarded as Western high chic by Japanese, was considered the height of Orientalia to the European and American fashioners of the style. The threads of influence from East to West and back again traversed the world so rapidly that they created a cultural snarl. Western clothes imitating kimono at the end of Meiji bring us full circle.

Japanese wearing yōfuku inspired by kimono is the appropriate image with which to leave the Meiji era. Taishō, the succeeding reign, began in 1912 and had a different feel from Meiji—not least in respect to the changing relative positions of wafuku and yōfuku. An article in *Fujin sekai* (Women's world) posed the question to the new era in 1914:[26]

> A man in swallowtail coat walks with a woman in crested kimono. His silk top hat is as shiny as her *marumage* hair-style. Where is this society headed, I wonder. Is traditional Japanese clothing gradually dying out? Will the entire Japanese race switch over to purely Western styles? Or, perhaps, is this just a passing fad that will be followed by a return to the clothing of our origins? Yet again, could it be that some new hybrid blend of Japanese and Western clothing will emerge and dominate the future?

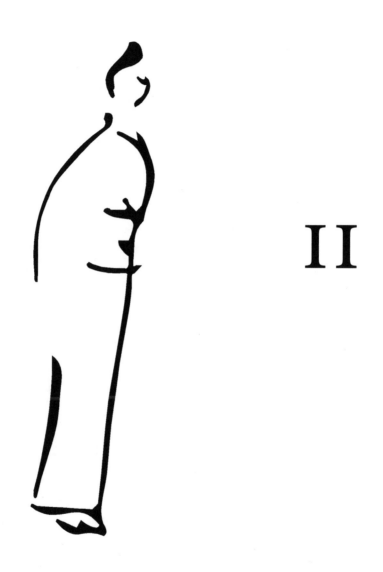

II

KIMONO IN THE MODERN WORLD

FOUR

WOMEN WHO CROSS THEIR LEGS— KIMONO IN MODERN JAPAN

I have often pondered why nowadays we so seldom see kimono worn beautifully. If you wear kimono yourself, it's obvious that the sleeves get in the way as soon as you do anything and that your steps are hindered by the narrow skirt. I suppose, too, that the soul of a woman who wears kimono is spiritually in a man's shadow as she walks behind him, suppressing any trace of her own ego. Since such women are rare these days, it's probably useless to hope to find anyone who truly loves to wear kimono.

—Kondō Tomie, *Yosoi no onnagokoro* (The feminine heart of dressing), 1985

MODERN JAPANESE WOMEN cross their legs, ride crowded subways, drive cars, and play golf. The cultural image of woman "standing spiritually in a man's shadow" has fallen out of favor in Japan. Fragility has given way to agility. The everyday activities of modern life are not carried out easily in kimono. Yet in spite of its commonly acknowledged disfunctionality, the kimono has not simply disappeared. As kimono's social sphere has contracted, its symbolic importance has intensified. Even though most women wear kimono a few times a year at most and men rarely, if ever, don one, Japanese regard kimono as the most beautiful native dress in the world. In its fabric is expressed the Japanese æsthetic sensibility to season and color; in its folds is layered the soul of Japan.

The paradox of modern kimono is this—although kimono is, profoundly, Japan's national dress, by no stretch can it be considered what Japanese normally choose to wear. Kimono made peace with Western clothing by conceding dominance in everyday work and play to pants and dresses, while clinging to the realm of high ceremony and formal sociability. Most of the time, most Japanese wear what everyone else in the advanced consumer societies of the 1990s wears instinctively. Consequently, a decision to wear kimono is not casual. Kimono-clad women on a Japanese street reflect neither the nonchalance of Hindu housewives in saris nor the set-piece sentimentality of Heidis-in-dirndls. To wear a kimono is, inevitably, to make a statement.

The kimono statement, these days, requires some finesse to make successfully. Contemporary kimono are marked by their limitations, not their potential. Even though the kimono class base has been broadened in principle to include all Japanese, over the past century its core constituency has also been halved, by practically eliminating men. Furthermore, among various historical kimono styles, only one, that of the samurai-turned-bourgeois, has become standard. As this kimono terrain has narrowed, it has simultaneously acquired stricter standards of what is and is not acceptable—not perhaps to the extent of becoming a stylized national costume, but to the significant detriment of free-wheeling variation. Connoisseurship and elegance are still possible today but are much harder to achieve, curiously, than in the decades when fancy kimono were forbidden pleasures under *bakufu* censorship.

The contemporary Japanese woman who wears kimono thus engages inescapably in a dialogue with others: the public at large, who notice the general effect, and other women attuned to wafuku's rules, who notice the subtleties. Not surprisingly, she can make mistakes. Some tension is usually attached to wearing kimono—uneasiness about overstepping bounds, fear of appearing flashy or awkward.

Ultimately, then, kimono today and the right wearing of them are redolent of the ever-present issue in Japan of being authentically Japanese. The cultural and historical roots of the shape and function of modern kimono are clear. They are embedded in the post-Meiji path trod by the Japanese in building a modern society. Along with other concrete manifestations of new, national values—standard language, education, beliefs about women's social role, and so on—kimono took its unifying inspiration from the ex-samurai elite who ruled Japan in the later nineteenth century. Subsequently that dress, that is, their kimono, was subjected to repeated barrages of criticism, internal and external, on functional, economic, and most recently feminist grounds. Through it all, even as the kimono has shrunk and changed in response to these pressures (and not always to the enhancement of its inherent æsthetic), it has embodied Japan. The world looked on in fascination when a cosmopolitan young woman named Owada Masako became affianced to crown prince Naruhito and began appearing in public (and even on the cover of *Newsweek*) wearing demure furisode. Masako's kimono was clearly worn to assuage the uneasiness of any Japanese who felt qualms about a Harvard-educated empress.

As such, modern kimono can express a wide range of nuance, from the propriety, continuity, and sense of belonging it confers on the wearer at family ceremonies to, at the extreme, its reference to the narcissistic tribalism of 1930s nationalistic ideology. Kimono equally inescapably marks the boundary of the foreign. Despite the inspiration European couturiers periodically rediscover in the kimono tradition, despite the ready-to-wear boutique 'kimona' and low-end lingerie in American import stores, the fact is that no foreigner can wear a kimono without looking silly, at least to Japanese. Women in Japan today may only be able to cross their ankles demurely in kimono. But they continue to feel a reason for so doing. Limited though kimono may have become, it is unlikely to be extinguished as long as Japanese remain Japanese.

The kimono that today claims the title National Dress of Japan is the ensemble of silk robe and brocade obi that a modern Japanese woman thinks of as a ceremonial alternative to a dress on her home turf—or as a way to impress foreigners when abroad. This kimono is the outfit in which a young woman chooses to be photographed for her official marriage dossier portrait. This kimono is the preferred dress for entrance ceremonies, graduations, and cultural pursuits where feminine character is on display. In this mode, kimono is not merely something-to-wear but rather an expression of mainstream Japanese culture, a kimono with rules. Its cultural mission is to reflect constructed yet traditional notions of genteel femininity. It is intolerant of variation and inimicable to experiment.

The Context of Official Kimono

In the late twentieth century, challenging the establishment Kimono has become nearly impossible. During the mid-1980s a new kimono magazine appeared on the crowded racks of Japanese fashion publications. Its goal was to breathe a new feeling of casual elegance into native dress. The editor-in-chief, Hibino Yōko, needed to position her experiment with a name just offbeat enough to escape the stiff nuance of official kimono. She called the magazine LE KIMONO, explaining that the usage was intended to extract kimono from its cocoon of "dignity, tradition, chastity, and etiquette."[1] There are several ways to depict neologisms in written Japanese, including so-called *romaji*, 'Roman letters.' Hibino used this technique to escape the associations that cling to both the characters and usual Japanese syllabic renditions of the word *kimono*. But LE KIMONO's message of whimsical chic was largely ignored, and the magazine folded after fewer than a dozen issues. The chaste and proper mainstream kimono, which LE KIMONO piqued with its artful photographs of avant-garde models, hardly noticed its demise.

The roots of official kimono go back to the Meiji high-city mode of bourgeois propriety, but its full manifestation is largely a post–World War II phenomenon. One result of Japan's postwar economic prosperity was to make traditional high culture available to all. The trite but exclusive upper-class image of a polished young lady became a goal within reach of almost everyone. Proficiency in flower arrangement, the tea ceremony, and wearing kimono demonstrated a girl's—and by extension her family's—cultural aspirations. Even today, after completing formal education, a Japanese girl will often mark time before marriage with lessons in various traditional arts, thereby polishing her desirability as a marriage partner. At this point she may even take a few lessons in how to wear kimono.

4.1   The modern *furisode* kimono

During her late teens and early twenties a Japanese young woman garners social approval by wearing, on special occasions, the ultra-long-sleeved, brightly colored *furisode* kimono befitting her age. Seven out of ten young women choose to be photographed in such a kimono for their engagement dossier portraits. Women who shun the process of parentally guided marriage arrangements are less likely to deck themselves in traditional array, but even they are not immune to the desire to own a furisode for the trousseau. Kimono makers may offer an installment plan to the office worker who buys one of these fabulously expensive outfits with her own salary rather than her father's yearly bonus paycheck.

Americans and Western Europeans have a steadily decreasing ability to appreciate the appeal of an organized concept of progression through life. Nurtured on centuries of exaltation of self-expression and individuality, a Western approach tends not to value conformity in dress or behavior except for utilitarian or, occasionally, sentimental reasons. The situation is very different in Japan. For better or worse, Japanese women in particular play out their lives on two planes: as individuals in ordinary domesticity, and as prefigured personæ manifested by stages or moments during which they fulfill their Japaneseness through precise modes of dress and deportment. All this may sound oppressive, and can be—but not always, and not necessarily.

Consider the role of stylization and kimono in the years during which a Japanese woman passes from adolescence to adulthood. The early twenties are the most carefree years for a Japanese woman. Finished with school, she earns spending money for herself and does not yet have to worry about the serious business of raising children. She probably dates but spends more time enjoying herself with female friends in a similar situation. Yet at the same time, marriage looms large in her mind, for she is approaching the wedding window of opportunity.

For women, the years between ages twenty-three and twenty-six are considered ideal for marriage. The window quickly lowers as the years progress. Heavy social pressure encourages women to marry at a seemly age in Japan. How then does a tennis-playing, fun-loving, fashion-conscious young woman deal with the upcoming demands of marriage? How does she show that she is at the same time athletic yet demure, conventional yet modern, independent yet docile? One way is to wear kimono. By putting on native dress she can demonstrate that besides being an up-to-date modern woman, she appreciates traditional values. The combination of cute with kimono appears to be quite effective as an appeal to prospective Japanese husbands.

Here then lies the reason that kimono are more in evidence at the marrying stage of a woman's life, than, say, after she has become a mother. Kimono embodies the characteristics deemed desirable in a Japanese bride and future wife. A willingness to sacrifice personal desires for family is a highly commendable trait in a wife. Compliance is better than independence. An attractive bundle of traditional accomplishments will be enticing to the groom's family by demonstrating that the girl has been properly brought up. These virtues hark back to samurai class values regarding ideal traits in women, and kimono worn according to present protocol hints at them all. Wearing kimono gives an impression of the wearer as sweet, docile, and conventional—in short, a good marriage prospect.

The advertising rhetoric of kimono aimed at this age group is couched in terms that go beyond fashion. "Change your clothes to the depth of your heart" is the caption on a typical page of a kimono fashion magazine. It continues: "It's the feeling of taking off your high heels and being different from your usual self. Today you're off to a party, brimming heart enfolded in your kimono—the joy of slipping on the kimono sleeves, the impression of becoming a completely different

心の奥まで着替えて。

4.2 Wearing kimono while serving ceremonial tea

person. You've changed your expression, your image—your self has a new allure."[2]

The tactic of encouraging young women to discover a new self in kimono is typical of the wafuku establishment. If anything, the new self is a stylized Japanese self a woman may not be fully conscious of possessing until she wears kimono.

The character of modern kimono may be judged not only by the impression it is designed to create but also by when it is worn. A late twentieth-century woman seldom wears kimono on a whim. Kimono is worn above all when occasion demands an icon of formality. Because kimono of the past entailed a hierarchy of fabrics and patterns deemed suitable to certain occasions, the modern practice of limiting the kimono to formal events also limits the type of kimono worn. Flowery patterned silks have become much more common than the mundane but charming striped cottons.

The occasions that call for kimono are crucial ceremonial points in the life cycle—birth, marriage, and death. Formal silk kimono thus appear at an infant's first presentation to the family shrine, weddings, and funerals. In between these ritual punctuations of a woman's progression through life are other milestones that prompt kimono. Graduations, the coming-of-age ceremony (January of one's twenty-first year), entrance rituals for school or company, retirement ceremonies, and New Year's Day are all good times to observe Japanese women displaying their Japaneseness.

These kimonoed occasions celebrate the cultural continuity that underlies individual beginnings and endings. They are social ritual, especially as a woman is surrounded by friends also experiencing the same process, wearing the same things. Wearing kimono today combines Japanese pride, traditional sensibility, cultural connectedness, and conspicuous consumption. At the same time, it is not mandatory for women to wear kimono as graduate, bride, mother, or mourner. Some women resist kimono's call. Yet the appeal of wearing kimono on these occasions, like the undertow at the new moon, remains uncannily strong.

A few nonceremonial occasions also prompt kimono-wearing, especially among middle-aged women. Ladies who pursue such hobbies as flower-arranging, tea ceremony, classic theater, dance, or music often do so dressed in kimono. In this special sense, the wearing of kimono per se may constitute a hobby for suitably well-heeled women. Coordinating kimono and obi according to color, pattern, season, age, and formality can be a great challenge. Like any engrossing hobby, it costs money and time, and gives great psychological reward when done right.

Kimono Academies

During the 1960s kimono academies sprang up all over Japan. Clever entrepreneurs saw money to be made in introducing kimono to young women lacking childhood familiarity with wearing it. Modeled on the schools of such venerable arts as tea, flower-arranging, and classical music, some kimono academies give courses in traditional sewing techniques, but far more important is the emphasis on simply learning how to wear the outfit. Kimono academies offer short courses, evening sessions for the working woman, and one-time exhibitions, as well as advanced seminars in obi-tying for the aficionado. The idea of earning a diploma in getting dressed is an indication of how seriously modern kimono takes itself.

To prevent wrinkles, a folded
towel fills out the upper chest

Cotton wool to fill cleavage
for full-busted women

Of course, not everyone who wears kimono needs to take lessons, nor is a license required to wear it. But the heavily advertised kimono schools and their influence on wafuku fashion magazines have significantly strengthened the current social consensus on how a kimono is supposed to be worn. At the same time, by turning kimono into an object of study, these schools have contributed to its stiff, mannered style.

The arts of tea, flowers, and music have long been organized and taught by hereditary schools. Each has its own traditions, rules, and codes. These pursuits are taught not as matter-of-fact skills but as disciplines that offer their practitioners spiritual insight.[3] The philosophy behind the exacting practice of these arts derives from the samurai regard for Zen. Over the centuries, however, the spontaneity so valued by Zen teaching has been smothered. Tea, flowers, and traditional music took on a second, narrower function, that of cultural and spiritual discipline for women. Today, the highest masters of tea, flower-arranging, and *koto* remain men, but the vast majority of adherents are women. The raison d'être of the schools is consistent across disciplines. These arts are considered excellent means to polish female character. The female ideal has historically been that of the indefatigably proper, internally strong, but outwardly submissive samurai daughter.

Modern kimono dovetails into this pattern of conservative femininity. The version of kimono propagated by the kimono academies is utterly dominated by propriety. The goal is to achieve a demeanor of equanimity and composure by dressing correctly. Women aim for beauty in dress, but not seductiveness. The modern kimono strives to be chaste, dignified, and proper, like the ideal samurai wife of the past. Students of the kimono academies are seeking advice in wearing the national dress of Japan, not frivolity. They aspire to wear kimono in a high-class way, and the academies respond to this desire by positioning themselves precisely as possessing the authority to dictate the Way.

Even as kimono academies urge women to find ways to squeeze kimono back into everyday life, the stiffness of the mode they promulgate undermines their efforts, æsthetically and functionally. They have devised elastic bands and alligator clips to hold the front overlap together, plastic rods to support the obi in back, bust suppressors and waist pads to even out the figure. This ingenious infrastructure helps an officially dressed woman achieve the proper, cylindrical line. It is not a relaxed figure. Because official Kimono is always concerned to stand on its dignity, efforts to work its way back to informal fabrics for every day are probably doomed to fail.

4.3   The infrastructure of modern kimono

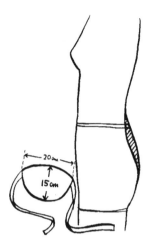

Pad for flat derrieres

Folded towel for thin waists

Folded towels at bust and waist for flat-chested women

Cotton wool for sloped shoulders

A man in anything but the most casual kimono is rare. In fact, unless he is a traditional artist, a male wearing full kimono is probably a bride-groom. And he, too, is unusual. Most grooms opt for tuxedos. The sexual segregation of kimono began in the nineteenth century. Men were quick to don the coats and trousers of the West during the 1880s as the clothing of the workplace and of official ceremony. Only after women began to take a greater part in public life did they begin to wear Western styles. But their public presence was limited and their numbers were few compared to women fully occupied in the home.

The first contingents of working girls were the mill hands in Japan's rapidly industrializing textile factories. But their arduous work did not require a public persona, and they continued to wear rationalized versions of native dress. Clothing in the private sphere of the home remained, for both sexes, kimono. Western clothes did not become marks of enlightened fashion consciousness for women until the mid-1920s.

'Home life' was a critical reason why women held on to native styles of dress when men did not. Home life was one side of the so-called double life of urban Japanese from the turn of the century through the 1930s. Double life referred to the convention of dividing the social universe into either Western or native things and activities. One sat in a chair at the office, but on a floor cushion in the house; drank coffee or beer in a restaurant, but tea and sake at home. One wore a suit to work, changing to kimono upon return to the family. The double life was fundamental to everyday Japanese culture during the first three decades of the twentieth century, but men experienced it more sharply than did women.

During the Meiji years, a girl of good family would have made her first major foray into the world outside the home to attend middle and high school. She would wear a modified version of native dress. Often a long-sleeved Western blouse was put on under the kimono, a simple narrow obi was tied over it, and a hakama skirt (previously male formalwear) was tied high at the waist. Western shoes rather than native footwear completed the schoolgirl's outfit. Graduation, adulthood, betrothal, marriage, and motherhood usually followed in quick succession. Each social step forward through life tended to bring a woman back to kimono. Those few who chose careers were the ones more likely to move on to dresses as well.

Traditional social roles usually required traditional costume for both men and women. The reason to wear foreign 'enlightened' garb was

4.4 Young Meiji women wearing kimono, hakama, and shoes

primarily to show that one was correspondingly modern in attitude, taste, and occupation. Before the mid-1920s, women lacked the opportunity in any numbers to make such a statement. When they did begin to work in new modern jobs outside the house, they put on Western clothing as men had done a generation before. But even Japanese career women still hold the orthodox female roles of wife and mother. Because being a wife and mother has always formed much more of a Japanese woman's social identity than being husband or father has for a man, the pull of traditional roles has been correspondingly strong in the continuing importance of female native dress. Women were drawn out of kimono far more gradually than were men, and less completely.

The Taishō Transformation

4.5 Taishō kimono (*above*), the 1920s silhouette, and fashionable hybrid (*opposite*)

Meiji ended in 1912. The thirteen-year reign period of the Meiji emperor's successor, Taishō, had a very different savor. Men and women of Meiji had gulped up Western culture with all the indiscriminate enthusiasm of new converts. By Taishō, Japanese sensibilities vis-à-vis the West were much smoother. This was Japan's political equivalent of the Weimar Republic in Germany, or the social scene of the American Roaring Twenties. Japanese born during Taishō would enter adolescence as modern boys and girls. Significantly, women opened their closets to Western clothing during this decade. Kimono has lost space ever since.

For the rest of the world the 1910s were marked by World War I, the first truly global conflict. During the war years, information about life, customs, and fashions of the West was widely introduced into Japan. By 1915 Japan was beginning to feel itself a world-class nation, more confident of its military strength and social development. Ordinary Japanese were inclined to look at their society in light of how life might be bettered by adapting foreign ideas, or made more interesting by acquiring foreign fashions. Borrowing from the West was of course not new, but it had now become a more reciprocal and respectable process. Had the West not complimented Japan in 1912 by borrowing the Oriental Look and kimono style into its fashions?

The war, the growing economy, and the popularity of moving pictures all impelled the Japanese toward Western modes. The economy was strong. The battlefields of World War I were far from home, and Japanese involvement had concentrated on exporting military supplies to the European combatants. For the first time, the common man and woman had a comfortable margin of money to spend on clothing. Mass-appeal bright colors and flamboyant styles appeared in kimono. Many more Western fashions became available. The craft of knitting took women another step toward yōfuku. Knitting enjoyed a tremendous vogue around 1918, soon manifesting itself in the sudden popularity of sweaters and shawls for women and Western-style knit garments for children. By 1924, girls' school uniforms began to move away from the kimono-and-hakama outfit to the uniform skirt and middy-blouse seen today.

These social trends encouraged Japanese women to try Western dress. But the great rise in numbers of working women during Taishō was definitive in establishing the other side of the double life. Some women made careers out of the new opportunities that opened in Japan's growing economy. Still more pioneered the contemporary practice of working for a few years before marrying and raising children. The requirements of working in such modern occupations as nurse, bus conductor, reporter, stenographer, waitress, theater usher, dance hall partner, and department store clerk demanded modern—Western—dress. Having experienced Western dress, a woman was likely to continue wearing it even after she married. If it was fashionable before marriage, why not after? If one wore a dress at school and at work, why not at home? In this way Western clothing gradually eroded kimono's ground.

Both Japanese and foreign social historians point to the Great Kantō earthquake of 1923 as marking a cultural change as seismic as the actual geophysical event. Before the quake, the city of Tokyo and urban culture in general were predominantly colored by native modes. Afterwards, Westernization gained the ascendancy. The heart of Tokyo was rebuilt in steel and concrete rather than wood. Western building styles became standard. Many people had lost everything, including their clothes, and some restocked their wardrobes with many yōfuku items. But the primary reason the earthquake boosted Western clothing styles for women was not just that dresses were cheap and kimono pricey, as is often asserted, but that Western styles were perceived as more rational. Voices proclaiming yōfuku's superiority to kimono had been raised before the earthquake, but the calamity gave the arguments more force.

The discussion of rational dress penetrated to underwear. Enlightened women were encouraged to wear *zurōsu*, drawers, rather than the traditional wraparound *koshimaki*, even under kimono. There was some resistance to pantiform intimate wear on the grounds that it was unfeminine.[4] Yet social reformers harped on the spectacle of hapless women caught in the conflagration that followed the earthquake, exposed in death by their disarrayed kimono. They even implied that victims might have been spared had they been wearing convenient *yōfuku* instead of the hobbling kimono. It is doubtful whether kimono liberation would have made any difference in the number of earthquake fatalities, but the psychological appeal to feminine modesty was effective. The embarrassment at the thought of exposure, even as a corpse, sent shudders down decorous female spines.[5]

Changing underwear was an interesting phenomenon. Intimate garments may be the most conservative elements of costume. For most of us, they are intimately tied to our conceptions of our bodies. We may play at fashion on the surfaces, but underneath we preserve psychological consistency with familiar underwear. Japanese women who wore the long Western skirts of the prewar era often continued to wear the traditional kimono hip-wrapping undergarment. But as hems rose in the 1920s, native undergarments were no longer feasible. Western dresses demanded Western underwear. A tubular, skirtlike woolen slip that could not flap open and cause embarrassment like the koshimaki was promoted as being warm, chaste, and modern. As women became accustomed to the slip, even kimono-wearers adopted it. Tube-sleeved undershirts, camisoles, and bandeaux soon followed. They continue to be standard for kimono underwear today. Kimono surely lost some integrity when women began to wear panties and brassieres beneath it.

In addition to the issue of rationality, an intense interest in quality of life emerged in public consciousness during the boom years of World

4.6   Sailorsuit-style children's wear, which became the basis for girls' school uniforms

War I. The sharp inflation at war's end added the question of economizing to the list of social reforms. How to improve life by modern means became the focus of much debate. In 1921 various reform-minded groups joined in a league to promote the betterment of life.[6] One starting point was to get women and children out of kimono and into Western dress.

During the early 1920s, the fashionable Western silhouette was a simple uncluttered line, a shift with a dropped waist. Since the amount of fabric used was less than for kimono, the reform league stressed the economy of such dresses. A woman did not have to be an accomplished seamstress to sew one, either. Western dresses that a woman made for herself were promoted as being more economical, easier to wear, and more conducive to freedom of movement than kimono. Even before the earthquake, an Asahi newspaper article reported that the popularity of home sewing had reached such a pitch that yard goods were practically flying off merchants' shelves. With the advent of warm weather these home-sewn dresses were appearing all over the city.[7] The contrast with the groping tailors of Meiji could hardly have been more marked.

4.7   Slips and pants

乳おさえ

自熱的大好評

本品に收良な加工を特に和装洋装の両用に適する樣幣の型に收良な加工を特に婦人の特製したもので左記特長の為め婦人力の大好評を得て居ります。工場にしに日本婦人の體格に合ふ樣に型に收良な加工を特に胸部の大きな御方でも衛生的品自在に御使用簡單にお乳の大きな御方でも伸縮絕胸部の大きな御方でもお姿の惡い御方でもお姿の整へ

御注文の方は鯨尺胸寸法御記入下さい
（價定）
胸製綿絹　一圓七十錢
上製（羽二重）　一圓七十錢
特製（錦）　紗（三　一圓八十錢
絹特製メリヤス製二圓八十錢
（ハガキ御申込次第代金引換で送る廿七錢增）
進呈　ハンカチーフを以て代用更紗裂樣つランスチリメンハンカチ裂姶さして呈上げます。
（殘女界社代理約でも知致次致します）

發賣元　東京市京橋區カブキ座前

製造　島元旦二商店

振替東京七一五八七番

4.9 Summer frock in Tokyo, 1920

4.8 "The Bust Suppressor—especially created for the Japanese figure, our product helps you attain the new shape popular in the West. Can be worn under kimono or Western styles both…"

By an accident of history, Western fashion during the 1920s emphasized a flat-chested, slim, straight look. It was probably not an accident that Japanese women in significant numbers began wearing yōfuku when Western dresses most closely approximated a familiar kimono line. Western fashions of the time embodied the ideals of ease of movement, economy of material, and simplicity of style that had become the hallmarks of modish modernity. At the same time, the flowerstem silhouette was much easier for Japanese to comprehend and assimilate than flounced and padded fin-de-siècle Western fashions. Oddly, the Taishō kimono and Western fashion came to resemble each other in looks even as the ideological wedge of functionality was being driven deeper between them.

By the late 1920s, then, most Japanese women had had at least some experience of Western clothing. Some wore dresses most of the time.

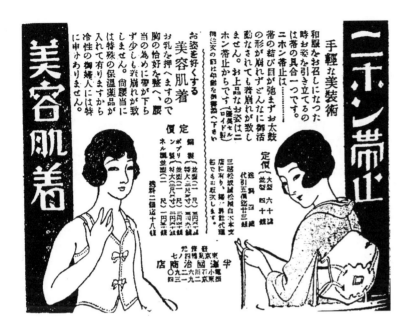

4.10 Whether in Western dress or kimono, the Taishō lady
looked to achieve the same slim, flat figure

Western dress even began to take the lead in women's fashion. The lowered thirties hemlines, the return of the belted waist, peplum blouses, T-strap shoes, and cloche hats all appeared in Tokyo almost as soon as they did on yōfuku's home turf. Without stretching truth, yōfuku by this time could claim urban Japan as part of its home territory. Kimono had lost the functionality competition and was on the verge of losing fashion as well. Fashion lives on change. Kimono was becoming more and more the representative of tradition. From Taishō on, yōfuku continued to change, according to fashion, while kimono froze into the set tableaux we see today.[8]

4.11 Summer frock in Paris, 1920

The War Years

The prosperity brought to Japan by World War I gave Western styles a boost. The devastation of World War II almost did in kimono. The strident cultural ultranationalism that accompanied Japan's military expansion called on citizens to shuck foreign styles, habits, and words in favor of native modes. As part of an official campaign to mobilize the spirit of the civilian population for Japan's war effort, showy dress was discouraged, cosmetics were banned, and permanent-waved hair was denounced.[9] Foreign fashions were frowned on, but wastefulness was deemed even more pernicious. From the beginning of Japan's war effort, extravagance per se was labeled an enemy.

A call for return to kimono might have been expected, but such was not the case. Wasteful of material, unconducive to labor, costly, and fragile, the kimono was effectively banned during these years, ironically enough, as an expression of unpatriotic indulgence in luxury. For

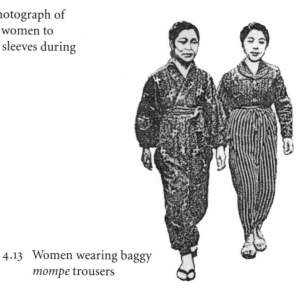

4.12 Newspaper photograph of poster urging women to adopt skimpy sleeves during the war years

4.13 Women wearing baggy *mompe* trousers

kimonoed women who had never made the transition to yōfuku, government policy urged short, non-draping sleeves. It is a mark of the depth of yōfuku's integration into Japanese life that no one seriously questioned its suitability for citizens. Yōfuku wasn't Western anymore. It was simply practical clothing for men and for women.

The year 1940 was the fifteenth year of Shōwa, the reign of Emperor Hirohito. Japan's involvement in the war was deepening. Deprivations were beginning to cut into civilian life. Food rationing began in 1941, and a year later clothing and material were rationed by a point system.[10] Because of fabric shortages, women sewed new clothing out of scraps of old. Turning necessity into virtue, some fashion-minded women and girls took pains in the design of their *yarikuri shitate* patchwork garments.[11] By 1943 there was no longer enough fabric in the country to fulfill rations. Baggy trousers called *mompe* became women's daily dress. Worn over a shirt or an old kimono, mompe was the civilian uniform of a generation of working women. Silk kimono remained in drawers during the war years. Some were bartered to farmers for sweet potatoes, others resewn into more useful clothing. By war's end, kimono's claim to wearability was gone.

Yet, after all, kimono was resurrected in the 1950s, and continued to grow in popularity during the 1960s in what Japanese called a 'kimono boom.' Kimono's revival was noticeable after about 1955, not as everyday wear but as ceremonial wear for the New Year's holidays. Department store sales in 1955 showed that four kimono outfits were sold for every six of yōfuku. Kimono that year were not the traditional sorts of seasonal colors, however. Strong color contrasts and abstract designs were common. This was the 'new sensibility' in kimono.[12]

As prosperity returned, kimono came back like robins in spring. Too extravagant to be worn during the ultranationalistic era, kimono had to wait for the economic miracle of the 1960s to find its new—small, and very formal—social niche.

[A Japanese woman] minces her steps
as tho' her legs were tied together at the knees.

—Townsend Harris, letter of 1856

Unless we abolish the obi and shorten the skirt, kimono cannot
be made practical. Yet if we do this, the result is no longer kimono.

—Designer Tanaka Chiyo, *Shin josei no yōsō*, 1936

The kimono: a combination of straitjacket and hobble skirt.

—Bernard Rudofsky, *The Kimono Mind*, 1965

That kimono is inconvenient for everyday activities is a modern truism. Kimono was ultimately convicted on its home territory on the charge of nonfunctionality. Given the matter-of-fact tone of the anti-kimono rhetoric now taken for granted, one wonders how Japanese managed for so many centuries.

The functionality argument has been made in two ways. One is that the kimono *was* practical in the context of traditional society (for example, for sitting on tatami) until Japan adopted the material culture of the West—furniture to sit on, in particular. Kimono then rapidly became unsuited to the demands of modern life. The other is to say that kimono by nature is, and always has been, inimicable to human activity. This is the feminist view.

One learns to be wary of functionalist criticism of clothing styles. The functionalist stick used to beat a particular mode of dress invariably turns out to be held by the fickle hand of fashion. Such Western clothing reforms as the condemnation of low necklines or the promulgation of bloomers were carried out according to moral or ideological concerns. As such they were quite straightforward. The functionalist argument, however, almost always has a hidden agenda. In the case of kimono, lines were drawn between old-fashioned and new, between feudalistic remnants in society and modern freedoms. As this dichotomy sliced everyday life, functional became fashion, and skirts got the nod. Feudalism was unfashionable. Kimono were denounced.

Kimono first came to be judged on the score of convenience, ease of movement, and economy during Taishō. Contemporary Western fashion was itself addressing the same questions in its revolt from the exaggeratedly padded and squeezed Victorian figure. The clothing choices of that era open to a Japanese woman were orthodox kimono, Western dress, and reformed native dress, *kairyōfuku,* which attempted to combine the best points of the other two. Reformed dress was an ideological creation—like Western bloomers during the 1880s. Basically unattractive, like bloomers, reformed dress faded on the vine of its functionality.

Reformed dress represented an effort to give native garments a fighting chance in the wearability competition. This was not an issue for men. Men simply wore pants and shirts to work and changed to casual kimono at home if they felt like it. The sole object of reformed dress was women's wear. Its main concerns were economy and mobility. Reformed dress advocated either tubular sleeves or the Genroku sleeve, a shorter sleeve attached to the body of the kimono rather than dangling free. Kairyōfuku could be worn with a half-width obi (about four inches), which was less constricting than the torso-swaddling full obi. The wide-skirted hakama, which female students had already adopted in the Meiji period, was suggested as a solution to the snugly wrapped kimono skirt. Fewer cords to wrap the kimono folds, the use of buttons and attached ties, one layer of kimono rather than the fashionable two or three—all were endorsed as ways to promote freedom of movement while remaining in kimono.

But reformed dress did not catch on. Even Tanaka Chiyo, a designer of the 'new kimono,' had to admit its failure: "Nothing has appeared to correct the basic deficiencies of kimono. The only thing that has happened is that kimono has gradually lost its beauty. We've corrected

4.14 Reformed dress

one or two points here and there, but have failed to come up with an overall scheme. With each partial reform we've only succeeded in making kimono look uglier."[13]

Most women apparently agreed. What was the point of looking awkward merely to remain in native dress? One could have one's kimono and wear dresses, too. The functionality debate merely increased the gap between Western dress and kimono. Ultimately, kimono lost the functionality competition. In so doing, it ceded the domain of active everyday life to yōfuku and retained only the consolation prize of formal beauty. Kimono began to be confined to the realm of the decorative—where, essentially, it remains today.

The main indictment against modern kimono has concentrated on its physical shape—the narrow skirt, constrictive obi, and dangling sleeves. But a second key element is economics. The truly fabulous expense appalls some women, discouraging

them from ever wearing wafuku—yet at the same time this very priciness proclaims the high cultural value placed on kimono. Even at the highest level of couture it would be almost impossible to put together an outfit of Western clothing that could match the price tag on a relatively fine kimono and obi ensemble. Japanese take no little pride in this fact.

A few displays and advertisements from the quarterly magazine *Utsukushii kimono* (Beautiful kimono) illustrate the sums involved for fashionable kimono dressing:[14]

> A young woman's long-sleeved furisode kimono in shades of pale green and pink silk crepe with embroidered fans scattered upon it—¥780,000 [$5,850]
>
> The obi is black silk brocade with gold, silver, red, and blue designs of cranes, drums, chrysanthemums, and other felicitous objects—¥690,000 [$5,175]
>
> A black, crested adult woman's kimono with designs of persimmons, chrysanthemums, and fans in embroidery and gold foil stamp on the skirt—¥580,000 [$4,350]. Gold and silver brocade obi—¥450,000 [$3,375]

These two ensembles represent the highest ceremonial level of kimono for an unmarried and a married woman, respectively. Just below them on the formality scale are visiting-wear kimono such as these:

4.15 Visiting-wear kimono

> A silver-gray satin kimono fading to peach with a hand-painted design of stylized floral sprays reaching to the shoulder—¥350,000 [$2,625]
>
> Salmon-color heavy silk obi with abstract floral design composed of a combination of hand-dyeing and gold embroidery—¥450,000 [$3,375].

The kimono itself and the obi doubtless are formidable items of expense, but neither are the accessories to be sneezed at. The Kyoto-based kimono company Keimeisyoji ran an advertisement for a fashionably coordinated set of kimono, obi, and all the accoutrements:

Black, white, and silver dyed visiting-wear kimono with
    orange and gold floral motifs — ¥380,000 [$2,850]
Multichrome brocade obi — ¥430,000 [$3,225]
Red satin insert collar [*date eri*] — ¥6,000 [$45]
Obi cord— ¥15,000 [$112]
Obi scarf — ¥10,000 [$75]
Zōri sandals — ¥26,000 [$195].

This list does not include the requisite silk underkimono (*nagajuban*), other types of kimono underwear, and white cotton tabi socks, all of which add another couple of hundred dollars to a bill already totaling more than $6,500.

At these prices kimono are more investment than vestment. Why are kimono so expensive? In spite of the relative simplicity of sewing involved, the production of a formal kimono is a highly labor-intensive procedure with many middlemen. To obtain a top-of-the-line formal kimono, for example, a woman goes to a retail shop where she chooses a bolt of white silk, decides the background color she will have it dyed, and picks the design to be painted and embroidered upon it. The shop will counsel a woman about appropriate choices and oversee the details of dyeing, design, embroidery, and sewing.

The process is as much commissioning a work of art as it is selecting a piece of clothing. Wives and daughters of wealthy families persist in purchasing their important kimono through traditional channels like these. Many of these kimono retailers do business the old-fashioned way, making housecalls with their samples of silk and swatches of color. Some families have been clients of kimono retailers for generations on both sides. For less ceremonial wear, a woman is likely simply to choose a bolt of fabric she likes and have the shop (or department store) sew it to her measurements. Informal does not necessarily mean inexpensive, however. A magazine display of a tan, nubble-textured silk kimono with a few stripes on the skirt—which would be appropriate only at a casual gathering—carries a price tag of ¥380,000, or $2,850. This is understatement to the nth degree.

Is it possible to wear kimono without spending such sums? One alternative is to purchase one of the various lines of prêt-à-porter new kimono made of fabrics like *shiruku*, a silk-lookalike polyacrylonatrile. Although the concept of buying a sewn garment rather than a roll of cloth is relatively new to the kimono business, a few modern kimono designers have eagerly taken this page from the yōfuku marketing book. A coordinated ready-to-wear ensemble of relatively informal kimono, obi, obi cord, obi scarf, patterned undercollar, and insert collar carries a price tag of ¥158,000, or $1,185. Although the idea of paying more than a thousand dollars for polyester makes one gasp, compared to the hand-dyed top-drawer silks this ready-to-wear set is a bargain.

Hype undeniably affects the inflated prices of silk kimono. In spring 1987 I attended a wholesalers' kimono show in Tokyo to observe companies and the clients they were wooing. The customers were middle-aged women buying for themselves and their teenaged daughters. The kimono samples and bolts of cloth were primarily the silks of high formalwear—brightly colored and patterned for young women, monochrome with hem designs for matrons. The atmosphere was as busy and noisy as a Loehmann's dressing room, and a far cry from the personal service of an established shop, yet the prices were not substantially lower. Acting as their own purveyors, these wholesalers were making a killing. Women pay these prices because the high price of a kimono in and of itself validates their feeling that they have purchased something of value. They look to buy an image of high cultural respectability. To buy it too cheaply would tarnish the image.

The kimono has a criminal record. For hundreds of years, up until the twentieth century, the kimono has unilaterally insulted the female sex and caused women to suffer. It has prevented free expression and impeded natural growth. When women finally removed their kimono, they burst the shackles of feudalism. But now the silky insinuating voice of kimono is heard again, seeking to confine women to the dim and cramped backstage of life. Who would say its appeal is simply due to a feminine desire for elegance? We must expose kimono for the pernicious device it is.

—(Male) clothing historian Murakami Nobuhiko,
Agura o kaku musumetachi (Girls who cross their legs), 1963

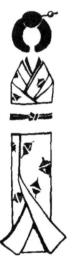

4.16 Restrictive dress

The feminist critique of kimono overlaps functionalist opinion, with extra vitriol. Since the late nineteenth century, Western judgment of kimono has divided between beauty and practicality. On the side of beauty and perhaps exoticism, kimono has been praised and admired. From the point of view of serviceable clothing it has been ridiculed. Prosper Mérrimée saw kimono-clad Japanese ladies at the Paris Exposition in 1867. He concluded that the only conceivable function imaginable for the obi was to confine the movement of women.

Part of such criticism clearly lies in culture-bound notions of comfort. The practical usually means the familiar. From today's perspective the obi is hardly less repressive than the wide crinolines of Mérrimée's France or the ensuing corset-and-bustle style in vogue throughout the West in the 1880s. Of course, all of these clothing styles are arguably oppressive to women and characteristic of societies in which women have limited economic and political authority.[15] Restrictive dress, especially when made of opulent fabrics, is a prime characteristic of the theory of conspicuous consumption. A woman rendered incapable of physical labor by her dress is more important as an indication of her father's or husband's status than as an economic contributor in her own right. She is a commodity. Kimono is surely conspicuously sumptuous, but its story is not explained by that alone.

Feminist detractors depict kimono ideology as glorifying a feudal ideal of woman as powerless chattel. Above the waist the bosom was oppressively bound in the same way a woman was bound ideologically by neo-Confucian strictures stressing obedience, docility, and subordination to father, husband, and son. Below the waist, kimono inhibited freedom of movement at the same time as it offered little protection to modesty. With kimono's lapover front, exposure was but a careless step away. The feudal woman was subject to enforced chastity in this view, yet she was also a sexual slave.

To evaluate this assessment of kimono two issues must be separated: kimono as it was when all Japanese wore it, and modern kimono as an item of wear limited primarily to women. It is easy to argue that the draping silk sleeves and the wide brocade obi of mainstream bourgeois kimono are utterly unsuited to active work or play. This kimono is ipso facto nonfunctional. But such condemnation ignores the evolution of the garment. Active serviceability is not kimono's purpose. Kimono today has other functions, more symbolic than workaday. Modern kimono descends from clothing worn by the upper classes for special occasions, one mode among many, decorative rather than daily wear, ceremonial not serviceable, and meant for display rather than work.

To assume, then, that modern kimono represents the prototypical kimono throughout history, and for all classes, is absurd. The kimono-wearing, bound and oppressed feudal woman of feminist criticism was hardly the norm. The wives and daughters of lords and samurai most closely approximated this feminist stereotype, but traditional kimono of the original working women—farmers, housewives, shopkeepers,

4.17 Working kimono

peddlers, laborers, students—were far from the stiff brocade cocoons that became the model for today's kimono.

When kimono was simply clothing, more relaxed versions were worn for everyday activities. These are infrequently seen now. Elements of casual kimono have become as rare as garter belts. There is a vintage kimono shop in Kyoto, for example, that has shelves piled with soft obi faced in black satin.[16] These are pliant hand-painted silks rather than brocade, worn through the 1930s as casually stylish everyday clothing. These obi are friendly, not forbidding. They are also obsolete.

Modern kimono, rejected by feminists as stilted and constricting, is also severe compared to the fancy formalwear of other classes of people—for example, geisha. The full-dress long kimono and obi ensemble of geisha would never claim to be sportswear. But it does achieve a flowing and æsthetically balanced line that is wholly absent in standard, modern, tubular kimono. A geisha is also able to wear an ordinary kimono with ease in a manner anything but stuffy. Part of this is due to sheer familiarity, since geisha are used to moving in kimono, but just as much has to do with subtle details of how the obi is tied and how the neckline is arranged. Stiff propriety is not a geisha's aim in dress.

By placing itself above practicality, modern kimono has tried to make itself immune to the functionalist critique by creating its own special, æsthetic realm. It has largely succeeded, yet because functionality is such an unquestioned virtue in post-modern society, some people still attempt to create practical versions of kimono, hoping to enhance its wearability. Examples of such endeavors include wash-and-wear fabrics and a flexible two-piece design in which the obi conceals the join. In a way, though, such experiments are irrelevant. Even in modern life some occasions demand silk, comfort is beside the point, and the expense is an integral part of the image. This is the realm of kimono today.

Kimono crystallizes Japaneseness. For this reason kimono can never be simply a matter of something to wear. Rightly or wrongly, Japanese regard their national dress as unique in the worldwide panoply of ethnic clothing.

Kimono is by no means the only aspect of their culture that Japanese view in this way. The Japanese compulsion to assert their uniqueness has received a great deal of attention from Western social scientists.[17] The overall phenomenon is called *Nihonjin-ron*, the 'discourse on being Japanese,' and most of the writings in this genre are for home consumption. It is fundamentally an internal monologue, not an attempt to persuade the world. Most Japanese have a gut feeling that they, as Japanese, *are* different from everyone else, and so the emotional arguments of the Nihonjin-ron speak to an audience already converted.

Higuchi Kiyoyuki is one of many authors who specialize in writing popular books about Japanese culture for a Japanese readership. In *Umeboshi to Nihon-tō* (Pickled plums and Japanese swords) his characterization of kimono is typical of the logic of the Nihonjin-ron, which posits a unique fit between culture, nature, and the Japanese psyche. Using the terms of the discourse on being Japanese, Higuchi explains everything about the kimono as functioning in complete harmony with the climate, social structure, physical body type, and æsthetic preferences of the Japanese.[18] The only issue Higuchi's 'kimono-ron' cannot explain is: if the kimono is so uniquely well-suited to the Japanese, why has it fallen out of everyday use?

In this view, the dangling sleeves, wide obi, and trailing skirt generally perceived as marks of kimono's unsuitability for modern life are in fact virtues. According to Higuchi, for example, the predominantly long-waisted Japanese female has a tendency to develop a pot belly, especially after childbirth. Nothing could be better suited to prevent this condition than the traditional wide obi wrapped around the torso. Similarly, kimono's long sleeves and the way they are sewn to the body of the garment leaves an opening beneath the armpits—ventilation, claims Higuchi, for Japan's muggy climate. The trailing kimono skirt (a mode not developed until the late eighteenth century) is supposed to provide æsthetic compensation for Japanese women's short legs.

Also, Higuchi continues, kimono has characteristics that make it superior to Western dress. Unlike Western clothes tailored to the individual, kimono can be given to others or passed down as a treasured keepsake. Western clothing affords no possibility of nuance compared to kimono. The Japanese preference for indirect expression of emotion can be indulged delicately, by how kimono is worn, rather than by speech or facial gesture. The example Higuchi gives is a woman flirting by loosening her obi—a gesture that might strike even a non-Japanese as pretty direct. Æsthetically, he states, kimono is the only clothing in the world that can be decorated with full-scale pictures as well as simply with patterns.

As bizarre as Higuchi's special pleading may appear to Westerners, his opinions are not considered nonsense by many Japanese. Slightly further toward the edge is a kimono consultant by the name of Yamanaka Norio, head of a large kimono academy, who every year travels around the world to "promote international understanding of the kimono." This kimono evangelist claims that kimono represents Japan's "unique spiritual culture" yet is something that women all over the world can be taught to wear and appreciate. To this end, Yamanaka's English-language *Book of Kimono* contains a mind-boggling sixty-step diagram of how to put on a kimono and obi.[19] The real message of this so-called kimono promotion is that the kimono is so complex that no one outside Japan could possibly master it. This echoes the darker chords of the classic Nihonjin-ron, which claims that the Japanese language, for example, is beyond the grasp of non-natives or that the physiology of the Japanese brain is fundamentally different from the brains of others. In whatever aspect of culture it focuses upon, the somber side of the Nihonjin-ron asserts that Japan is not only unique, it is ultimately superior. It is all well and good to be proud of traditional clothing, but kimono chauvinism is, ultimately, ugly.

Like Japanese themselves, kimono revels in cultural connoisseurship at home but is somewhat stiff and unsure in an international context. Does it measure up to Western modes? Is it *better* than Western modes? Both arguments have been made at the extremes—the functionalist stance positing kimono's inferiority to yōfuku, and the Nihonjin-ron position, which elevates kimono to a summit of rationality and beauty at the expense of the clothing customs of the rest of the world. The sense of hierarchy so deeply ingrained in Japanese culture makes it hard for Japanese to judge themselves with a feeling of equanimity—if something is not inferior, then it must be superior.

The kimono is neither better nor worse than yōfuku. You can't cross your legs in kimono, but you can become absorbed in its colors, textures, folds, and designs, and in the social and cultural meanings that reverberate through the combinations.

FIVE

THE OTHER KIMONO

Kimono with its official pedigree stands at the cultural core of contemporary Japanese dress. Yet at the same time, forms of indigenous clothing that have been overshadowed by the robe-and-obi had much to recommend them in their day, both as functional wear and as items of beauty.

Under genteel preservation today as folk art, these nonKimono are a useful reminder of the politics of clothing. So thoroughly does kimono now represent native dress that even Japanese forget that numerous folk styles could equally well claim to be the traditional dress of the Japanese people. That they are largely ignored is evidence of the successful campaign waged by kimono (through its upper-class wearers) to smother variant native styles and gain undisputed recognition as Japan's national dress par excellence.

Yet it would be wrong to conclude that folk clothing has been eradicated—it has simply been consigned to museums and the occasional edifying television program. This fate has not been unique—the nonKimono are not the only objects of cultural domination from the center in recent Japanese history. Together with such things as the regional dialects of the Japanese language, the local products (*meibutsu*) of various prefectures and towns, and local festivals, folk clothing is still suffered to exist, on the margin, perhaps as a symbol of the nonstandard, nonTokyo aspects of life. The only quality these cultural variants lack is potency.

No matter how faintly, however, ethnological differences persist within the facade of uniformity, constituting something of a problem for the deadly serious 'discourse on being Japanese.' Official Japanese Culture generally responds either by treating such divergences as curiosities or by absorbing them into the mainstream rank-and-reward process through the creation of special categories of merit and the cooptation of their practitioners. Self-consciously or not, this has made nonKimono irrelevant to most people, and certainly a cipher in the evolution of modern Japanese dress. For our intent, these more practical versions of traditional Japanese clothing serve the purpose of marking the outer boundaries of the context of modern kimono.

THE PEOPLE'S KIMONO

Modern Japanese will readily slip into saying *wafuku* when they mean 'kimono,' even though, historically, wafuku has been represented by many things besides the kimono robe. Almost all items of native Japanese clothing share some design characteristics clearly recognizable as kimonoid, but 'people's kimono' over the centuries has been nothing if not functional work clothing.

Until about the middle of the present century, there was a strong and varied set of regional traditions of work clothing, especially for women. Two factors have almost eradicated these local styles at present. The first is the widespread availability, convenience, and cheapness of Western pants and tops for working clothes. The second is a precipitous decrease in the agricultural labor force. Inexpensive Western clothing has made local clothing uneconomic, while the decline in agricultural labor has weakened village cultural traditions. Regional work clothing (*noragi*) could have claimed the title of native Japanese dress with as much justification as did kimono, but it did not. Instead, noragi became extinct with barely any public notice. Modern Japanese regard old styles of working wear as they might snail darters—insignificant victims of inevitable progress.

Yet folk clothing did find a champion in the person of Segawa Kiyoko, a disciple of Japan's premier ethnologist Yanagita Kunio. As a young woman, Segawa traveled throughout the countryside in the 1930s, gathering information on styles of folk clothing that were even then beginning to disappear. Her informants, old women in remote villages, showed her the clothes they wore for work and festivals and told her the dialect terms that described them. Segawa's work was included in Yanagita's many volumes on regional terminology and folklore and was also published under her own name in 1946 in a small newsprint volume simply entitled *Kimono*. Here Segawa pointedly used the term to mean 'things-to-wear.' Her mission was clear—with Margaret Mead-like zeal, she set out to record a vanishing tradition.

But Segawa was not simply collecting museum pieces. Like her mentor, Yanagita Kunio, she exhorted Japanese not to lose their roots in the folk traditions of an agricultural community. In her introduction to *Kimono*, Segawa wrote:[1]

> Ethnology may not be particularly fashionable, but even so our countrywomen have been extremely remiss in their responsibility as clothing conservators over the past century. In the early 1800s, most Japanese clothing was still made by the women of each household. Each woman spun the thread, wove the cloth, and sewed the clothing. Every aspect of clothing was her creation—the thickness of the cloth, color, design, and the ultimate shape of the garment. But then a change occurred. When individual households stopped spinning and weaving, women lost their perspective on clothing. They began to defer to the shallow judgment of arbiters of taste. In this century, the advantages of traditional work clothing have been utterly

5.1 Mid-twentieth-century farm woman in traditional working dress

5.2　Farm woman
　　　gathering dried grass

ignored. Even the village women who wore it are on the verge of throwing their tradition away. This state of affairs should give us pause.

We are not dolls who have to put up with kimono we cannot work in. We can no longer view our clothing with the perception of dolls, either. Among those who believe that in the future clothing must be more active, many contend that Western clothing is more convenient than the kimono with its long sleeves and wide obi. The fact that Western dress has much in common with rural farmers' dress should make us examine our folk clothing traditions seriously for the first time. The proper recognition of the place of peasant dress as authentic 'kimono' can become the basis for the design of our national dress in the future. It is high time we began to study our legacy of folk clothing, which has been adapted and refined through experience over the course of two and a half millennia.

Intense study of the 'people's kimono' was part of Yanagita Kunio's greater mission to record the cultural lives of the common man and woman in the face of the broadening centralized bureaucratic control that had been exerted over the country since Meiji times. Segawa noted with disappointment that already when she was working, many wafuku research organizations did not recognize farmers' clothing as legitimate representatives of wafuku.[2]

In the face of a tendency to identify Japan with the hierarchical, military-dominated, nationalistic values of the elite, Yanagita and his group argued for the equal validity of local traditions and the village-based morality of the common people. Communal village solidarity, Yanagita believed, was being destroyed by a policy of national centralization using the instrument of emperor worship. The effects of this cultural homogenization were visible in material culture as well as in social life. The identification of kimono as *the* native dress was both sign and symbol of the political dominance of elite traditions. It was against this background that collecting data on traditional work clothing assumed its importance.

Japanese historians of dress see a single outstanding morphological division within the category of native clothing—the one-piece type (essentially the kimono), and the two-piece style characteristic of archaic clothing and peasant working dress. The ankle-length, long-sleeved, obi-wrapped gown that we think of today as Japan's national costume has usually taken the high side of the social dichotomy. On the dimension of work, two-piece clothing was for labor, kimono was for leisure. On the dimension of ceremony, two-piece wear was for ordinary time, kimono for festivals. Socially, kimono was high-class, two-piece low-class. Kimono was urban, two-piece rural. In the nineteenth century, kimono was native, two-piece foreign. Beginning in the modern period, kimono was for women, two-piece was for men.

It is not hard to see how kimono received the mandate to represent native dress. The balance on each dimension tips in kimono's favor as the repository of more concentrated or more preferable cultural values. Nevertheless, the range of native work clothing provided the relevant backdrop that defined the figure of kimono for centuries—until Western clothes gave kimono a new significant other. Since then, the undisputedly practical and arrestingly simple designs of traditional work clothing have gotten short shrift.

5.3   Gathering tea leaves in Shiga Prefecture

Despite great differences in fabric, function, and social standing among different types of native dress, all traditional Japanese clothing shares similar construction techniques. The *ur*-kimono pattern comprises only a limited set of stylistic elements that are reflected in the dress of peasant and princess alike. Unlike the sophisticated urban silks, however, Japanese folk clothing has always addressed the problems of mobility, warmth, economy, and protection. Some folk styles are undeniably expressions of consciously worked beauty, yet the hallmark of the beauty of folk clothing is always rooted in its functionality—for example in the embroidery technique called *sashiko,* which originated as a mundane attempt to add strength to fabric.

From among all the possible ways to encase the human torso in cloth, the Japanese choice since historical times has been of front-wrapping, left over right, jacketlike construction. The history of Japanese clothing admits no pullovers, back-closures, side-fastened, or indeed buttoned garments of any sort. The collar has also been remarkably consistent in style: a band of cloth folded lengthwise, attached most of the way around the front edge. The length and shape of a sleeve can vary, but it is always attached in the same manner by a straight seam at the edge of the garment. Sleeves were never inset, dropped, dolmaned, cuffed, or sewn into any of the other contours theoretically possible in the universe of arm coverings. In fact, variation in Japanese sleeve shape can mostly be accounted for by simple folds rather than by cutting.

Fastening is the job of strings and cords, occasionally sewn on but more often separate from the clothing. Modern kimono is cinched by two or three strips of cloth before the obi is tied around. The obi may be held together by another cord. Work clothing is held in place by a narrow obi, or else by the ties from over-trousers or apron strings. Lacking fixed fasteners, and constructed along straight lines, Japanese garments are 'fitted' to their individual wearers in only the loosest sense.

5.4 Farm woman in a
medley of stripes

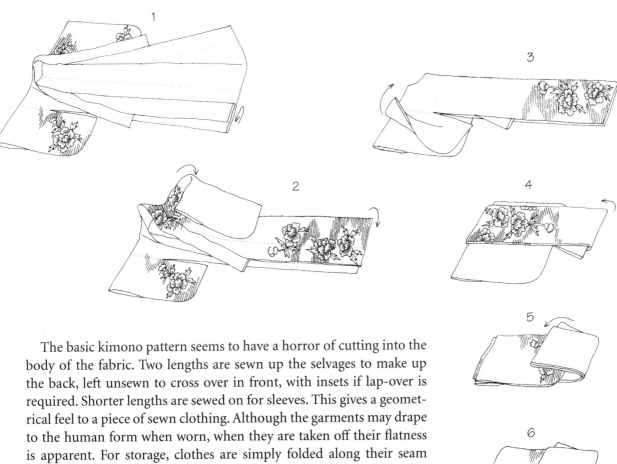

The basic kimono pattern seems to have a horror of cutting into the body of the fabric. Two lengths are sewn up the selvages to make up the back, left unsewn to cross over in front, with insets if lap-over is required. Shorter lengths are sewed on for sleeves. This gives a geometrical feel to a piece of sewn clothing. Although the garments may drape to the human form when worn, when they are taken off their flatness is apparent. For storage, clothes are simply folded along their seam lengths. The sewn pieces may be taken apart and rearranged when one area becomes worn. Traditional clothing thus is almost modular, in the same sense as Japanese architecture. Rooms in a post-and-beam structure can be created wherever one places a sliding paper door. Likewise, the pieces of fabric in a garment are not fixed by design but can be rotated from back to front or shoulder to hem if necessary.

5.5   Steps in folding a kimono along its seams

Traditional clothing for a working woman started with a kimono-shaped robe that reached mid-calf.[3] Perhaps made of indigo-dyed cotton, native bast fibers, or tough wild silk, such a garment was made for economy and mobility. Its sleeves were modified to stay out of the way, either by their sewn shape or by a looped cord called a *tasuki,* which kept a 'normal'-sized kimono sleeve from swinging. No woman was expected to work with bags of cloth hanging from her arms.

Depending on local tradition, additional clothing was worn on the lower body. For ease of movement, warmth, protection, and modesty, there were scores of variations on trousers, some worn under the kimono-robe, some worn over it. Segawa claims to have distinguished more than three hundred versions of *mompe.* No farmer would have been hobbled with a long tubular skirt of cloth constraining her steps. Another common solution to the problem of the kimono skirt was to hike it above the knees and tuck the ends into the obi. A one-piece kimono could be transformed instantly into working or traveling mode simply by tucking up the skirt.

Extra layers of single, lined, or padded jackets were also worn. In general such tops are known as *mijika,* a term etymologically related to the word for 'short.' A *hanten* was the folk equivalent of the more aristocratic haori worn over kimono. Another common item of working apparel was the *sodenashi,* or 'sleeveless'—a simple straight vest, with or without a collar strip. On the lower body, wide aprons made of panels of fabric attached to a belt were commonly worn atop kimono or pants. As well as protecting clothing, these *maekake* were areas of display for regional weaving and embroidery techniques.

For particularly heavy outdoor work, additional items of clothing were added to protect the extremities. Leggings (*kyahan*), arm wrappers (*udenuki*), hand-protectors (*tekko* and *tebukuro*), and lengths of cloth called *tenugui*[4] to wrap the head were all functional accessories to a

5.6 Housewives (*opposite*) and farmers kept sleeves out of the way with a looped cord called a *tasuki*

5.7 Farm woman from Yamagata prefecture wearing an apron, headgear, and *jika tabi*

working woman's wardrobe. Cloth worn on the head also displayed an array of social distinctions. Young women had one style, their mothers another; the people of village *X* wrapped theirs this way, village *Y* that way. In some rural areas, special headgear rather than color, material, or shape of kimono indicated ceremonial dress.[5]

Western clothing styles were slow to be absorbed in rural Japan. Mompe adopted the convenience of elasticized waistbands, and certain Meiji-esque hybrids eventually integrated into rustic working dress. Once in place, they proved tenaciously conservative. Western-influenced aprons and bonnets are still seen at rice harvest in the countryside. From about the turn of the century, rubber boots with a separate space for the big toe, called *jika tabi,* became standard working footgear for both men and women. These field sneakers are a cross between a Japanese sock and a Western rubber boot.[6] Before the importation of rubber, straw sandals were ubiquitous as footwear for farmer or laborer.

Peoples' kimono thus consisted of pants, tops, leggings, vests, jackets, and aprons, as well as short kimono-shaped robes. The dictates of mobility, climate, and economy were paramount in shaping this clothing, but its actual production, in the hands of the women who made it, could express a fine sense of craftwork that still commands admiration when we find a rare surviving piece of it today. The textiles, the dyes, the stitchery of folk clothing have come to be appreciated as art forms on their own, even as the forms of dress to which they once applied disappear.

5.8 Modern farm woman from Chiba Prefecture wearing bonnet, apron, *mompe* and *jika tabi*

Ever since the term *mingei,* 'folk art,' was coined in Japan in the 1930s, the art world has become sensitive to the æsthetic of the unknown craftsman. Japanese folk pottery, in particular, has caught the eye of collectors around the world. Pottery, sculpture, and even painting have mingei representatives. So, too, does fabric. But the problem with the fabric of folk clothing is that its use was in the wearing, and in the wearing it wore out. Relatively few examples of textiles in folk craft museums can match the age of wood, stone, or ceramic artifacts.

The æsthetic tenets of mingei require first and foremost that an object be crafted according to its ultimate function. Adornment is secondary. The object is not primarily an expression of the artist's ego but of materials brought together according to tradition by an anonymous craftworker. This is the classic definition of mingei according to Yanagi Sōetsu, founder of the mingei movement.[7] Modern mingei, however, has developed heroes. The Ministry of Culture designates 'living national treasures' who are hardly anonymous. It could even be argued that the social conditions of the modern industrial age render true mingei impossible. We can have artists who create 'in the style of mingei,' but their relationship to their materials and the consumer is now market-directed.

In effect, the concept of mingei was destroyed as soon as it was created. It could only be recognized as an æsthetic force on the eve of its disappearance. Mingei was the unselfconscious craft of the preindustrial age, only perceivable as an art form when the coming of machine mass production threw it into relief. Previously, the only relevant contrast to folk craft was the art of aristocratic tradition—to which folk art had been presumed irredeemably inferior. True mingei is frozen in time in those objects that are now museum pieces, whispering of a time nostalgic today precisely because it is irretrievable. The door of modernity closed on that life sometime in the mid-twentieth century.

One of the last bastions of classic mingei was folk clothing. The craftspeople were as anonymous as it was possible to be—they were women, the farm women who made and sewed the cloth into traditional work clothing.

Many aspects of folk textile traditions that are now hailed as folk art were originally inseparable from utilitarian concerns. The peasant penchant for deep blue had an incentive even more compelling than fashion—indigo dye preserved the cloth from the ravages of insects and mold, and it wore well.[8] In Japan the color metaphor for true-blue love is homonymous with indigo (*ai*); its opposite is fickle and quick-to-fade scarlet (*kurenai*). Farm woman Chiba Ayano, designated an Important Intangible Cultural Property by the government in 1955 when she was sixty-five, was recognized for preserving the technique of producing a naturally fermented indigo-dyed hemp cloth. From planting the seed, cultivating and preparing the dye, and spinning the thread to weaving and dyeing the cloth, Chiba sustained a self-sufficient rural mode of production that had all but died out in twentieth-century Japan.

The strong and warm serviceable silk called *tsumugi* is another material of folk clothing that has since gained recognition as folk art. Tsumugi is the cloth that peasants wove for themselves from the broken filaments of wild cocoons after the moths had emerged, or from the leftovers of the cultivated crop that had been spoiled or broken by hatching the seed moths that would lay the eggs for the next season's crop of silkworms. The cloth is nubble-textured because of the unevenness of the thread. Tsumugi, in other words, was a frugal cloth, a way to use scraps and wastage. The feudal sumptuary restriction on peasants wearing silk did not apply to tsumugi. Today tsumugi is a staple of the quest for understatement so prominent in traditional Japanese æsthetic modes. A kimono of tsumugi silk is limited by its fabric to informal occasions. But its expense and the manner in which it may be dyed give

5.9   *Egasuri* of eggplant, hawk, and Mt. Fuji— good fortune in New Year's dreams

it drop-dead cachet in the world of kimono fashion one-upmanship, where the expensively unobtrusive is highly appreciated.

Sashiko is the name of a quilting stitch that creates a strong, warm cloth by incorporating two or more layers of fabric within a network of hand stitching. The classic sashiko piece consists of white thread sewn into indigo cloth. The thread follows straight lines in its simplest version but may describe geometric forms, wave patterns, or free-form designs in more elaborate styles. On close inspection, an Edo fireman's jacket collected in Japan in the 1890s by scientist Edward Sylvester Morse and preserved in the collection of the Peabody Museum of Salem, Massachusetts, can be seen to be made of sashiko cloth. Inside the coat is a hand-painted design of dragons and waterfalls, antiflammable talismans next to the skin. The sturdy sashiko stitching provided as much protection as the dragons. Sashiko also provided a way to reuse old cloth that was beginning to fray. Sandwiched within a web of stitchery, even rags could be recycled into a vest, jacket, or back pad.

Another embroidery technique, which developed a distinct regional style in northwest Japan, is *kogin*. Kogin is more purely decorative than sashiko. It fills the surface with interlocking diamond-shaped designs in white thread on indigo cloth, indigo on white, or occasionally colored thread on black cloth. Kogin works from a sense of beauty very different from the classically Japanese. Its bright colors and busy geometrically symmetrical designs seem more like South Asian textiles. Panels of cloth worked in kogin were sometimes made into kimono, but more often they were used in treble-paneled aprons that served the function of an obi for working dress. The apron strings held the outfit together.

5.10 *Egasuri* weaving in a pattern of tigers and bamboo

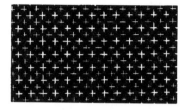

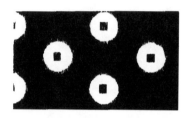

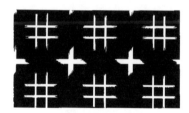

5.11 Some common traditional ikat weaves: mosquito, coins, well-crib

During the eighteenth and nineteenth centuries, cotton was the cloth of choice for work clothing. Until Japan opened its doors to the West in the 1860s, and cheap imported cottons proceeded to smother the native industry, most peasant households were self-sufficient producers of their clothing needs. Cloth for work clothes and bedding was woven at home, mostly in a-thousand-and-one variations on stripes. The choicest men's wear was dyed the darkest hue of indigo and woven in stripes so narrow that from five steps away the garment appeared a solid blue. Women favored lighter degrees of indigo, as well as brown, gray, and light blue. Women's stripes were typically slightly wider and had more variation in spacing. The widest stripes and lattices (a warp and weft stripe, in effect) were used during Meiji for bedding fabric, but these more exuberant stripes later crept into the kimono cloth of early twentieth-century work clothes. A work outfit was frequently a medley of stripes: a vertically striped, short-sleeved kimono cinched with a horizontally striped obi, over a striped underskirt, and finally a striped apron over all.

A Meiji farm girl usually wove her own dowry. Most of the kimono and haori she sewed were dark, simply striped garments that she could expect to wear for the rest of her life. During Taishō, the plain, dark, naturally-dyed peasant hues went out of fashion in the face of aniline purples and orange. Absorbing fashion trends from the cities, rural stripes ran riot. Many late Meiji trousseaux have been preserved simply because their small dark stripes dropped out of fashion before they could be worn.

Along with her endowment of cloth, a bride-to-be would take to her husband's home a sample book of striped swatches. This *shima-chō*, or stripe album, was her feminine heritage—weaving patterns to which she would add and pass on to her daughters. Ethnographer and textile researcher Fukui Sadako tells of her attempts to gather old stripe albums for preservation and research:[9]

5.12 Casual combinations of ikat and stripes: male servant (early twentieth century); nursing mother (eighteenth century)

During these expeditions to find shima-chō, my first impression was of great old thatch-roofed farmhouses. As long as an elderly grandmother was alive, there would be a stripe album tucked away somewhere. These women could page through the hundreds of swatches and tell me who wove them, when, and for what occasion. One old woman gave me hers saying, 'Now that I've safely bequeathed my shima-chō, I can die in peace.' But more often they would refuse to part with the books as long as they still drew breath. I had to respect how precious these ragged books were to their owners, and I was grateful for a mere look at them. But I'm afraid my reticence did not serve the research well. Returning to this area several years later, I found that the old women with whom I had spoken had gone to their graves, and their precious stripe albums had been lost or discarded.

Stripes are the simplest form of design that can be woven in fabric; the ikat weaves known as kasuri are among the most complicated. In ikat weaving, the pattern is dyed into sections of the thread lengths before it is woven. Warp or weft alone may carry the pattern, or the pattern may be created by the intersection of dyed warp and weft. The simplest expositions of the design possibilities of kasuri are cross shapes, arrows, hexagons, and the double cross well-crib design. These relatively regular repeating patterns are most common in kasuri woven for clothing. More ambitious large-scale 'picture kasuri' (*egasuri*) were originally

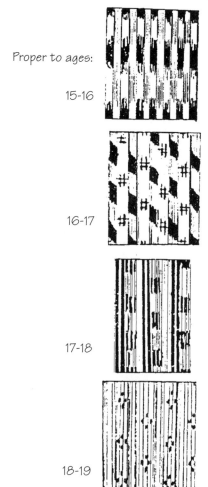

Proper to ages:

15-16

16-17

17-18

18-19

5.13 Kasuri patterns varied by age until the early part of this century

made in four to five panels for bedding coverlets. As peasant clothing moved from the somber colors, narrow stripes, and small patterns of Meiji, kimono kasuri adopted more intricate pictorial designs as well.

Social distinctions have always been woven into Japanese clothing. Different kasuri designs were appropriate for young and old, male and female. The common well-crib figure, for example, was supposed to be smaller the older the person. Increased density of a design like crosses or hexagons raised the social status of the garment. The supreme example of a kasuri pattern remains, even today, the pattern called mosquito kasuri. Its minuscule spots of white, where warp and weft cross on an indigo background, require the ultimate in a weaver's skill.

The sudden popularity of gauzy ramie kasuri kimono among fashion-conscious urbanites in the late eighteenth century provided a new market for the handwoven goods of countrywomen. The northern province of Echigo and southern Okinawa became famous for production of kasuri. In these areas women wove to order for commercial purpose, but exercised ingenuity and creativity in the cloth for home consumption. Some of these domestic pieces are preserved in the Museum of Kasuri in Kurume, Fukuoka prefecture. But as the curator explained when I visited, "So much has been lost. When a kimono became worn, it was taken apart and sewed into futon covers. When they became worn, they were cut into aprons. When the aprons got worn, they were made into diapers. Nothing makes such a soft diaper as a piece of well-worn kasuri cloth."

During the early twentieth century, technological developments in dyeing and weaving equipment made cotton kasuri widely and cheaply available all over Japan. Machine-produced kasuri became the equivalent of blue jeans today—serviceable, comfortable, and fashionable for town or country, student or farmer. Older women today have somewhat mixed emotions about kasuri because the baggy mompe pants they had to wear during the war years were usually made of it. Still, a kasuri cotton unlined kimono for summer has great appeal and is often a young woman's first experience of wearing wafuku.

Stripes and kasuri, then, have been the woven staples of folk clothing. They are sometimes found combined in the supreme examples of peasant frugality, patchwork garments. Patchwork has always been a measure of economy, but it has also created one of the most striking folk costumes in Japan. Fukui Sadako gives this account of finding a patchwork kimono early in her career of cataloguing textiles:[10]

> This was a single garment overlaid with one hundred and forty separate scraps of cloth in unplanned arrangement. When it emerged from the great bale of old cotton clothes we were analyzing, I was struck dumb. My eyes started crossing and I couldn't focus on the whole thing at once. My assistant Kagetsu Setsuko had the same reaction. We just sat there speechless for a while, and then I whispered, 'This is the true image of the Japanese peasant.'
>
> I had been collecting people's discarded cotton cloth and old tools as artifacts for some time, but I had never come across an item like this. That one piece of clothing expressed a tenacity to life and depth of human emotion that was terribly moving. Each and every scrap in the medley of kasuri and striped cloth was hand-loomed. Even as they blended together, they transmitted a lingering warmth from within. This was a cherished woman's garment that spanned three generations in workmanship.

The garment that so amazed Fukui in its embodiment of the frugal, disciplined peasant acceptance of life originally came from Hiroshima prefecture. It was probably worn in the evaporation fields where salt was harvested, protecting its wearer from the wind blowing in from the open sea. The "true image of the Japanese peasant" that emanates from this remarkable congregation of cotton is certainly as much a part of Japanese culture as are the painted silks and woven brocades that assert Kimono's claim to national pride.

5.14 Patchwork garment known as *hagi tōjin* from Nagasaki Prefecture

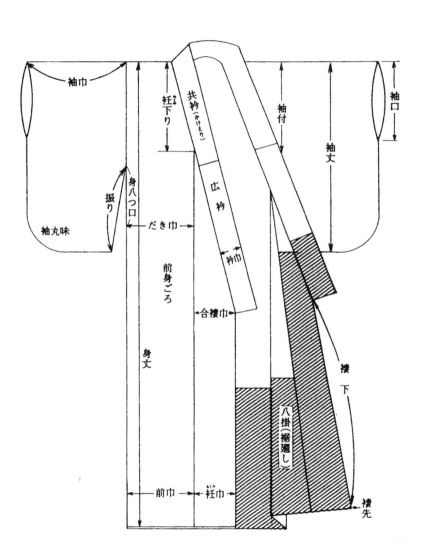

袖巾

袖口

衽下り

共衿（かけえり）

袖付

袖丈

身八つ口

広衿

振り

袖丸味

だき巾

衿巾

前身ごろ

合褄巾

身丈

褄下

八掛（裾廻し）

前巾

衽巾

褄先

SIX

THE STRUCTURE OF KIMONO

We can tell many things about people just by looking at their cast-off kimono. The material, form, color, the way it is thrown off, give us messages at an unconscious level—yet we have not made an effort to understand this scientifically.

—Segawa Kiyoko, *Kimono*, 1948

EVEN WOMEN WHO CROSS THEIR LEGS occasionally wear kimono. Once they do, a great many rules come into play. Modern kimono is constrained by a corset of convention. Even in the present era of fashion experimentation, Japanese have a strong sense of what is and is not appropriate when dressing in wafuku. Manuals, magazines, and kimono academies all promote a culturally consistent line on kimono protocol.

The relative stability and widespread acceptance of a canon makes it possible to think of the domain of kimono as a system. Without such a systemic understanding, in fact, one cannot appreciate the way a woman wears a kimono and obi ensemble in any but subjective terms. A woman standing in a hotel lobby in early November, wearing a licorice-black kimono patterned with mountains in pale green and gold on the hem and five white rondels at shoulder and sleeve, makes a precise statement in 'kimonese' of who she is and what she is doing.

Dressing in wafuku may be complicated, but it is logical. Unlike the terrain of Western clothing, which is constantly altered by upheavals of fashion, the kimono system today is relatively fossilized. As we have seen, wafuku in modern Japan maintains its small bailiwick within the larger domain of dress, surrounded on all sides by Western clothing. The preceding chapters have paced out the boundaries of kimono's domain. We shall now map its inner territory.

We get our bearings for exploring the topography of kimono from Japanese names for clothing types—words that are good indicators of socially important distinctions in dress. In addition, I will make explicit the hidden compass that defines in cultural terms the directions choices may take. During the fifteen years in which I have had experience wearing and trying to understand kimono, I have constantly checked the categories of my observations with professional wearers and makers of wafuku. I feel confident that the analysis I apply to kimono is not far removed from the process Japanese themselves use when deciding who wears what kind of kimono when. This is not to say that any Japanese has ever laid out the system in the way I present it here. Yet when shown this scheme, a kimono wearer's reaction typically is not only that it works but also that it brings an order to her or his extensive practical knowledge of native Japanese dress.[1]

Here, then, are the cultural underpinnings of Japanese clothing. Every kimono and obi ensemble worn can—must—take into account distinctions on each of the following dimensions:

Life / Death
Gender
Formality or Occasion
Season
Age
Taste or Class.

We might think of these categories as pegs upon which are hung particular social messages. Sometimes the choice is straightforwardly x or y, as in the case of gender—since a kimono outfit is either for a male or for a female. The dress of living persons and corpses is another simple dichotomy. In other dimensions, the options are many. In the category of formality, for example, there is an extensive and finely graduated series of choices. Season is relatively unambiguous, although the clothing seasons are not identical with those of nature. Age is signified both by two fundamental divisions (child or adult) and by many graded ones. What signified class in an earlier era is, in present-day society, something closer to what we might call taste. This category is the most subtle, but nevertheless is clearly distinguishable at crucial places such as the nape of the neck and set of the obi.

The egregiousness of clothing mistakes corresponds to this list. At the extreme, a corpse cannot be faulted for a lapse of taste, but a living person in solid white kimono and obi could only be an actor in the role of a ghost. Likewise, to mistake gender would be so odd as to redefine the entire social situation. A person dressing in kimono of the opposite sex is either proclaiming transvestism or play-acting. Outside such oddities, wearing kimono at the wrong level of formality is probably the most excruciating clothing mistake a person can commit in Japan. Being out of season, or dressing too old or young are mistakes on the level of the faux pas. Where one ties the obi or how much of the nape is exposed send more subtle messages of taste, evoking the raised eyebrow or quiet smile.

How does kimono convey its messages and meanings on all these dimensions? It employs a vocabulary of fabric, color, pattern, and form. Kimono's ability to convey a wearer's age, for example, is based on several things: most obviously colors (brighter for younger, more subdued for older), but also placement of the design. In this formula, the younger the wearer, the higher the hem pattern reaches toward the waist. In the vocabulary of seasonality, an unlined kimono in the airy leno-weave silk fabric called *ro* is marked as a summer garment by its fabric.

But the kimono and obi ensemble is not flat terrain from which social meanings are broadcast with equal intensity. Some kimono elements are more saturated with meaning than others. Sleeves, for example, distinguish gender, proclaim formality, and define age distinctions. The question of taste attaches strongly to the set of the collar. Hems are an important canvas for formality. The different parts of a kimono and obi ensemble combine according to rules to make a clothing statement.

6.1 Parts of the modern
kimono/obi ensemble

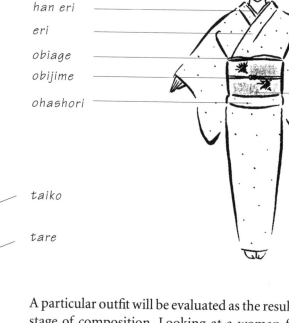

han eri

eri

obiage

obijime

ohashori

obi

taiko

tare

tabi

obijime

A particular outfit will be evaluated as the result of choices made at each stage of composition. Looking at a woman fully dressed in kimono, a Japanese views an ensemble of parts and interprets its meaning. Violations of an expected rule will stand out—brilliantly if done with knowledge and taste, embarrassingly if not.

To be able to interpret meaning in the first place, however, it is necessary to know the range of choices involved. We can appreciate kimono only as a bundle of gorgeous textiles or as another exotic ethnic costume unless we have some idea of the possible types of kimono robe there can be or the range of obi from which a particular obi has been chosen. Meaning results, in part, because the choice by definition excludes all those items not chosen.

The systemic nature of the domain of kimono reveals itself in many places, highlighting a logic that projects onto the social world. Here is an example so inconspicuous that even most Japanese are probably not conscious of it—the shape of the lower outside corner seam of the kimono sleeve. Men's kimono sleeves are square-cut, adult women's are slightly rounded, unmarried women's sleeve seams are more rounded, and children's seams are roundest of all.

A set of details having no conceivable function follows a continuum of round to square, and corresponds to a distinction among clothing meant for children, girls, women, and men. The social markers of this continuum are gender and age, while the message projected by sleeve corners indicates degrees of sameness and difference among these categories of people. In this 'seaming' of meaning, the more socially accountable the wearer, the sharper the corner. Thus children, girls, and women are perceived to be more like one another than any of them are like men. But at the same time degree of squareness indicates that women are more like men than are girls or children. Few, I think, would argue with this depiction of traditional Japanese society. How interesting to find it hidden in people's sleeves.

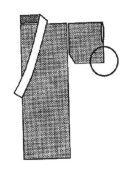

Adult male

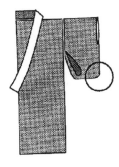

Adult female

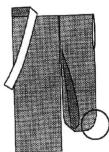

Single female

Child

6.2 Construction of kimono sleeve according to age and gender

When we observe all the places on kimono where similar distinctions are made, signifying gender, formality, age, season, and class, the ultimate effect can be complex and subtle. A kimono composition can of course be trite, as can a poem, yet it can also obey all the rules and still be striking and original. This kind of analysis may seem initially to drain an object of its purely æsthetic aspect, but in the end, it makes possible a fuller appreciation of the higher levels of kimono connoisseurship, reflecting, as it does, the way Japanese themselves appreciate kimono.

GENDER

6.3 Informal obi for a man (*above*) and a woman

Let us now examine how the language of kimono works on each dimension in turn, beginning with gender. The basic cut of the modern kimono differs little between the sexes, yet there is nevertheless no mistaking a woman's kimono for a man's. The most obvious difference is color. The modern male kimono is the drabber of the species. Charcoal grays, brown-toned blacks, seaweed greens, and wine-dark cyans constitute its hues. If there is a pattern at all, a man's kimono will sport a subdued small-scale repeat. The sole design will be the crest at mid-back and shoulder, and only on the formal kimono. A few men indulge love of color and pattern through painted silk linings, which do not show, or inside the haori jacket, where a glimpse can be discreetly flashed. How different this is from the early seventeenth century, when brightly colored, dramatically patterned robes were so similar for men and women that in woodblock prints it is often difficult to tell the sexes apart.

A man's kimono falls straight from shoulder to ankle with no excess length to be tucked up. A woman's kimono must be longer than her height and adjusted to ankle length by blousing over a tie at the hips. American women, on average taller than Japanese women, can use antique kimono as lounging robes that conveniently come right to the ankle. The other main gender difference in garment construction is found in the sleeves. Men's kimono sleeves are shorter and they are sewn closed on the side that touches the body, whereas women's sleeves are open from underarm to bottom edge.

A man's obi is distinctly different from a woman's in its narrower width, subdued colors, and manner of tying. In ceremonial wear, men secure kimono at the hips with a stiff, two-inch-wide *kaku obi*, which ends up hidden by the pleated skirtlike hakama they add to complete the formal ensemble. For yukata or other casual kimono, men wear a soft, scarflike *heko obi*, similar in style and comfort (although not color) to children's wear. Women cannot wear a heko obi, but only an obi of greater or lesser wide stiffness. This again reflects a social distinction. Men and children are considered somehow similar, in distinction to women. The interpretation of this statement, clearly, is the degree of relaxed freedom that is socially permissible to men and children but not to women. All the cords, clasps, and scarves worn as obi accessories occur only with women's kimono.

Traditional sandalform footwear are also shaped by gender. Men's *zōri* and *geta* have squarish corners, while women's are rounded—which is exactly what we would expect, given the cultural logic we see underlying gender differentiation. In Japanese culture as in many others, curves mark female, straight lines male.

6.4 Man's *kaku obi* tied in 'clam's mouth' knot (*top*); informal, soft *heko obi* in a simple bow

6.5 Footwear for men (*left*) and women

When most people dress for funerals they consider what the mourners, not the corpse, will wear, yet there are culturally important distinctions between kimono for the quick and the dead. Later I shall discuss the special articles of wafuku marked as mourning wear (*mōfuku*) for the living, but for the moment we are concerned with necrofashion. Although nowadays there is a movement toward dressing the deceased in the clothing preferred in life, the traditional corpse will still wear a pure white cotton or hempen kimono and obi sewn by female relatives.

Significantly, the only person besides a corpse who wears a solid white kimono is a bride.[2] Ceremonial bridal white is relieved by the gold and silver brocade of the obi, and a bride may wear a colorful padded robe over the white kimono. Despite the gilding, however, there remains an undeniable similarity between brides and corpses: both have ended one life and are embarking upon another. Ideally, sins or idiosyncrasies from former existences should not color lives to come—as buddhas or daughters-in-law. Immediately after wedding cups are exchanged, the bride changes to a colored kimono, marking her official passage into the groom's family.

The kimono of a corpse is distinctive in another way. Instead of the usual overlap left side over right, a corpse's robe is crossed right over left. This explains why a foreign woman wearing a cotton hotel yukata on a provincial Japanese street may fall afoul of an old woman who reproachfully attempts to rearrange her bosom. In the West, right-over-left signifies gender: women's coats and blouses button to the left, men's the opposite. In Japan, the cultural polarity of life and death, rather than male and female, governs the handedness of clothing.

Gender and quickness are so clear-cut that in these areas it is hard to make clothing mistakes. By the same token, their readability as social statement is strong. For example, articles of male traditional wear were incorporated into women's dress during the Meiji period in order to create a new form of public, nonfrivolous working garb for women. In hakama or haori, women were not merely borrowing clothing, they were putting on social weight previously reserved to males.

We now take up the most important, most differentiated, and most problematic dimension of native dress for the modern kimono wearer—formality. The first distinction that Japanese make when talking about kimono hinges on this question: a kimono is either *haregi*, 'special, formal wear,' or it is *fudangi*, 'everyday-wear.' Japanese propriety produces infinitely graduated levels of formality defining people's places in particular settings. These are the sorts of distinctions that dress is ideally suited to demonstrate. Indeed, the primary reason for the kimono wearer's obsessive concern with formality is that formal styles of wafuku dominate the contemporary kimono repertoire. The whole wardrobe of everyday-wear has been replaced by Western clothing. It is precisely on formality that kimono pins its modern existence.

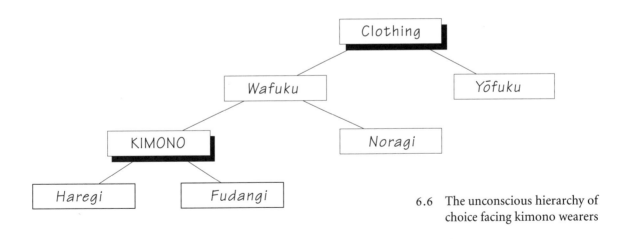

6.6 The unconscious hierarchy of choice facing kimono wearers

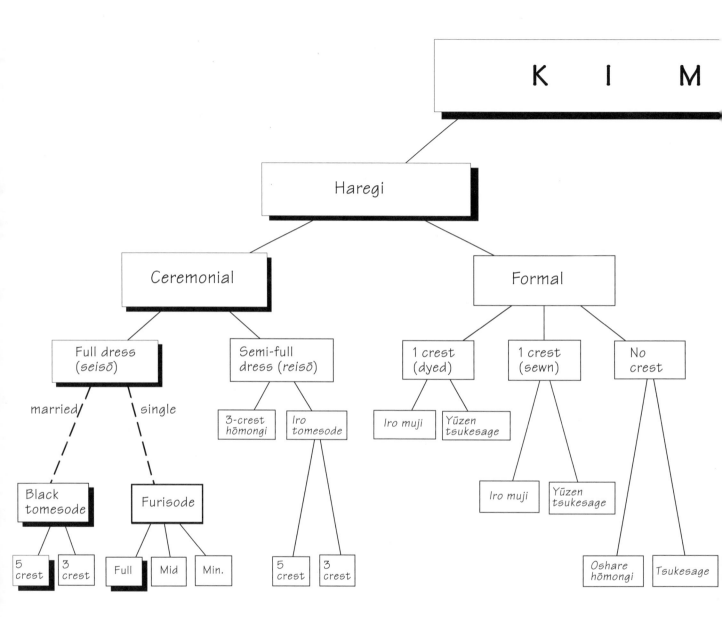

KIMONO IN THE MODERN WORLD

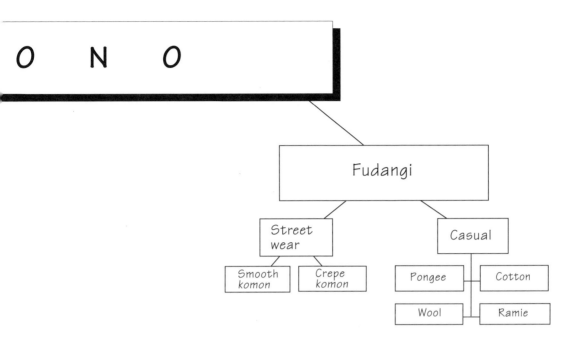

This tree diagram closely follows Japanese linguistic distinctions. At each node, formality defines the type of kimono. The more formal branch is on the left, so with modern wafuku's formal tendencies the tree has become quite lopsided. The nodes indicate noncontroversial ensembles—they both describe and prescribe items of wear for specific occasions. Much magazine discussion aimed at the kimono-wearing woman takes such nonproblematic safety zones for granted, focusing instead on the gray areas that fall between. Uncertainty lurks where an outfit has not been completely predetermined—when a woman must combine elements from the base types on either side to create the effect she wants. The extremes of the rules are always clear. The middle ranges—the stuff of everyday life—require a fair amount of individual adjustment to create the proper effect.

6.7   Formality hierarchy of kimono

The Formal Kimono

Formality is expressed on the kimono, on the obi, and in footwear through the media of fabric, pattern, and color. It is literally impossible to dress in kimono without simultaneously electing a precise level of formality. Every natural fiber used for kimono—silk, bast fiber, cotton, or wool—has a level of formality inextricably woven into it. The same is true for the obi, and of course the two must be properly coordinated. Degree of formality is also indicated by placement of the design painted or dyed into silks, by the garment's color, and by family crests. We shall examine how all these elements work together.

Kimono Fabric

By cultural fiat, formal kimono must be made from glossed dyed silk. Unglossed silks and fabrics other than silk are informal. This distinction between fabrics, though technically imprecise, is commonly referred to as *somemono* (dyed things) versus *orimono* (woven things).[3] Furthermore, there is a hierarchy among fine silks: weave-patterned damask is more formal than plain-weave habutae, which in turn is higher than silk crepe. Even silk per se is not a clear-cut sign of formality. Orimono include raw silk, tussah, pongee, or wild silk, as well as wool, fine hemp, and cotton. Wild silk from cocoons where the moth has hatched and broken the threads or textured 'pulled silk' (*tsumugi*)—while beautiful and expensive—may be used only for ordinary-wear kimono.

A refined ploy in wafuku fashion one-upwomanship is to have a rough tsumugi silk kimono hand painted or dyed in the yūzen manner more commonly found on smooth silks. Expensive as it is, such a kimono, because of its fabric, cannot be anything other than fudangi, 'ordinary wear.' But it is exquisitely ordinary.

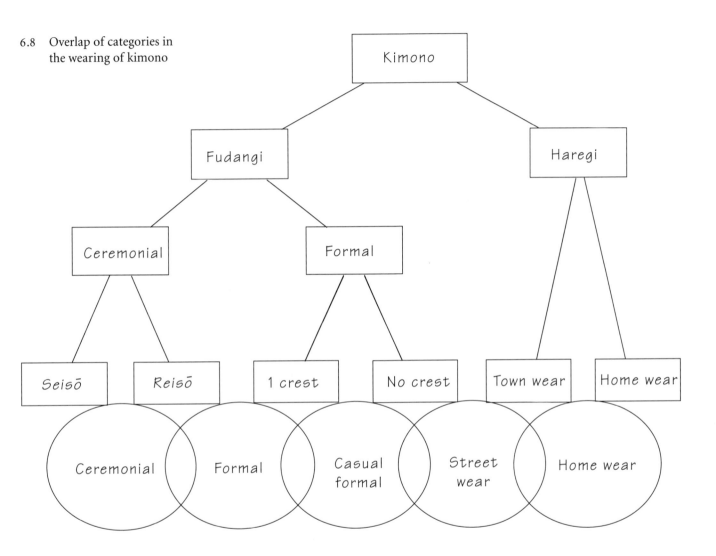

6.8 Overlap of categories in the wearing of kimono

Kimono Patterns and Their Placement

A hand-painted wisteria blossom trailing down from the shoulder, or a pattern of gold-embroidered wavelets lapping a hem, can also signify a kimono's degree of formality—by virtue of where it occurs. At least three categories of kimono are defined by pattern placement, each representing a precise level of formality.

A kimono grammatical rule seems to be in operation here. The more pervasive the pattern, the less formal the garment. Thus at the lowest, most informal level, stenciled or painted repeat patterns cover the entire garment. This patterning, *komon*, provides the name for this type of kimono. One step up is the *tsukesage*, a garment with an asymmetrical pattern appearing on its left shoulder and hem only. An all-over patterned komon kimono cannot be dressed up by adding a crest, but the tsukesage can be, and so jump to a higher level of ceremony.

A crested tsukesage begins to encroach on the turf of *hōmongi*, visiting wear. Hōmongi has higher cachet because its asymmetrical patterning continues without break across the side seams to the back hem. Such kimono are made from bolts of silk provisionally stitched up into the

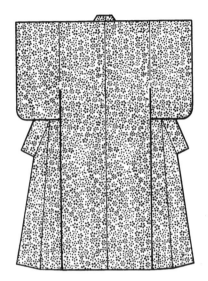

Komon

Tsukesage

finished length and then hand painted, taken apart, dyed, and resewed. In contrast, a tsukesage, much the same in overall effect, can be made straight from the bolt. The most formal kimono in this pattern index is the *un*patterned monochrome kimono (*iro muji*), with one, three, or five crests.

The subjects of the designs and patterns are more a matter of seasonality than formality, but traditional Japanese designs are felt to be more suitable for formal kimono, while 'foreign' flowers like roses or cattleya orchids are left to more casual wafuku.

The rules governing pattern have fostered hybrid kimono among the pattern types. One such is the *tsukesage komon*, an overall pattern dyed so that the direction of the motifs will be the same, back and front, when the garment is sewed—a trellised wisteria pattern that trails down both sides, for example, or a wave pattern gradually increasing in scale from shoulder to hem. Such a kimono comes precisely midway between a komon and a tsukesage in formality.

6.9   Pattern as a signifier of formality

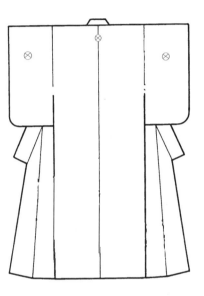

Three-crested iro muji

Hōmongi

Kimono Color

Color signifies formality in a dramatic and clear way through contrast. Colors per se do not hold meaning as they did in ancient days, when reds and purples per se were marks of high status, forbidden to all but royalty. In modern kimono parlance, the *distinction* between black and colored is significant. Among crested, ceremonial kimono, for instance, the difference between semi-full-dress and the highest full-dress level of wafuku rests on whether the ground color of the gown is black or colored. Black is the most formal, colors by fiat less so.

Thus the accepted definition of a woman's most formal full-dress kimono is black, patterned on hem only, with five crests. The current colored version of this kimono (*iro tomesode*) aspires to the highest reaches of formality but still defers to black. At a wedding, for example, the female relatives of the bride (whose participation is socially 'heaviest') are usually dressed in black, whereas her friends (whose position is 'lighter') dress in colored versions of crested, hem-patterned kimono.

Formality can also be signified through the sleeves, as in the case of the swinging-sleeved (*furisode*) kimono worn by unmarried girls. Sleeve length primarily indicates gender and age, but the so-called mid-deep sleeve (*chū-furisode*), a relatively recent development, can be worn in opposition to the full, ankle-length swinging sleeve. This creates a category of semi-full-dress for unmarried women. Because long sleeves equate to high formality, the logic of shortening them slightly to deformalize the outfit is apparent to all.

6.10 Women's highest ceremonial wear: mother of the bride in black five-crest kimono; younger sister in *furisode*

No one layers kimono any more. Underkimono are always white and absolutely dull. I've been thinking for the past five or six years that I would really love to combine some different colors and patterns, but I haven't had the courage to do it yet.

—Kondō Tomie, *Yosoi no onnagokoro*, 1985

Modern layering of kimono is a skimpy version of what used to be. Kimono layering reached full and glorious expression during the Heian period a millennium ago. A mere century before the present a woman's ceremonial kimono consisted of three full layers, and in the 1920s and 1930s, two were normal. Today a two-layer look can be faked in a single garment for highly formal wear, or a kimono-neck dickey may be inserted under the gown. At least an artificial layered look means that layering still has the potency to make something more formal, but the great Heian tradition echoes only faintly today.

6.11 A kimono collar dickey creates the effect of an extra layer

Mourning Kimono

In modern Japan, occasion and formality tend to define each other. Nevertheless, some occasions demand a particular form of traditional dress, apart from the question of formality as such. Bridal dress, which most women wear but once in their lives, is an example. Mourningwear is another, and one mourns more often than one marries.

The kimono tree diagram depicted earlier included only special wear of a felicitous sort. If the chart had three dimensions, we could construct a parallel branch of 'infelicitous' formalwear—that is, mourning dress, the important distinctions within which are illustrated here. Again, the left side of each branch is the weighted form. Rather than formality per se, in this instance the marked version expresses either degree of kinship to the deceased or temporal proximity to the time of death.

6.12 Special wear of an infelicitous nature (*mōfuku*), according to its formality hierarchy

Like Victorian mourning ritual, Buddhist funerary ceremony occurs in stages. Degrees of mourning are expressed by color. A widow wears solid black at her husband's funeral, but at the ceremony on the

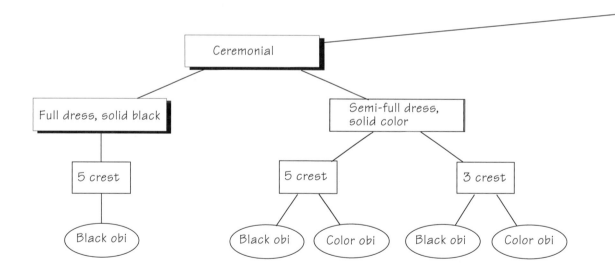

forty-ninth day after his death she might wear a mauve kimono with a black obi. The husband's female secretary, however, would wear mauve and black at the funeral itself, having been (one would hope) more distantly involved with the man. In fact, were she to wear solid black, tongues would wag. Blackness thus is most intense for family members, and most intense at the time of the funeral. In this context, color is associated with normal life, black with nearness to death.

In the most intense expression of mourning, a solid black kimono tied with a solid black obi is worn with black obi accessories and sandals. Monochrome, unpatterned kimono can be turned into 'light' mourning wear by the addition of a subdued obi and a black obi cord. The black obi cord is the last vestige of mourning. When it gives way to an ordinary colored one, mourning has ended. By the same token, black can never be used as a fashion color for an obi cord.

6.13 A totally black full mourning ensemble, and the lighter version of semi-mourning

```
                    ┌─────────────────────┐
                    │  Mourning kimono    │
                    └─────────────────────┘
                               │
                        ┌─────────────┐
                        │   Formal    │
                        └─────────────┘
                         /            \
              ┌─────────────┐      ┌─────────────────┐
              │ Solid color │      │  Hem-patterned  │
              └─────────────┘      └─────────────────┘
                    │               /              \
              ┌─────────┐     ┌─────────┐     ┌─────────┐
              │ 1 crest │     │ 3 crest │     │ 1 crest │
              └─────────┘     └─────────┘     └─────────┘
               /      \        /      \        /      \
          (Black  (Color  (Black  (Color  (Black  (Color
           obi)    obi)    obi)    obi)    obi)    obi)
```

Formality and Crests

A discussion of the signifiers of kimono formality would be incomplete without that punctuation of punctilio, the family crest. The Japanese crest (*mon*) is a stylized motif, usually within a rondel, combining the functions of heraldry, logo, and sheer design. A single crested kimono displays the mon at the mid-back seam just below the collar. A three-crested garment adds two crests to the back of the sleeves, while a five-crested kimono adds two more to the front of the garment, placed just below the collar bone.

The presence or absence of crests is the clearest indication of whether a kimono is considered formal. While there can be uncrested formal kimono, there are no crested informal ones. In modern Japan, the actual design on a crest is less important than the fact that it is there.

The social significance of crests has varied throughout Japanese history. Heian nobility used motifs on carriages and personal articles, although not, apparently, on clothing. During the Kamakura era, and with the rise of the samurai, crests were writ large on banners, armor, tents, and other military paraphernalia, identifying friend and foe on the battlefield. During the Tokugawa period, crests were divided into heraldic and decorative usage. Regional lords and samurai adopted certain mon as family insignia, but at the same time townspeople developed the inherent design possibilities of crests purely for fashionable clothing. These two aspects of the crest commingle today. Every Japanese family is entitled to use a crest, but its pedigree may go no deeper than great-grandfather's partiality to the oak leaf motif.

The wearing of family crests (*ie mon*) and regulated crests (*sadame mon*) was restricted to members of the samurai and noble classes in the feudal era. Certain crests, such as the hollyhock mon of the ruling Tokugawa shogunate, were forbidden to all but members of specific families. There were about four hundred official crests. Many underwent meiosis when branch families formed, however, so that when variations are included, the number of crests reaches seven or eight thousand.

The plum blossom motif alone has at least ninety variants. From about the mid-eighteenth century, woodblock-printed family crest directories were published annually. They served as a *Who's Who*, listing out the current status of crests and their rightful bearers.

Apart from samurai, kabuki actors and courtesans in the floating world used mon as individual logos, almost trademarks, within their professions. The mon of Kabuki actors eventually became like family crests. They were identified with a particular line of actors and passed on to successors. Prostitutes, however, chose flamboyant renditions of parasols and paper lanterns, changing them on a whim. Printers published crest directories for them, too. Customers used them as catalogues.

The use of one version of a crest for public occasions and another for private also stems from feudal times. The official version of a crest is called the recto crest (*omote mon*), full-sun crest (*hinata mon*), or dye-reserved crest (*somenuki mon*). These terms refer to a crest design in a circlet of the white of the fabric that was reserved before the garment was dyed. By contrast, for less formal occasions the same design could be dyed intaglio as the verso crest (*ura mon*) or shadow crest (*kage mon*), or embroidered as a *nui mon*.

The embroidered crest overlaps the realm of crest as decoration, becoming the *date mon*, the direct descendent of mid-Edo period fashionable crests worn by townspeople. A crest design discreetly embroidered in white thread is still an official, albeit less formal crest, but if executed in different colors, or applied on a slightly larger scale, the embroidered crest becomes decoration rather than decorum, and its subject matter is not limited to the family design.

It is perfectly permissible for a woman to wear her maiden crests on any kimono. Called *onna mon*, women's crests are inherited matrilineally, and a woman is not obliged to change to her father's or husband's design. In premodern Japan, a bride's trousseau was prepared with the crest of her natal family (father's or mother's crest). Her family would

6.14 Crests: variations on plum blossoms (*opposite*) and bamboo (*above*)

6.15 Different versions of a gingko leaf crest: full-sun (*top*), shadow (*middle*), mid-shadow (*bottom*)

Hinata mon

Kage mon

Nakakage mon

also have supplied her with crested robes for her babies when they were first presented to the shrine deity, and later for the children's festivals. The bride's continued use of her maiden crests was supposed to be a visual reminder to her husband's family of her connections and a preventative against bride-bullying, a favorite sport of traditional Japanese mothers-in-law.

Questions as to how many crests and what type to have on a kimono are not easily resolved at the boundary between the merely formal and the truly ceremonial. Kimono magazines are replete with advice to the woman eager to wear wafuku correctly. In an article concerning *iro muji* (unpatterned monochrome) kimono, we find the following specialized advice:[4]

> Five crests on a monochrome kimono make it formal, suitable for occasions like weddings and betrothal parties. Yet, a full sun style with five crests will stand out too much, so it is advisable to have the crests dyed in a mid-range shadow style. The same holds for three crests. A one-crested monochrome kimono, on the other hand, just makes it into the category of formal wear, so it can use the added weight of a crest dyed in its full sun version.

Distinctions among levels of formality are often couched in terms of an outfit's 'hardness' or 'softness,' concepts that reflect attitudes toward official things in general. An outfit that comes across as overly official will be as psychologically uncomfortable as one that is not up to formal par. The balancing act just shown represents a typical attempt to bridge the gap between 'hard' propriety and 'softer' style. This is the area of greatest difficulty in wearing wafuku. This is what scares many modern women who don't trust their own judgment about their 'native dress.' This is what kimono schools and magazines capitalize on, and this is what, when done right, is most appreciated by kimono connoisseurs.

The modern incarnation of the obi is nearly the equal of the kimono, inasmuch as kimono and obi work together to create the total wafuku effect. Choice of kimono, however, automatically influences the range of obi that can be worn.

The hierarchy of obi types follows a set of fabric rules similar to those for kimono. At the highest level of formality are brocades, metallic or colored, followed in order by dyed silks, woven silks, and non-silk fabrics. In general, metallic, patterned brocade obi accompany the most formal kimono; colored brocades are appropriate for semi-full-dress. A dyed obi goes with formal kimono, while an orimono obi, its patterns produced on the loom rather than painted by hand, goes with everyday wear. Raw silk, cotton, hemp, and wool are, by the nature of their fabric, limited to everyday wear.

Kimono-obi grammatical rules proscribe, for example, the wearing of a gold brocade obi with an informal komon pattern kimono. Nor is it possible to combine a lowly dyed obi with ceremonial wear—but you could intensify the formality of a 'visiting wear' formal kimono by adding a brocade obi. As we have seen, the extremities of these categorical rules are set, while the middle ground leaves room for choice. This becomes an important factor in a modern woman's decision to buy a kimono. Few women maintain the extensive kimono wardrobes that were considered a bride's due as recently as two generations ago. Nowadays, a woman thinks in terms of getting the most wear from the one or two kimono she stashes away behind her Chanel suits. One reason for the popularity of the tsukesage hem-and-shoulder–patterned kimono is precisely that it can be dressed up or down by choice of obi, thus equipping its owner for a wider range of social occasions.

Types of Obi

When kimono were worn every day, they could be tied with a great variety of obi. Many of the informal obi styles, like the soft, black-satin faced *chūya obi*, have disappeared. Nowadays, concern about the appropriateness of obi revolves largely around the issues of material and brocade mentioned above.

However, the obi is also defined in categories based on its construction. The most formal obi is the *maru obi*, now almost obsolete by reason of its sheer bulk. A maru obi consists of more than four yards of solid brocade cloth twenty-seven inches wide—precisely four times the width of a tied obi. The maru obi is folded in half along its entire length so that each side is right-side-out brocade. (Its only practical virtue is that if you happened to stain it with soy sauce on one side, it could later be reversed.) Its edges are lapped together over an inserted facing, and since this doubled layer is again doubled where it goes around the waist, a maru obi creates a great bulk of cloth around a woman's middle. Except for bridal kimono, the maru obi is almost never worn today.

6.16 Types of obi and their relative sizes

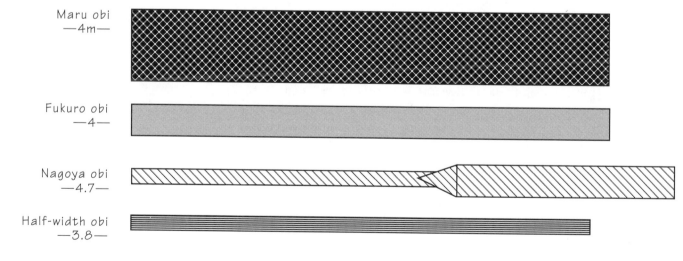

Maru obi
—4m—

Fukuro obi
—4—

Nagoya obi
—4.7—

Half-width obi
—3.8—

The most formal obi in practical use today is the *fukuro* (pocket) obi, consisting of a piece of brocade cloth slightly less than half the width of the maru obi. A backing of brocade or plain silk is sewn to it without stiffener. A fukuro obi is the same length as a maru obi and just a tad narrower. Since it is less bulky, easier to tie, and practically indistinguishable from the maru obi when worn, the fukuro obi has displaced the maru obi in modern kimono life. It, however, is not reversible, so a soy sauce stain is forever.

The pocket obi is further hierarchized according to its design patterns.[5] When totally patterned, repeat-motived brocade covers both sides of the entire sash. A two-thirds–patterned pocket obi, when laid flat, reveals a gap in the brocade amounting to a third of its total length. This section of plain silk is hidden around the waist. Less brocade makes the obi less bulky and somewhat cheaper. Yet when worn, it is hard to distinguish from a fully patterned obi. Finally, the taiko-patterned pocket obi carries a design placed so as to be centered in the back when the obi is tied in the taiko style, the most common tying method for adult women. A smaller version of the design appears in the front, torso-wrapping section of the obi.

In terms of construction, the Nagoya obi is becoming the obi women feel most comfortable with.[6] The part that wraps the body is sewn into its worn width rather than folded like the fukuro obi, while about a third of its length (the tail part, or *tare*) is left unsewn for tying in the taiko style. Its dimensions and appearance do not differ substantially from the fukuro obi, but it is easier to tie and more comfortable to wear.

The *Nagoya obi* is a relatively modern invention, created by a seamstress in the city of Nagoya in the late 1920s for use as casual wear. This obi became popular in the geisha quarters of Tokyo for informal kimono. From there it spread to fashionable use as streetwear—a notch up from casualwear—for fashionable urbanites. Technically, a Nagoya obi cannot make the transition from formal to truly ceremonial, but in fact

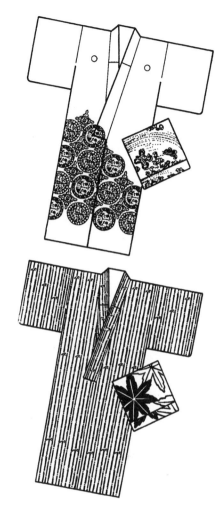

6.17 Pairing a crested robe with a high-level brocade obi (*above*); contrasting an old-fashioned *komon*-patterned kimono with a modern obi

Obi Accessories

most kimono primers grudgingly approve it for use with the lower levels of ceremonial wear if the brocade is up to snuff.[7]

For modern women, more formal has come to mean more uncomfortable. This explains why the fukuro obi has displaced the maru obi, and why the originally informal Nagoya obi is now allowed into the ranks of the ceremonial sashes. Much as purists would like to prevent this process, such accommodations have been necessary since most women no longer wear kimono every day and thus have never attained facility in wearing it.

Given the obi logic that wider is more formal, it is no surprise that narrow sashes (the six-inch-wide *han haba* and *ko-fukuro obi*) can be worn only with ordinary-class kimono, with cotton yukata, or under a haori jacket when the haori is worn for effect and the wearer does not plan to remove it in public.

It is now possible to feign proficiency in obi-tying by cutting the obi into two sections. The narrower part simply wraps around the waist with two cotton ties sewn to its ends, while the wider tail part is perched on a metal or plastic taiko-support inserted at the back. The obi-cord then holds the whole rig in place. The two-part obi was originally created as a concession to women with arthritis, but because it is impossible to detect when worn, many women cheat and have a Nagoya obi cut in two. The fact that cutting an obi restricts its tying style to the taiko is of little concern, because women rarely wear anything else.

As the obi grew from a cord into a sash and then to a great wide girdle of cloth in the late 1700s, it lost some of its original function—to hold the kimono in place. When the obi widened to more than twelve inches, the tie itself needed a tie to be secure. This task was taken by the obi-cord (*obijime*), the most important modern obi accessory. An obijime is absolutely necessary to keep the popular taiko package together.

Obi-cords are of two basic types—narrow sausages of silk cloth (*kukehimo*) or belts of braided silk thread (*kumihimo*), either of which may be tubular or flat. The stuffed cloth kukehimo have largely vanished from adult wear and are seen, if at all, only with high-level crested kimono. They are still in common use for children's kimono, however. Women today usually choose braided cords, about the width of a little finger, which loop through the back of the taiko and tie in a simple square knot in the front middle of the obi. Compactly woven flat cords of metallic gold or silver thread are worn with formal dress. Other than the metallic cords, the best obijime are hand woven of pure silk floss. Round ones are higher on the formality index than flat, and plain or monochrome are higher than patterned.

Obi-cords can be any color but black, which is limited to mourning, and are often chosen to provide an accent by contrast to the color of the obi. The need for the obijime only vanishes at the very bottom of the formality hierarchy when one puts on a cotton yukata or a wool kimono tied with a half-width obi.

The obi-scarf (*obi-age*) is an accessory that, like the cord, is closely tied to the popularity of the taiko. A scarf-length rectangle of thin silk, the obi-age discreetly circles the top of the obi around the torso, disappearing in back under the taiko. The obi-scarf says more about age than formality. But since it is required whenever a full-width obi is worn, it conforms to a version of obi rules, coming in monochrome patterned damask and intricate tie-died nubble-textures for ceremonial wear, and colors and designs on flat-woven plain silks otherwise. The obi-scarf is not worn with the casual half-width obi.

The obi-clasp (*obidome*) is the single piece of kimono jewelry. Obidome are decorative broochlike pieces that thread onto the obi-cord and are centered where the square knot would normally come. The obi-cord is knotted and hidden in the fold of the taiko when a clasp is worn. The obidome originated in the early Meiji years with a host of other Western

6.19 How to tie the obi-cord

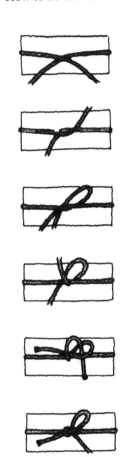

influences on Japanese clothing. Necklaces, gloves, and fringed shawls were eventually dropped from post-Meiji wafuku, but the obi-clasp remains a legitimate kimono accessory. Rather than denoting formality per se, it functions as a thoroughly Veblenesque item of conspicuous consumption. It may be carved of wood or lacquer for casual kimono, or it may be an emerald surrounded by diamonds—not for ceremonial wear, but for evening wear. A slight whiff of the overdone clings to jeweled obi-clasps. Kimono purists like geisha tend to disdain them.

Formality and Footwear

Footwear, not surprisingly, is also affected by rules of formality. Any color but white for the split-toed cotton socks called *tabi* is now rare, and highly informal. Two broad categories of thonged footwear are distinguished along the dimension of formality. Leather or cloth-covered flat-soled *zōri* are formal, whereas wooden, prong-soled *geta* are casual. Geta are worn sockless with yukata, although nicer ones, worn with tabi, may go with stylish casual wear. Until the middle of this century, geta were probably the most common footwear of ordinary folk, but they seem slightly déclassé today. Geta are definitely outdoor footgear. With the proliferation of modern public buildings in which footwear is not removed, clunking geta have become anathema to hotels, theaters, and department stores. Zōri, however, can pass as shoes.

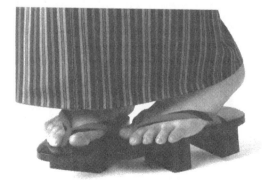

6.20 *Zōri* (*above*) and *geta*

Zōri require socks. How formal they are is set by the material of strap and side. Cloth-covered zōri are more formal than leather, and again, gold and silver brocade is chosen for ceremonial kimono. Higher platforms also raise the formality level of zōri.

When a woman adds a wafuku jacket, or *haori*, over her kimono or a pleated skirtlike *hakama* above its lower portion, she declares herself to be in a certain type of formal situation. Haori and hakama give kimono a serious tone. Both were adopted from male wafuku styles in the late nineteenth century and express what had been considered masculine characteristics. A woman can wear one or the other at one time, but *not* both. That combination is the definitive male version of formal wafuku.

In the early years of Meiji Westernization, hakama were worn by female teachers and students, thus they picked up academic associations like lint. At present, an arrow-patterned kimono overskirted by hakama is as much a graduation cliché for women as tasseled mortarboards are for students in the West. Women who perform recitals of traditional Japanese music on stage also wear hakama, presumably to stress their studious pursuit of art.

Geisha were the first women to borrow the haori from the male wardrobe. Looking for a way to proclaim their seriousness as artists, the geisha of Fukagawa in Edo chose this item of male apparel to make the point that their arts were not of the bedroom variety—at least not primarily. Around 1895, in direct imitation of male formalwear, black crepe haori with crests were adopted by ordinary women for high ceremonial wear. By the 1920s different colors and patterned haori had come into vogue, leading to the modern sensibility in choosing a haori to accessorize a kimono as an ensemble. A black haori can be worn over a subdued kimono as simple mourning wear.

Formality in Jackets and Skirts

6.21 Haori over kimono

All in all, a haori formalizes a woman's kimono in the same way that putting on the jacket makes a suit proper. In fact, this use of the haori probably reflects Western notions of formality filtered through early Western influences on Japanese men's clothing.

This elaborate and minute attention to details exemplifying formality in kimono may appear astonishing to Americans for whom 'degree of casualness' has come to characterize most social occasions. Still, the use of clothing to indicate social occasion makes sense to anyone—from New Guinea highlander to California valley girl. Formality and ceremony are exceedingly important in Japanese culture, and whenever something is culturally significant it tends to be highly ramified. Edwardian English culture had at least as many clothing indicators for levels of social occasion as does contemporary Japanese.

Interestingly, Japanese clothing rules ignore time of day, the fundamental formality boundary used in the West. "There I stood, ten after six, wearing the brownest shoes a man could wear"—a Japanese would be hard pressed to understand the discomfiture implied. We do not wear cocktail dresses before 5:00 P.M., and evening dress by definition is formality after dark. A morning coat, though now rarely seen except on state occasions, has the time of day built into its name as well.

Time of day creates headaches for the wives of Japanese diplomats, who feel, as representatives of Japan abroad, that they ought to wear native dress to official gatherings. The difficulty comes in translating the kimono formality hierarchy into the Western one. If one wears hōmongi to black-tie dinners, then is a komon-patterned kimono appropriate for a luncheon? Finding every other lady in the higher, visiting-wear style at lunch, a komon-clad dignitary's wife regretted her miscalculation of the formality equation thus. At least one Japanese consul general's wife wishes that the Foreign Office would issue an official 'kimono formality equivalence guide' to its cultural emissaries in foreign countries.

6.22 Male formalwear: haori and hakama

We now take up an equally important dimension of female kimono, the signification of age. To be appropriate, a woman's kimono must consider her age and social station as much as it does the formality of the occasion.

Several years ago I attended a reception for Japanese and American guests on the East Coast. A fortyish married Japanese woman who had been living in the United States for many years appeared in a mint-green, floral-patterned, swinging-sleeved kimono. She was surrounded by Americans who admired its lively colors and gorgeous embroidery. But the Japanese guests seemed not to know what to make of her. Clearly over forty, perhaps she had been in America too long?

There was method in the woman's apparent madness. She had chosen the brightly colored unmarried girl's long swinging-sleeve style of kimono specifically to appeal to American sensibilities, not Japanese. Her problem was that the Japanese social messages proclaimed by the outfit were not silenced by her intentions, and they were read as inappropriate by those guests conversant in 'kimonese.'

Kimono evolves throughout a woman's life. Age is interwoven with station, reflecting distinctions between child and adult—or married and single, which traditionally cleave along age lines. At about age eighteen a woman in pre-twentieth-century Japan made the transition from child to adult through her engagement and marriage. She would put away her swinging sleeves (in some cases, actually cutting or hemming the extra length) in favor of the shorter-sleeved adult kimono. Boys had coming-of-age ceremonies, too, but they were never marked by the abrupt clothing changes of women. In modern wafuku, only size and some shoulder tucks differentiate a boy's formal outfit from his father's.

Unlike men, women in kimono are constrained to conform to life's stages. This is one reason why wearing kimono rankles some modern women—they don't wear their hearts on their sleeves, so why must they announce their age and station there? In addition, few modern women marry as early as eighteen, so the contemporary fit between age, marital status, and kimono sleeve is less than perfect. A thinking woman looking for a manner of expressing 'Ms.' in kimonese can do so in various ways. To understand her choices, let us look at the conventional social categories that apply to women in Japanese culture and their reflections in the kimono system.

Japanese women pass through three broad stages after childhood. According to extensive popular kimono literature, their dress ought to represent this progress. Because of the perceived feudalistic odor clinging to the native terms for unmarried woman and wife, post-war Japanese women like to use the English loanwords *Misu* (Miss) for unmarried women, and *Misesu* (Missus) for those who are married. Young Miss and Young Missus are subsets of these. The words may be faddish, but the terms correspond to traditional concepts. In the older reaches of the Missus designation, at some mercifully vague point, a Missus will be considered a *nenpai no kata*, a nongender-specific term meaning an aged person.

6.23 Gender, age, and kimono— infants wear the same baby wafuku, but by age five, boys and girls wear different styles; variations in women's kimono continue to proliferate

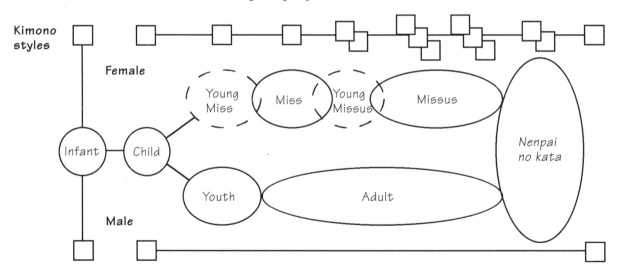

A girl becomes a Young Miss at puberty, traditionally marked by a ceremonial visit to a shrine on April 13 of the year she turns thirteen. For this ceremony, the *Jūsan mairi*, a girl wears a fully cut (*hondachi*) kimono for the first time, with shoulder tucks if it is too large, and she pairs it with an adult-length obi. If her mother has chosen her kimono with care and the pattern is not too childish, she can continue to wear it up to and including the adulthood ceremony (*seijin shiki*), which she will celebrate when she turns twenty.

The ideal Young Miss is innocent, reserved, obedient, and cheerful. Her kimono, when worn properly according to modern wafuku convention, should express this. Even in Japan, some teenagers would rather die than be thought innocent or obedient. These girls are excruciatingly uncomfortable in a modern furisode kimono. Through its recent stylized evolution, modern kimono has lost the ability to express anything other than spruce, chirpy propriety for young girls.

By the time a girl graduates from high school at seventeen, she is squarely in the Miss category. She is presumed to be interested in boys, at least in fantasy, and to be thinking about a professional or money-earning activity to keep herself occupied until marriage. Her six to eight years of being a Miss will probably be the freest and most adventurous period of her life. Adulthood, officially conferred at age twenty, does not occur fully for a woman until marriage and is not utterly clinched until she becomes a mother. As long as a girl/woman is unmarried, she is a Miss. The pejorative Japlish 'Old Miss' labels the social anomaly of a thirty-year-old unmarried woman.

The Miss

6.24 A Young Miss in full length swinging sleeves

Miss Kimono

Ceremonial kimono worn by unmarried women stand out by virtue of their sleeves, vivid colors, and busy designs. Kimono length of sleeve refers to a dimension that Western clothing lacks. For us, long or short sleeves mean the total length of the tube of sleeve material. For kimono, that dimension is standardized just above the wristbone; the 'depth' of the bag of the sleeve is the important, variable part. Miss's ceremonial kimono takes its name, furisode, from its deep fluttering sleeves. In full-blown furisode, sleeves reach to the ankles. There are also ko- (little) and chū- (mid) versions of furisode, reflecting lesser degrees of formality.

Sleeves are deep pockets of significance in kimono's scheme of meaning. Gender and formality distinctions are expressed through sleeves, and so is age or stage of life. The cultural dimension of social responsibility varies in inverse proportion to the depth of one's kimono sleeve—the more responsibility (adult males), the shorter the sleeve. Sleeve depth has an implicit logic. Just as with the gradations of square

6.25 Length of the kimono sleeve according to age, gender, and formality

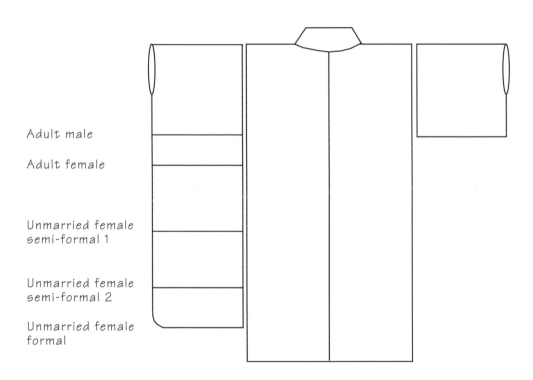

Adult male

Adult female

Unmarried female semi-formal 1

Unmarried female semi-formal 2

Unmarried female formal

and rounded outer seams, the absolute sleeve depth of traditional clothing reinforces a traditional message that opposes adult males to children, with adult women in an intermediate category partaking of aspects of both—like children as opposed to men, but like men as opposed to children.

A Miss's kimono stands out not only by virtue of its long fluttering sleeves but also by its colors. A furisode is allowed the brightest colors and showiest patterns of the kimono lexicon. Because the furisode is permitted such intense hue and design, it can all too easily become gaudy. Adding the vividly brocaded obi it requires sometimes tips the furisode dangerously close to tackiness. As signals of youthfulness, radiant color and fanciful pattern must become progressively more subdued as a woman ages.

Because a furisode is comparable in formality to adult women's black crested ceremonial wear, it partakes of some of the same design elements. It has a main background color (which can be bright pink, acid green, or sky blue in modern fashion) with an asymmetrical pattern clustering on hem and left shoulder. The hem pattern of a furisode kimono reaches all the way up to a girl's waist, diving under the obi only to spring out and continue up the left shoulder. Modern furisode are rarely crested since their long sleeved-ness in itself marks high formality.

The extent of pattern coverage on formal kimono is a good indication of the wearer's age. The waist-deep florals, butterflies, and swirls gambolling upon a Miss's furisode drop down to upper-thigh level on a formal kimono for a Missus. From there, pattern slowly sinks toward the hem in a subtle progression that whispers a woman's age.

Youthfulness is further indicated by how a Miss wears her kimono, especially at the collar and front overlap. The kimono collar is usually made to set back off the nape so that it angles away from the body. How far it is set back, however, makes a tremendous difference in the ultimate effect of the outfit. Napes are a primary erotic focus of the

衣紋の抜き

余り抜かないとき
指3本ぐらい

標　準
軽くこぶしひとつぐらい

多めに抜くとき
こぶしひとつがすっぽり

6.26 Gauging the set of the collar: "set back a little, an average amount, and a lot"

female body in Japan, fully the equivalent of breasts in the West. The modern young Japanese Miss is not supposed to be an erotic being—she is expected to be shy, sweet, and cute. Thus she is to wear her collar demurely close to her nape, set back 'no more than the width of an upright fist' in popular advice. A collar set flat on the nape ruins the kimono line, however, and merely betrays an inexperienced wearer.

The way a kimono overlaps at the bosom is a fine point. The left side of the gown crosses over the right, forming a V highlighted by the overlapped white collar of the under-kimono. For a Miss, this V-shape should be relatively wide and high toward the throat. The contrast with a Missus, who overlaps her kimono to create a deeper and lower V-line, makes a subtle statement of age and sophistication.

6.27 A married woman (*below*) and a Miss (*right*), wearing the same kimono and obi

 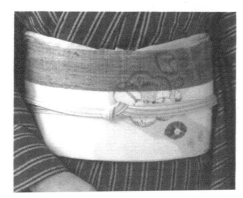 

Miss Obi

The brightness and profusion of colors allowed on a furisode kimono are also found on the obi a Miss ties around it. Accepted æsthetic judgment holds that the main color and obi pattern ought to contrast with that of the kimono. When the kimono is embellished with a naturalistic floral motif, the obi pattern can be geometric. All the obi formality rules concerning material and brocade also come into play because the furisode, by virtue of its high position on the formality ladder, requires a brocade obi.

The most striking thing about a formal obi for a Miss is that it can be tied in many styles. Whereas a Missus wears her obi in the taiko style most of the time, a Miss may have hers arranged in a thick butterfly, a great boxy bow, a facsimile of sparrow wings, or a modern rendition of a daffodil. Kimono schools have seized upon this area to display limitless invention. A Miss fully done up in a bright swinging-sleeved kimono cinched with an equally colorful obi tied in a fat bow gives the impression of an exquisite piece of gift wrapping. Since this is the age of

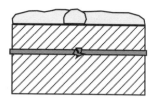

Unmarried girl

obi-scarf

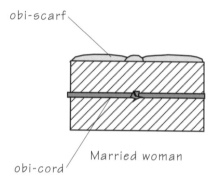

Married woman

obi-cord

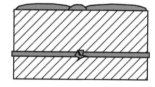

Older woman

6.28 How the obi and its
accessories indicate a
woman's age

marriage negotiations—during which young women often wear their furisode—the image of the beautifully (and traditionally) wrapped package is probably quite apt. If he is tempted to unwrap the package, the groom-to-be will propose.

The fanciful bundles of brocade are clear markers of youth, but there are more subtle age indicators in the tying of an obi. How high or low the obi is tied around the torso carries a simple message—the younger, the higher. An unmarried girl's obi is tied high on the ribcage, just below her armpits. A married woman wears hers centered on her waist, while the older woman ties hers closer to the hips. In absolute terms, we are considering a matter of two inches either way. But as in the era of miniskirts, two inches can be vital.

The height at which the obi is tied also evokes the related dimension of modesty/sexiness. The higher on the torso, the primmer the effect. As we know, modesty is an attribute expected of the Miss, and another reason her obi will be tied high on the bosom. It's hard to know which came first in Japan, youth or primness, but in the modern language of kimono the point is moot—they are inextricably linked.

The female bustline, so focused upon and erotically charged throughout the history of fashion in the West, almost disappears in the kimono-clothed body. Not only are breasts de-emphasized, they are a positive nuisance, for they spoil the line. Like flappers in the 1920s, some women must bind their chests to achieve the right look. Wearing the obi high, in other words, is not simply a maneuver to conceal the erotic interest of the bosom, for that is something it traditionally never had. An obi's primness or sexiness is fully expressed in the paradigm of high to low: young, sexually inexperienced women wear the obi high, sexually experienced women wear it lower.

Obi accessories, especially the obi-scarf, also indicate age. Not only is the scarf more brightly colored for the Miss, as we would expect, it is worn conspicuously lapped over the top of the obi. Accordingly, it comes as no surprise that the Missus wears her obi-scarf just peeking above the top of the obi, while the elderly woman pushes hers down so that it is barely visible. Likewise with the obi-cord: a Miss wears hers in the upper third of the obi, Missus in the center, and the older woman in the lower third.

6.29 Fancy obi styles for unmarried women

Origami-style crane

Iris

Turtle

The Missus

The Missus is an ideal type. But in Japan, an amazing number of women manage to make themselves into a faithful version of this ideal. Above all, she is what the Miss becomes once she marries. The category of Young Missus helps women bridge the transition in the early years of their marriages, but becoming a Missus remains the most significant, hence most clearly marked, social step a woman takes. Aging may be gradual, but one changes from Miss to Missus in a single ceremonial swoop—marriage. An unmarried woman may wear ordinary-length sleeves on her less formal kimono, but a married woman will never wear her swinging sleeves again.

What characteristics should a Missus cultivate? The words 'calm,' 'composed,' 'dignified,' and 'elegant' appear over and over to describe her.[8] She has shed the frivolity of her younger days, as the more subdued colors of her dress indicate. She shoulders the responsibilities of social adulthood—marked, as we saw earlier by her shorter, less rounded sleeves. Modesty still becomes her, for she is a respectable wife, but she is not shy like the Miss. She is sexually mature, as indicated by the placement of her obi and accessories, and she has some choice as to how much of her nape she lets her kimono collar expose in back.

We have anticipated the form of the Missus version of kimono by implicit contrast to Miss kimono above. The two define each other and in the process set up a series of meaningful oppositions that continue to define age-appropriate wear for older women. The kimono sleeve is the most clear-cut age signifier of women's kimono. *Tomesode*, the name of the shorter sleeve, becomes the name of the garment.

A woman's transition to social adulthood is dramatically expressed by the series of clothing changes performed by the bride during the wedding ceremony. In the classic style of wedding, a neo-traditional mode that became popular in the 1880s and continued through roughly the 1920s, after which it was somewhat simplified, the bride enters the

年配の人 ——貫禄と品位をもたせて——

◈ 衿は抜きかげんに
◈ 首の短い人は衿幅をやや広く、短い人は細めに仕立てるとよい
◈ 胸元は、余裕をもたせて打ち合わせる
◈ 帯あげは、ほとんど出さない
◈ 帯は少し低めにしめる
◈ 帯じめは、帯巾の上位の位置に

ミセス ——ゆったりと上品な感じに——

◈ 衿の抜きかげんは、横にしたこぶしが一つ入る位に
◈ 帯の位置は、ミスより少し低めに お太鼓は高い帯枕をさけて、低めに丸みを持たせる
◈ 半衿は1.5cm位見せる。
◈ 衿元はゆったりと首のつけねで合わせる
◈ 帯あげは、少しだけだす
◈ 帯じめは、帯巾の中央よりやや低めに

6.30 Figures from a kimono manual demonstrate points for an older woman (*left*) and a missus to keep in mind when dressing in kimono

room in a pure white furisode kimono; dons a scarlet over-robe (*uchikake*) for the ceremony itself; then changes to a multicolored furisode and finally to a black, crested adult tomesode kimono for the continuing festivities. The woman's ceremonial metamorphosis from Miss to Missus is plainly indicated by her changes of kimono.[9] The transformation of her dress from white to red to multichrome to black is the visual focus of this custom, which takes a maiden in long white sleeves and transforms her into a madam in short black ones.

Whereas sleeves are unambiguous markers of the gap between Miss and Missus, aging per se—its gradual character—can be expressed by fine gradations in color and pattern. The Young Missus must wear a tomesode kimono for formal occasions, but its designs can be fairly brightly colored and extend relatively high up the skirt. As she adjusts to the life of a Missus, and as her children and husband's salary grow, the kimono she buys will typically become less intense in color.

In wearing her kimono, a Missus 'lowers' each area discussed above. The back of her collar is pulled further from her nape. The taiko fold of her obi sinks slightly. The front of the obi lies lower on the torso, the obi-cord settles to the center, and the obi-scarf ducks behind the obi. The kimono's crossover front overlap forms a deeper, narrower V-shape.

Once this pattern of 'the older, the lower' is established, it continues to determine how an elderly woman wears her kimono. The patterns on an older woman's hem and obi, as well as placement of the obi-cord, continue to sink. As with any coherent system of meaning, a considerable amount of redundancy is built into the language of kimonese. These indicators of age have some interesting social ramifications. The progression from high to low is a one-way street. A woman may wear 'older,' but she can't dress much younger than her age permits. This is why a forty-five-year-old woman in a bright furisode appears ridiculous. A woman in a purely Japanese social context would never do anything

so extreme—but through her choice of color and pattern, she might try to shave five years or so off the impression she gives of her age . This is a difficult trick, although of course some women are always attempting it. The danger is that as soon as it becomes evident, it becomes pathetic.

The opposite tactic, dressing older, is one way of saying 'Ms.' in kimonese. A Miss can bypass the childishly prim effect of the furisode ensemble by wearing a subdued tomesode instead. This route is taken by unmarried women in their late twenties who have begun to feel foolish in long swinging sleeves. A young woman can also lean toward darker colors to project a quality of sophistication that her age-designated color choices do not permit. If she rejects the traditional sensibilities and social messages the kimono inevitably projects, however, an independent-minded young woman will shun kimono altogether.

6.31 A woman's most formal kimono—the black crested—worn by a young missus, a missus, and an older woman

TASTE—
THE GEISHA DIMENSION

The signifiers of taste and class are very similar to those that mark age. By 'class' I do not mean social class, which is remarkably homogeneous at least in Japanese self-perception, but rather the more ineffable quality of demeanor the Japanese call *hinkaku*. Our closest equivalent is in such expressions as 'a classy lady' and 'she's got class.'

The ideal of the Young Miss as expressed in kimono is heavily laden with modesty. On the opposite end of the scale stands the kimono worn by geisha, who embody the traditional ideal of the sexily attractive woman. Between these two poles lies a range of possibilities in the way kimono may be worn. How a woman chooses to put these elements together will express her character, demeanor, sexy modesty, or modest sexiness—in a word, her taste.

The signifiers of sexiness in the language of kimono are obvious. For this reason, they must be invoked with care, since sexiness as such may not be the social message a woman wants to convey. A kimono and obi outfit that has been put together with thought to convey social station, season, and occasion receives its ultimate judgment by the way it is worn. If the back of her collar dips a tad, her obi is tied closer to her hips, or her obi-cord is lower than those of other women, people's perceptions will shift accordingly. A woman who arranges her kimono as just described does not project the image of a proper middle-class wife. People may wonder whether she has spent time in the entertainment world, where sexiness in dress is avidly cultivated.

The kimono-clad Young Miss is prim and the geisha sexy because their manner of dressing is reciprocally defined. A dropped nape and a low obi is sexy because a hidden nape and a high obi is prim—and vice versa. The distinctions of age and taste share many signifiers. What happens when they cross? The costume of the maiko, the young apprentice geisha of Kyoto, provides an interesting example of how to express both poles of this continuum simultaneously.

A maiko's full-dress kimono sports many youthful characteristics—bright colors, deep swinging sleeves, the front of her collar overlapped high and close to the throat, the obi tied high on the torso with the obi-scarf showing conspicuously, obi-cord tied slightly above center. But when the maiko turns around, the back of her collar is pulled down as far as any adult geisha's would be, exposing her nape practically down to her shoulder blades. Napier is definitely sexier.

This example shows clearly how kimono signifiers can be rearranged and combined according to a logic of relations in order to express different combinations of social characteristics—in this case youth and sexiness, a combination that has been largely erased from standard Japanese middle-class life.

6.32 Front and back views of a maiko in traditional costume

January–February
pine
plum
bamboo

March–April
cherry
butterflies
wisteria

May–June
iris
willow
birds

Seasonality is a concept familiar in Western clothing but is more highly ramified and rule-bound in the domain of wafuku. Given the long-standing Japanese cultural obsession with the fine nuances of seasonal change in nature, it is not surprising that the time of year plays an important role in the constitution of a kimono ensemble.

The functional notion that garments ought to adapt to climate and weather is the foundation upon which an elaborate cultural edifice has been constructed to portray kimono seasonality. Summer kimono consist of a single layer of light silk, and winter ones are of heavier material with linings. This is just the beginning of the process by which a kimono displays awareness of season.

Kimono today come in one of two basic types according to time of year—*hitoe*, a single-layer (unlined) kimono, or *awase*, lined kimono. Hitoe kimono are summer garments, worn from the beginning of June through the end of September. During the rest of the year kimono are lined. The traditional custom of *koromogae*, wardrobe change, takes place on the first day of the sixth month. Lined garments are put away and unlined ones taken out of mothballs, while on the first of the tenth month the procedure is reversed.[10] We speak here of proper kimono, which are always worn over an underkimono. The cotton yukata (cotton is associated with summer) is a special instance of an unlined garment worn next to the skin. Japanese make a clear distinction between yukata (literally 'bathrobe') and kimono. Whereas Westerners might describe a yukata as 'an unlined cotton kimono' because of its shape, Japanese do not consider yukata to be kimono at all.

It is useful to think of kimono seasonality as calibrated by a set of nested dials. The outermost fixed circle is marked off with seasons and months. At the center is a moveable dial representing lined and unlined kimono. This dial has about ten degrees of leeway in its movement. If the weather turns hot in May, it is permissible to rush the season for hitoe by two or three weeks, and likewise in early autumn chill, to wear lined kimono slightly before the first of October.

Ringing the lined-unlined center dial is another concentric dial representing types of material. Its scope of movement is much freer, although its range is also fixed at certain points. Outside the cloth dial is a color dial, which also has relative freedom of movement. The outermost ring is the motif dial, which contains numerous designs and patterns considered to have seasonal connotations. This hypothetical seasonal synthesizer works as follows: one first sets the main dials and then fine-tunes the more freewheeling ones, allowing for precisely graduated expressions representing the actual month, the cultural season, the day's weather, and subjective personal sensibility.

Let us take an example. October is culturally part of autumn, yet the weather (variable, as in the proverb 'A man's heart is like the autumn sky') may well still be hot. One may twist the lined-unlined dial to its limit and wear a hitoe kimono during the first part of the month, but the color dial would have to be rotated to darker, richer colors, while the motif dial should turn to grass orchids, flying geese, or even maples.

Another example: if the weather in the middle of May turns hot, it is permissible to wear an unlined kimono, but it should be made of crepe or an otherwise solidly woven silk. May is still too early to wear light silk gauze, or the semitransparent weaves of full summer hitoe. As June approaches, a woman will remove the winter collar from her under-kimono and attach a fresh one of *ro*-weave silk. Further into summer, the obi she chooses will also be of a lighter, open weave, as will her obi-scarf and the material of her underkimono. By midsummer, the unlined kimono itself should be one of the gauze silks.

July–August
plovers
waves
shells

September–October
plumed grass
maple
chrysanthemum

November–December
bamboo in snow
pine needles
gingko

Thus do color, pattern, motif, accessories, and the kimono material move, each within its own range of seasonal expression. Each has an intensified essence, expressing a particular season par excellence. At the height of each season all the dials line up as shown in the chart below.

Winter is an interesting exception. From early in kimono history winter has received short shrift. It is usually treated as a part of spring—that is, there is one long winter-spring season, with the first month of the year set apart for the important festivities of New Year's. Seasonal awareness also governs the æsthetic by which kimono and obi are

6.33 Expressions of the essence of each season

	Spring	Summer	Autumn	Winter
Month	March	July	November	January
Layers	Awase	Hitoe	Awase	Awase
Fabric	Satin	Gauze	Crepe	Damask
Colors	Cool, pale	Light	Warm, dark	Bright
Motifs	Cherry blossom	Clematis	Persimmon	Pine / bamboo / plum

combined. The classic ideal requires a matching of formality levels but contrasts in the areas of color and pattern. For example, during the New Year season, for which the pine/bamboo/plum combination is a classic motif, a plum-patterned kimono should not be tied with a plum-patterned obi. Kimono and obi motifs may, however, refer to each other in more subtle fashion: a floral summer robe can be paired with an obi pattern of flowing water, or a wave-patterned kimono with an obi decorated with a stylized water-loving plover.

6.35 Examples of coordinating patterns between kimono and obi—images may have meaning associations (e.g., cranes and tortoises together symbolize longevity) but the visual aspects of the designs ought to contrast

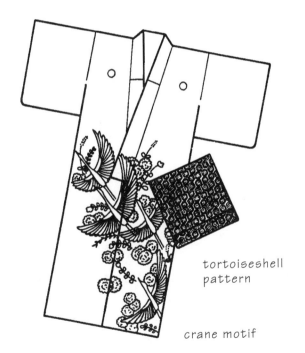

tortoiseshell
pattern

crane motif

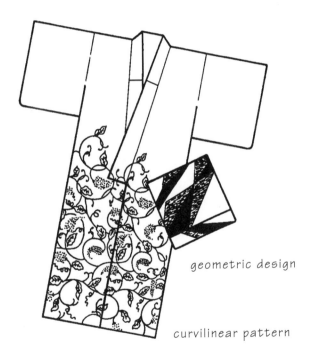

geometric design

curvilinear pattern

Kimono worn in the month just preceding the start of a new season (again, except winter) anticipate the upcoming change. Thus May, the month before summer officially starts, brings out lighter colors, iris and flowing-water motifs, and the occasional unlined kimono. September prefigures autumn with darker colored unlined kimono and fall-flower motifs like chrysanthemums, maples, bellflower, and yarrow. In general, seasonal anticipation by floral motif is a hallmark of wafuku fashion sense. By the time a flower has actually come into bloom, it is too late to wear it on kimono.

Seasonal sensibility may be traced back at least to the eleventh century. In her list of 'depressing things,' the soignée Heian writer Sei Shōnagon included plum-pink colored robes (connoting early spring) worn on into the third and fourth months, and a white under-robe worn in the eighth lunar month. In both cases, the colors were technically correct for the season, but the wearer showed a depressing lack of sensibility in not anticipating the approaching seasonal change. In terms of our dials, it appears that the outermost ring of motifs ought to be permanently set just slightly ahead.

What about women with limited kimono wardrobes? After all, only a geisha or the most avid kimono hobbyist today can change her wardrobe to reflect the season so exquisitely. Again we discover one of the reasons for the popularity of the solid-color unpatterned kimono. It is relatively seasonless and can fit many circumstances merely by changing the obi. Abstract patterns are another way of broadening the seasonal scope of a garment, as are combinations like cherry blossoms, chrysanthemums, iris, pine, grass orchids, and maple leaves—all on the same kimono. Our motif dial has a completely free-spinning outer edge for such unseasoned and pan-seasonal motifs.

Practical as all-purpose kimono may be—and necessary, too, for the woman who just has one or two—they nevertheless must æsthetically defer to more seasonally specific outfits. Practicality, after all, is not the name of the modern kimono game.

> Having grown up in the old downtown section of the city near the geisha quarters, I have always been especially sensitive to the sight of a beautiful person. It is the same with beautiful kimono. For over fifty years I have kept the memory of a young geisha I once glimpsed, dressed in a summer outfit of transparent black Akashi silk.
>
> In the nineteen-twenties, when women still dressed to please the eyes of men, the purpose of a woman's summer dress was not so much to keep her cool as to make her appear cool to others. The joy of wearing thin Akashi silk must have been the joy of knowing that you yourself would appear as a poetic composition on a summer theme.
>
> —Kondō Tomie, *Yosoi no onnagokoro*, 1985

III

KIMONO

CONTEXTS

SEVEN

THE CULTURED NATURE OF HEIAN COLORS

> Whenever the colors of a robe do not match the seasons, the flowers of spring and the autumn tints, whenever they are somehow vague and muddy, then the whole effort is as futile as the dew. So it is with women…we are all pursuing the ideal and failing to find it.
>
> —Remark by Tō no Chūjo to his friend Prince Genji
> during a desultory afternoon discussion

KIMONO FIRST ATTAINED A RECOGNIZABLY JAPANESE FORM at the Heian imperial court in the ninth to eleventh centuries. For the preceding two hundred years, the ruling class had been keen observers of Chinese culture, first via the Korean peninsula and later directly from the Sui and Tang courts. Welcoming cultured Chinese and Korean immigrants and sending their own students abroad, Japanese immersed themselves in Chinese civilization. They studied everything from Buddhism to city planning, from the administration of empire to jurisprudence and the ordering of time by the calendar. Most basic, the Japanese learned to write. Everything assimilated from China was applied to the emerging task of building a proper kingly culture in Japan.

During the Asuka and Nara periods of the sixth and seventh centuries, Japanese courts looked very Chinese. Yet, as has so often been remarked, the Japanese absorbed what appealed of mainland high culture, disregarded other elements, ultimately creating their own synthesis. The same cultural elements may have been present, but in such a changed configuration that the gestalt was totally new. Nowhere was this æsthetic shift more apparent than in clothing.

Heian writers paid an extraordinary amount of attention to descriptions of dress. This reflects the importance that nuances of clothing held for contemporary readers, but it is one of the hardest things for a translator or a modern reader to contend with. Ironically, the more central something is to the heart of a culture, the more likely will its basic tenets be unspoken. Writers always presume a common base of knowledge supporting the terms of their discourse. Although a veritable closetful of clothing references survive in Heian documents, there is little overt explanation as to what it all meant. The gentle Heian reader knew, of course, but the subtleties she would have relished are largely lost upon us. My goal here is to explore explicitly some of those implicit understandings within the Heian courtly world.

A NEW ÆSTHETIC SYSTEM

Dress touched every aspect of Heian aristocratic life. Court rank was expressed in clothing and colors. Cloth and clothes were major forms of economic exchange. Heian literature is full of references to artistically chosen robes, the descriptions of which limned personality, setting, and emotional tone. Romantic relations between men and women could not help but be influenced by the voluminous envelopes of clothing worn by the beau monde. Romance was expressed through poetic convention in images of tear-damp sleeves and spread-out robes.

Although the prototype of Japanese court clothing was Chinese, during the Heian period the kimono-shaped robes worn by women of the aristocracy achieved a distinctly Japanese form, and came to be worn according to a specifically Japanese æsthetic sense. Colors came to be combined into discrete named combinations known as *irome no kasane*. This sensitive layering of colors developed full and subtle bloom over the course of three hundred years. There was little Chinese about it. As an actual mode of dress, kasane fashion passed away with courtly society, but its influence on kimono style has had echoes down to the present day.

Of the many possible ramifications of the clothing system of this period, color especially stands out. Color combinations were displayed first and foremost on clothing, although furnishings, drapery, and paper also attracted exquisite attention. Color names and layered colors are woven throughout Heian poetry and literature, serving to pull together nature, season, person, and incident into a poetic whole. In the *Pillow Book* of Sei Shōnagon, that arch observer of Heian mores, we find this passage (Shōnagon is in her carriage, waiting to catch a glimpse of the procession of the High Priestess of Ise):[1]

> Though we had been told that there might be a long wait, the High Priestess and her retinue soon arrived from the Upper Shrine. First we could see the fans come into sight, then the sprout-green robes of the gentlemen from the Emperor's Private Office. It was a splendid sight. The men wore their under-robes in such a way that the white material stood out against the green of their outer robes, and I was reminded so much of the saxifrage [*u no hana*] blossoms in their green hedge that I almost expected to find a little cuckoo.

Returning to the palace, Shōnagon passed an actual saxifrage hedge and told her runners to break off branches to decorate her carriage.

Shōnagon's reference to saxifrage was not just chance observation. *U no hana* is the name of a specific layered color combination, white over green, displayed here on the robes of imperial officials. It is also a seasonal reference to early summer, and as such complements the singing cuckoo (*hototogisu*). Echoing this seasonal imagery several paragraphs later, Shōnagon picks a branch of the flower mentioned previously regarding clothing.

This offhand paragraph is typical of the way Heian writers cluster references to nature/color/clothing/occasion. The effect is an orchestration of related themes recalling one another, producing a coordinated sensory and literary impression.

The fashion of layering colors is a marvelous example of how a cultural system can exploit natural metaphors, and it raises the entire issue of the nature of nature in Heian culture. The ultra-refined sensibilities of Heian courtiers were not simply reactions to beautiful natural phenomena. By this time, nature had been completely acculturized by tradition—in poetry, ritual, and especially clothing, so that nature in Heian culture came to form an independent realm, not just an epiphenomenon to the weather and the great outdoors. Richard Bowring's comments on Murasaki Shikibu's diary apply equally to clothing:[2]

> [Murasaki's] inner world and the outer [natural world] are linked by a series of points where they intersect. The selection of these points is governed not by accident or personal whim but by a whole set of conventions common to her culture. It is the sight of birds on the lake, of fading chrysanthemums, of snow in a dilapidated garden, that trigger such responses. All these are moments sanctioned and sanctified by literary tradition. More than anything else this is what marks Murasaki as a Heian woman.

Heian women were not making creative individual fashion statements by combining colors that appealed to their whims or enhanced their complexions. The changing color combinations of women's clothing were based on a shared system of cultural assumptions in the same way that the quotidian composition of poetry was based on literary tradition. That is, both poetry and dress were woven of allusions—allusions to a larger literary-æsthetic system, familiar hence impalpable, and as necessary to social life as air is to physical.

The ideal of personal beauty among Heian aristocracy combined physical and cultural features. A full face, high forehead, and white skin were beautiful. A stately bearing was appreciated in both men and women. Both sexes painted and powdered their complexions white and stained their teeth black. In addition, women shaved their eyebrows and painted feathery replacements high on their foreheads. By far the most important element of a Heian woman's purely physical beauty was her hair. Faces are seldom described beyond being pleasingly plump (the ideal), but even a thin face was but a minor flaw provided hair was up to par. Every woman described as exemplary had glossy floor-length black hair. Aging Heian beauties were as afraid of thinning hair as modern women are of thickening bodies.

Heian women gained notice using their selves the way men gained recognition using their minds. But this did not mean relying simply on a pretty face—or even pretty hair. A woman's physical presence was appreciated as an expression of her sensibilities, as were her surroundings: the poems she wrote, but also the paper she used and her calligraphic style, the blend of incense with which she chose to perfume her rooms and clothing, and the color combinations in her layered robes.

The accomplished attributes of beauty were even more important than the physical. One can imagine an ugly woman with the proper cultural refinements being able to cope in Heian society, but the reverse, a beautiful boor—such as the Omi Lady in the *Tale of Genji*—seems only to have furnished contemporaries a source of malicious amusement.[3]

All the usual reasons for the social, cultural, and personal importance of dress were magnified in Heian court ladies' robes, because robes were literally all there was to see of them publicly. A lady's sleeves and skirts extending from behind blinds and curtains proclaimed her social persona. Not surprisingly, the layered colors of sleeve edges and hems came to be the æsthetic focus of female Heian dress.

This faceless display was called *uchide* or *idashiginu*, 'putting out one's robes,' and the arrangement of these waist-down tableaux of cloth was prescribed as follows:[4]

> One should display two [women in their] ensembles in each bay. The colors will depend on the occasion. The ladies are advised to pull out one leg of their long trousers fairly fully, then align the front of the inner robes and the chemise, pull two or so of the inner robes well out, and arrange the ensemble right up to the edge of the base lintel. Otherwise, if one pulls everything out at once, the edges of the inner robes will turn under and look bad.
>
> If there are thick and thin inner robes, compress the thick ones. For thin robes, pull out the basting thread and cut it. Fluff the padding and use weights to anchor them behind the pillars.

7.1 *Idashiginu* in a building (*above*) and in a carriage

This prescription applied to formal seating within the palace. A lady could also display her self (that is, her clothing) in her carriage. This led to the custom of making gowns with inordinately wide sleeves on the side to drape outside. Sei Shōnagon, for one, had little patience with this fashion: "I cannot stand a woman who wears sleeves of unequal width. If she has on several layers of robes, the added weight on one side makes her entire costume lopsided and most inelegant…yet nowadays everybody seems to have their clothes cut like this.…Fashionable, good-looking people really dress in a most inconvenient way."[5] Riding in the carriage must not have been particularly convenient, either, since the sleeves had to be supported by a hidden thread attached to a stick of bamboo skewered behind the seat.[6]

Convenience, however, was the last thing Heian ladies expected in clothing. Dressed like butterflies but having the mobility of caterpillars, they may well have crawled within the confines of their quarters as much as they walked.

The world of the kimono wearers of the Heian court was, in Ivan Morris's words, "an extreme form [of] features that are common to small aristocratic groups everywhere. Members of the upper class are almost all related to each other. They are totally uninterested in everyone outside their own charmed circle and exceedingly sensitive in judging the precise social level of each person who does belong."[7] The Heian system of clothing, in which robes became a prime expression of social grace, was sustainable only by persons who held the all-important criterion for social recognition at the time—court rank.

The lives of Heian people of rank were regulated to an extravagantly detailed degree. The nuances of which appurtenances were permitted to whom could only have been appreciated in a society ingrown to the extent of the Heian ruling class. Rank was the prerequisite, but beyond it, artistic sensibilities definitively shaped one's career and standing in the eyes of peers. The wedding of high rank and poetic sensitivity, personified by Genji, the Shining Prince, was the Heian ideal—while a mismatch was the stuff of pity or tragedy.

Rank, not surprisingly, dictated what a person could wear. This code was carried out primarily in colors in a system adapted from the Chinese court. Men's formal costume indicated the wearer's rank by color. Women's clothing was constrained by the law of forbidden colors (*kinjiki*), which reserved several shades of red and the color deep purple to imperial ladies. Such colors, as well as certain weaves and patterns of silk, were allowed only occasionally to individual ladies of lower rank as a mark of imperial favor.

The fascinating paradox about the clothing system of Heian Japan is that even though the robes were of standard cut, changed by rigid rule of season, and made of fabrics assigned by rank, an irreducible element of personal choice was involved in the combining of colors. In the end, either this judgment expressed an individual artistic soul, or it failed.

Again, we find a parallel in poetry. The exchanging of verses, both public and private, was a Heian preoccupation meant to reflect a person's sensibilities through the juxtaposition of season, occasion, classical allusion, and personal sentiment. Orchestrating an outfit likewise had to demonstrate awareness of similar conventions pertaining to season, rank, and occasion. In poetry or in clothing, observance of the rules came first. Upon that foundation there lay a tiny, circumscribed but crucial arena for the skillful display of nuance. Sei Shōnagon again:[8]

> One evening during the reign of Emperor Murakami, when it had been snowing very heavily, and the moon was shining brightly, His Majesty ordered some snow to be heaped on a platter. Then a branch of plum blossom was stuck into it, and the Emperor told someone to hand the platter to Hyōe, the Lady Chamberlain. 'Let us have a poem about this,' he said to her. 'What will you give us?'
>
> 'The moon, the snow, the flowers,' she replied, much to His Majesty's delight. 'To have composed a special poem for the occasion,' he said, "would have been the ordinary thing to do. But to find a line that fits the moment so beautifully—that is really hard.'

This is the heart of Heian æsthetic appreciation—to find an appropriate line from the existing corpus, or to choose an exactly appropriate set of colors, the name of which was redolent with seasonal and poetic associations. This rich self-reference was appreciated far more than sheer originality.

LAYERS OF COLOR

A great distance in time and culture separates us from the world of Heian-kyō. Some uncertainty regarding the shimmering and striking layered color combinations is thus inevitable. No actual Heian period courtly garments survive. No one can definitively say what tints the color names described. Inescapably we are obliged to deal with reconstructions and interpretations, of greater or less certainty. Compounding the problem is the difficulty of translating the names into English and the underlying dilemma that in both languages and cultures, one person's persimmon is another's orange.

Beyond their astonishing multiplicity, the most interesting aspect of Heian colors was their set combinations, called *irome no kasane*. These sets had poetic names that referred to natural phenomena, especially flowers. The naming of sets of layered colors began early in the Heian period and continued to develop as courtly fashion for several centuries.[9] The colors used in each named combination were generally consistent, though the absolute number of combinations and the fashions of layering changed over the centuries.

Since we are working with text, not textiles, it is worth noting that names are our subject. Insofar as the color-name *murasaki* had attributes *x*, *y*, and *z*, we are entitled to speak about the meanings of murasaki—no matter what shade of purple murasaki actually was. Thus we begin with the way colors were named.

Color names often derived from plant names and may refer to the plant either for its dyeing properties:

murasaki (gromwell), purple   *suo* (sappanwood), maroon
akane (madder), red   *kurenai* (safflower), scarlet-pink
tsurubami (acorn), black   *kihada* (philodendron), yellow

or for the color of its blossom:

fuji (wisteria), lavender   *sakura* (cherry), pale pink
momo (peach), pink   *sumire* (violet), mauve.

A dyecolor, *some-iro*, took its name from the substance which dyed it. But color names could also refer to the effect produced when two separately dyed pieces of material were superimposed. This was called an 'overlay color,' *awase-iro*. The color named 'willow' is an example—

a frosty green arising from layering semi-translucent white material over dark green. Occasionally, a color was named because of its woven properties (*ori-iro*)—the color effect created when warp and weft are different hues.[10]

From about mid-Heian, represented by the world of Prince Genji, fewer than twenty color combinations are mentioned, with just five or six appearing most frequently. These Heian kasanes were all overlays. Sakura was the most common, a 'cherry-blossom' muted pink arising from the layering of white over red. Later, the term *kasane* was extended to mean set pairs of discrete non-overlapping colors. Thus the kasane combination called *matsu* (pine) meant green plus maroon, *tachibana* (mandarin orange) was old-leaf tan plus pure yellow—and so on. Today *irome no kasane* is generally understood to mean these named color pairs, of which there are approximately one hundred.[11]

During the late Heian era, the concept of layered colors was extended again, to the set of five robes (*itsutsuginu*) constituting the basic apparel of noble ladies. The color of each robe, its lining, and the unlined chemise worn under them was specified and the entire set then called by a kasane name.[12]

AN IMPERIAL WARDROBE

Five-layer cluster names survive in profusion in a text describing the wardrobe of court ladies at the time of Senior Grand Empress Tashi, a late twelfth-century paragon of Heian fashion. To appreciate this amazing wardrobe we must understand how Heian women wore their robes, interpret the colors employed, and probe a bit of Tashi's unusual background to understand how it happens that we have a document cataloguing the clothing she would have worn.

In the year 1150, ten-year-old Fujiwara Tashi was married to eleven-year-old Emperor Konoe. Widowed at fifteen, Tashi was elevated to the rank of Grand Empress a year later during the reign of Konoe's brother Goshirakawa, and subsequently to the rank of Senior Grand Empress. In 1159, her brother-in-law abdicated the throne to his eighteen-year-old son Nijō. The following year, Nijō made the utterly unprecedented move of marrying his aunt, Senior Grand Empress Tashi—who was all of twenty-one at the time. This unusual marital history gave Tashi the epithet Nidai no Kisaki, 'Empress of Two Generations.'

Tashi was a Fujiwara woman—an unspoken prerequisite for a candidate for imperial spouse in Heian times. Yet there were divisive factions within the Fujiwara clan. Tashi's adoptive father and sponsor, Yorinaga, had been ousted from clan leadership during the reign of Emperor Goshirakawa. Why did Emperor Nijō call Tashi back to court as an active imperial consort? Since her political connections were hardly in good repair at this time, perhaps it was simply that Nijō loved her—a possibility striking in its directness during an age when political machination lay behind every important courtly action.

Tashi had enjoyed a reputation as a lady of great elegance and refinement, but she nevertheless must have been put in a delicate predicament when she left her previous elevated titles behind her to answer the imperial summons to matrimony. Marrying the emperor did not automatically make one an empress. The various titles for imperial spouses were bestowed at the emperor's discretion as steps in a predetermined hierarchy. Tashi was unique in that she rose to the most elevated rank of Senior Grand Empress once and then started all over at the bottom of the royal ladder as a consort and climbed it again.

It was at this point, some speculate, that Tashi received avuncular advice from Minamoto Masasuke, another Yorinaga protégé who had been in service in Tashi's household. Masasuke was a master of court ceremony, a walking encyclopedia of Heian court ritual. To help Tashi avoid a faux pas of dress in her sensitive situation, Masasuke wrote out a list of robe combinations for each season. This document, "Colors for a Court Lady's Dress," found in the *Masasuke shōzokushō* (Masasuke's notes on court costume), is annotated with what some scholars believe to be Tashi's own comments.[13]

The document lists ensembles of named color sets in appropriate materials spanning a complete annual round of the seasons—the closest we could possibly come to an overt, self-conscious description from a native informant. It tells us the categories that defined meaningful distinctions in dress, season, and color. As a late Heian text, it works with a full palette of the layered clothing combinations available to women of the highest rank.

The Clothing

Heian women's dress is often referred to in later ages as *jūni hitoe*, 'the twelve layers,' although the actual number of robes varied. After a period of excess in the early eleventh century, during which women sometimes bundled themselves into as many as twenty layers, sumptuary statutes limited the basic set to five. The term *kinu* (gown) in its most general sense meant a garment, long or short, worn on the upper body, as opposed to such things as pants or skirts that covered the legs. Ladies' kinu were cut in the same basic kimonoid shape but differed in material and placement in the total ensemble. From under to outer, a Heian gentlewoman would have worn trousers topped by five generic types of kinu. These elements of costume were:

> *Hakama* or *haribakama*, long trousers. This was a divided-leg lower garment worn as nightclothing with a chemise and under all else during the day. Attached ties secured it at the waist. Hakama were visible at the front parting of the gowns from just above the knee down to the floor, where they trailed. The trousers were made of unglossed (somewhat stiff raw) silk material for everyday, and

glossed silk for special occasions. Women wore them in bright scarlet pink, while unmarried girls wore dark purplish red—a reversal of modern Japanese notions of age-appropriate colors. In her *Pillow Book*, Sei Shōnagon described this scene: "It is dawn and a woman is lying in bed after her lover has taken his leave. She has a beautiful glossed silk lavender robe lined in violet pulled up over her head. She is asleep. She wears an apricot-colored chemise, a yellow raw silk robe, and a scarlet-pink unlined robe. The cords of her long trousers hang untied by her side."[14]—Just as her lover left them, is what Shōnagon means, with a hint of the arched eyebrow. This is the limit of Heian deshabille.

Hitoe, chemise.[15] This was an unlined gown worn next to the skin. The hitoe was cut larger than the gowns layered upon it, so it protruded prominently at sleeve openings and hem. The color of the chemise was crucial to the ensemble's effect. Unlike modern kimono, the sleeve openings of all these gowns were unsewn all the way down the front edge.

7.2　Basic elements of a Heian noblewoman's dress

Uchigi, robe. These robes, each cut successively smaller to show the edge of the one beneath, were layered by hue and formed the basis of Heian color schemes in dress. The fabrics, like certain colors, were also constrained by rules of class. Only those of highest rank could wear patterned silk uchigi. Ordinary court ladies wore unpatterned weaves similar to modern habutae. The color parfaits of uchigi were visible at the sleeve openings, at the front overlap, and at the hem of an ensemble.

At this point, a lady would have been suitably dressed for informal situations in her own quarters with her familiar ladies-in-waiting. Other gowns were worn atop this basic set when a male visitor came, when another ranked lady visited, when madame went out, or when the occasion demanded slightly greater formality. Naturally, the æsthetic rules that informed color combinations would have applied to those garments as well. Among the most common of these other kinds of outer robes were:

Ko-uchigi, dressing gown. This was a patterned small-cut robe that could be thrown over the layered uchigi to give a slightly more dressed effect. It was not worn if the succeeding full formal upper layers were put on.

Uchiginu, beaten silk gown. The uchiginu was a stiff silk garment that hardly showed. Like a shirt cardboard, it provided stiffener for the formal gowns worn on top of it.

Uwagi, over-robe. This gown topped all the layers. Again, its fabric was prescribed by rank. For women permitted intricate woven patterns, the uwagi was the place to display them. The length of hem and trailing effect were also a function of rank. The higher the rank, the longer the uwagi.

Mo, apron-skirt. Sometimes the mo is called a 'train' since it trailed in back. The mo made an outfit formal and was de rigueur for palace women on official duty. The Heian mo, with its ancient history and associations, was a ceremonial vestige dating from Asuka times.

Karaginu, Chinese jacket. Worn in conjunction with the mo, this was a short brocade, embroidered, or painted jacket with relatively narrow sleeves. Like the modern haori, the front sides did not lap, but hung straight. The back of the collar could be worn pulled slightly down off the nape for a soigné effect.

This list by no means exhausts a Heian noblewoman's wardrobe, and I do not plan even to open the Heian male's closet door. Heian ladies filled in this outline of basic costume with their palettes of colored silk.

Overlay color
Willow
(white over green)

Color pair
Pine tree
(scarlet-pink over green)

Woven color
Lespedeza
(lavender warp, green weft)

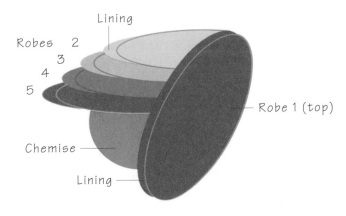

Robes   2
3
4
5

Lining

Robe 1 (top)

Chemise

Lining

Five-color set
Pine tree

The Palette

Ten colors appear most frequently in Empress Tashi's wardrobe. My English interpretations rely on three sources—Japanese definitions based on knowledge of what hue particular dyestuffs would produce, my sense of what the color swatches in Uemura and Yamazaki's *Encyclopedia of Japanese Color Terms* would be called in modern American English, and the notion that a plum blossom of today probably looks like a plum blossom of a millennium ago.

Ao
(blue-green)

Ao is one of the four oldest Japanese colors, appearing in the earliest Japanese poetry and prose texts along with black, white, and red. Although its modern meaning is blue as distinct from green, in the Heian period, as earlier, ao referred to a wider blue-green chunk of the spectrum. The range of cool tones during Heian may be subdivided into ao (blue-green), moegi (sprout-green), kon (deep blue with a red cast), and hanada (sky blue). Ao corresponds most closely to 'turquoise-green' in the Schwan forty-eight-color pencil box. In modern Japanese, the traffic signal green is called ao, an archaic holdover that confuses preschoolers.

Cyans

The term *midori* also existed in Heian times—it was the color of the sixth court rank—but it was never used as a kasane color. Likewise, the truest red, *ake*, the color of the fourth rank, occurs but rarely in ladies' dress. Probably the official connotations of these colors rendered them unsuitable for fashion.

Moegi
(sprout-green)

Moegi was clearly a variety of green. Whether it was a pale bluish-green or jaundiced is a matter of some argument. Etymologically, moegi is related to the sprouting (*moederu*) of herbs in the spring. Some sources write the -*gi* of moegi with the graph for 'tree,' others with the graph 'yellow' (both are pronounced *ki*, voiced *gi*). Since the green of new growth is often characterized by a slight yellowish cast, I have chosen the yellowish-green interpretation. Moegi could also be called grass-green or apple-green.

Kurenai
(scarlet-pink)

Reds

The warm spectrum of Heian colors was the most diverse. There had to have been numerous subtle distinctions in the hues to match the plethora of sanguine color terms. Kurenai was a bright, slightly yellow-toned pink produced from the benibana, 'safflower' (*Carthamus tinctoris*), an herbal dye source with very ancient roots. Kurenai was the closest thing to red in the fashion palette, since the truer red, *ake*, was primarily used to indicate rank. It was second only to murasaki in the hierarchy of forbidden colors. Kurenai is usually translated as scarlet or crimson, although during the Heian period it seems to have been less harsh or aggressively red than those names suggest in English—hence 'scarlet-pink.' Kurenai provided a popular metaphor for inconstant love since it was a notoriously ephemeral dye.

Kōbai
(plum-pink)

Kōbai is written with the two characters 'safflower' and 'plum.' It was most likely a light red with a purple cast. Plum-pink is a happy gloss for kōbai, since the English color name 'plum' means a reddish purple. We should remember, though, that this is coincidence. We think of plum primarily as the purplish fruit, whereas in Japanese plum refers exclusively to the flowers of a variety of *prunus*—one whose fruit we would probably call an apricot. As a 'woven color,' kōbai referred to a material with purple warp threads and a scarlet-pink weft. 'Rose pink' might also work as a gloss, although no translator can resist preserving the plum.

Suo
(maroon)

Suo was another red, wandering in tone from purple to brown to orange. It is the name of the tree (sappanwood) from which the dye comes. Depending on how the fabric was mordented or what the dye was combined with, a great range of warm tones was possible. During the latter Heian period, suo appears to have been maroon, russet, burgundy, an oxblood red, a chocolate red.

Ao

Kon

Midori

Hanada

Moegi

Kurenai

Kōbai

Suo

Ki

Yamabuki

Kuchiba

Kaki

Murasaki

Koki

Usuki

Keshi

Ebi

Fuji

Yellows

Ki
(yellow)

Ki was the purest yellow, without admixture of red or brown which make the other yellows golden, progressing toward tan. Ki, like ao, is one of the basic colors that appear in every culture after the primitive black-white-red distinction.[16] 'Lemon yellow' or the Schwan pencil simply designated 'yellow' seems to be the ki we are looking for. It is the color of the sour-grass oxalis flowers that are the first thing to bloom in the northern California spring.

Kuchiba
(old-leaf tan)

This name means rotted leaves. Like all the more colorful color terms, its development was relatively late. As a dye color, kuchiba is described as being simply the color of decaying leaves, a subdued tan. As a color pair, Kuchiba means old-leaf tan over yellow. If kuchiba were a bit brighter, it would approach mustard.

Yamabuki
(golden-yellow)

Yamabuki is a tree-shrub, the *Kerria japonica*, with a roseate yellow blossom. As a simple color name, it is one of the least problematic: a golden yellow like the color of the yamabuki flower or (today) the common freesia.

Murasaki
(purple)

We know that the dye for murasaki, from the root of the gromwell, was difficult to work with and that its products were always restricted to those of high rank. It was a fragile color that tended to fade, thus providing a poetic image throughout Heian literature for genteel aging. A range of purples included shades called *fuji* (wisteria), *keshi murasaki* (a grayed mauve), *ebi* (red-violet), and the esteemed *koki* (deep violet) and *usuki* (pale violet).

Sometimes the word *iro*, color, when used alone, was understood to mean the color of colors, purple. In this usage, koki, meaning deep or intense, by itself meant specifically koki murasaki—purple being understood. Likewise its opposite usuki (thin, pale, weak) stood for lavender. Murasaki was the premier Heian color; high-ranking, beautiful,

Purples

白

White

黒

Black

Shiro
(white)

The Text

fragile, full of meaning. It is no accident that the heroine of the *Tale of Genji* (eponymously, its author as well) was named Murasaki.

White is white. More than twenty percent of the layered colors used white on top, and half of the two-layer summer combinations used it underneath. White was basic to Heian fashion coordination, but it was also, along with its primal opposite, black, full of religious and ceremonial significance. A new empress wore a white Chinese jacket and white apron-skirt at her investiture ceremony, and a woman approaching childbirth wore white robes. An aristocratic newborn was surrounded by ladies all in white for the ceremonies that took place during the first week after birth. Reversion to color (*iro naoshi*) took place on the eighth day, when women donned their colorful combinations again.

If white was the color of purity and beginnings, it makes cultural sense that black was the color of death and mourning. Black robes, in various shades, proclaimed but one thing—bereavement. This message could not be overridden by fashion, which is why black did not appear in kasane colors. In Heian times, as in Victorian, mourning dress was graduated into stages of deep and light as life went on for the bereaved. In both societies this was socially indicated by clothing of progressively lighter shades of black.[17]

We are now ready to open Empress Tashi's closet, where we find close to five hundred separate robes layered into at least seventy-five different ensembles. The kasane colors were inspired by the tints of blossoms and leaves, bundled together into sets recognized by name as chrysanthemum, gentian, iris, and so on. At this point, however, the sets were named according to cultural convention rather than natural resemblance per se. In fact, literal resemblance was probably shunned as unsubtle by men and women of taste.

It seems to me that these ensembles can be analyzed as compositions of color. The major tone of each ensemble was supplied by the color of the top robe or robes. The minor tone, or foil to the most prominent color, came from the chemise. Although the chemise was worn under everything else, it was cut larger to show at sleeve and edges. Within the framework of major and minor tones, color accents occurred either on the least conspicuous middle and last robes or on the linings.

In analyzing each ensemble of robes in terms of its major and minor tones with accents, we see a color composition that, like a musical phrase, has its own character. The context of that color phrase is in the ensembles that precede and follow it in the yearly cycle. Phrases are often related in the manner of a theme with variations. Sometimes a theme plays itself out and is followed by something utterly new. At other times, a new phrase develops by picking up the accent colors from the previous kasane, amplifying them into a new major tone.

Masasuke divided the ensembles into ten sections according to the time of year they were to be worn. As in modern Japan, the two main seasons were winter-spring and summer-autumn. The year was clearly bisected at the beginning of winter by the change to padded glossed silks and at summer by the switch to light silks. The progressions from winter to spring and summer to autumn were more subtle. The shift between these particular seasons was not a sharp break—rather, it manifested itself by the appearance of new colors and seasonal kasane names.

As with so many arts in the Heian period, the art of dress had become a matter of correctly recreating classic compositions rather than inventing one's own. How could a woman's taste be judged if matters were predefined? Perhaps we should think of Tashi's text as a musical score to which the ladies of the court added their own interpretations when performing it. We have the score. We can only imagine the performance.

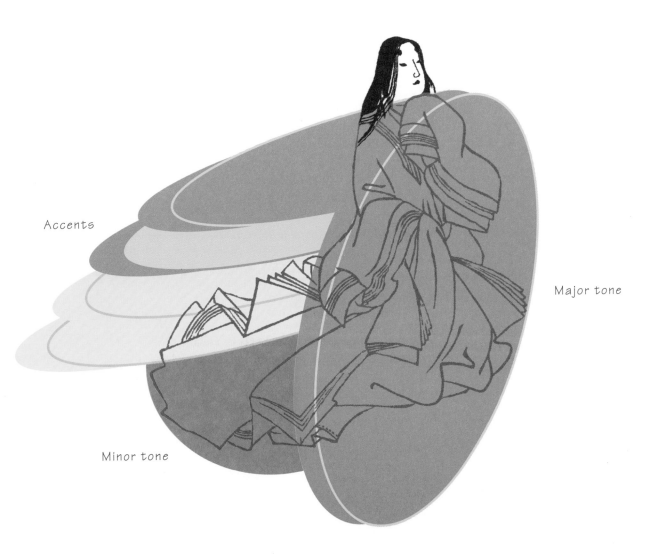

Accents

Major tone

Minor tone

Colors for a Court Lady's Dress

The text is little more than a list. It is divided into ten sections, each labeled with the time of year and type of robe appropriate to it. A varying number of kasane outfits are given for each section. The description of the kasane lists the color for five robes ordered outermost to inner, noting the color of the chemise at the end. Sprinkled throughout are short comments, attributed to Tashi.

I THINGS FOR SPECIAL OCCASIONS

The things for special occasions seem to be wardrobe classics. This is the only section that does not refer to a specific time of year.

> Deep maroon linings (*ura koki suo*)
> All five robes are colored a mid-range maroon, lined with a darker shade of maroon. The chemise is blue-green.

One of the most striking aspects of Heian color duets is color contrasts, such as the warm major tone maroon and cool minor blue-green in this kasane. This is a dramatic color æsthetic that even now continues to rule the assemblage of kimono and obi.

> Shades of maroon (*suo no nioi*)
> The robes are graduated shades of maroon, beginning with the lightest on top and deepening in hue to the innermost layer. The chemise is blue-green.

Arranging hues of graduated intensity of a single color was known by the term *nioi*, a visual concept later applied to an olfactory one—the word *nioi* now means fragrance. The gradual intensifying or fading of a color is metaphorically akin to the nose's experience of an odor.

Pine tree (*matsugasane*)
> The top two robes are deep maroon and light maroon. Robes three, four, and five are in shades of sprout-green ordered light, medium, dark. The chemise is scarlet-pink.

Tashi is probably correct. Among the various sources mentioning Pine, which combined a shade of green with a complementary warm tone (either maroon or purple), only Masasuke's puts the red tone on top. Convention later assigned each month a named color pair, establishing Pine as the duo for the first month of the year. During the Heian era, the layered set reflecting the reddish trunk and green needles of the pine was considered especially fine at the New Year but was by no means limited to it.

Tashi's marginalia: "It seems to me that I recall seeing the Pine combination with blue-green for the upper layers. Perhaps I am mistaken?"

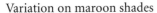
Variation on maroon shades
> Three maroon robes in the order dark, medium, and light, with a white robe and a deep persimmon-colored robe worn underneath.

These first four kasane ensembles seem to constitute a theme and variations. In all four, the major tone is maroon, the minor is a green shade, and the different accents provide diversity. The next three kasane begin a new color phrase, sharing a sanguine tone set off by different minor notes.

Shades of scarlet-pink (*kurenai no nioi*)
> A robe of scarlet-pink for the top layer, with each successive robe in a lighter shade, fading to pale pink. The chemise is plum-pink.

This ensemble was an unrelieved orchestration of scarlets and pinks, wearable only by a woman permitted the forbidden colors. Its dramatic impact would have lain in its proclamation of high status.

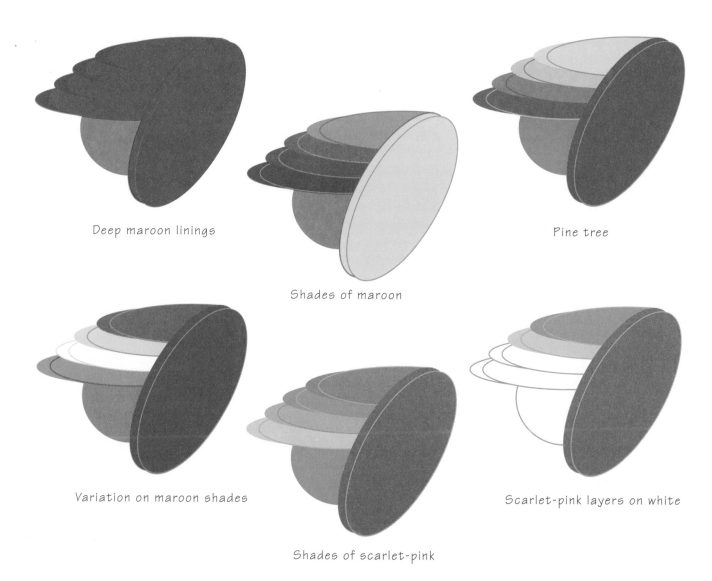

Deep maroon linings

Shades of maroon

Pine tree

Variation on maroon shades

Shades of scarlet-pink

Scarlet-pink layers on white

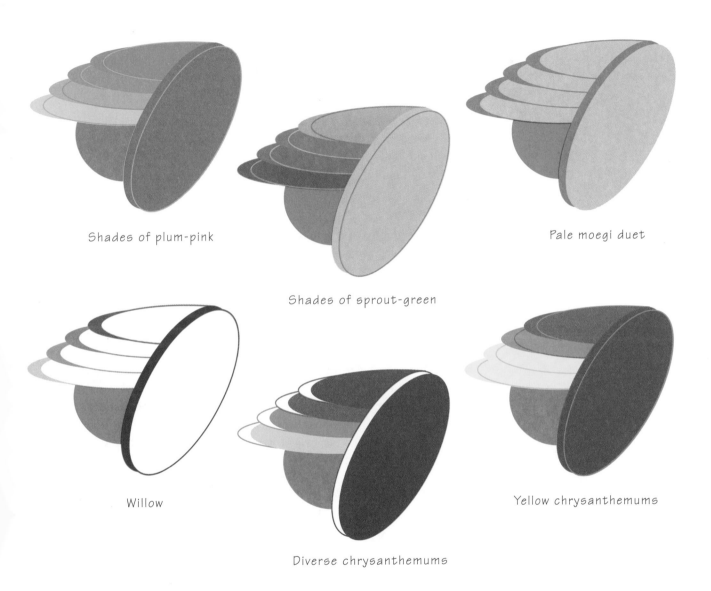

Shades of plum-pink

Shades of sprout-green

Pale moegi duet

Willow

Diverse chrysanthemums

Yellow chrysanthemums

Scarlet-pink layers on white (*kurenai no usuyō*)
> The top three layers are shades of scarlet-pink in the order dark, medium, light, and the next two layers are white. The chemise is also white.

The term *usuyō*, 'in the pale style,' means shades of a single hue over two inner layers of white. Usuyō occurs with pinks and purple only. This scarlet-pink over white combination was particularly favored and was recreated in different weights of silk for every season.

Shades of plum-pink (*kōbai no nioi*)
> All five robes are plum-pink, going from the palest hue on top, deepening to the innermost one. The chemise is either blue-green or deep red.

This order of plum-pink hues going from light to dark with a green chemise appears to have been a longstanding classic. It was mentioned in *The Confessions of Lady Nijō*, written approximately a century after Tashi consulted her manual.[18] After she had become a mendicant nun, Nijō was summoned by a provincial lord whose wife was trying to put together an outfit from material sent by the court. Her rustic ladies-in-waiting had gotten it all wrong: "The layered gowns had been assembled with the lightest layer properly on the outside, but immediately under it was the darkest one, so that the layers became successively lighter rather than darker toward the inside. It was quite incongruous"—wrote the nun, in a somewhat unseemly display of worldly erudition.

At this point in the cycle, the pink-dominated major tone shifts to shades of green, although pink continues to provide the minor note. There is nothing in Masasuke's text to indicate the separation of spring from winter, but the dramatic appearance of these green-toned kasane, one having a specifically vernal name—willow—probably served that purpose.

Shades of sprout-green (*moegi no nioi*)
> All robes are in shades of sprout-green. The top one is the lightest, and each robe deepens successively through the fifth. The chemise is scarlet-pink.

Here is another example of a nioi, a color scheme that intensifies like a fragrance. Because most colors were made by repeated dippings in a dye, the nioi æsthetic could be created systematically by regulating the number of dye baths for each robe of a combination. The pink chemise gives this ensemble its æsthetic balance and continues the pink motif from the previous set of kasanes.

Pale moegi duet (*usu moegi*)
> All five robes are pale blue-green [ao] lined with slightly darker blue-green. The chemise is scarlet-pink.

Moegi is a glaring example of the ambiguity of Heian color names. If we decide that moegi is green with a yellow tinge, then how can we account for the fact that this combination is specifically noted as two shades of the color ao, blue-green. Perhaps moegi is not jaundiced after all? But then why use a term separate from ao? Presumably the ladies of Tashi's court would have known.

Willow (*yanagi*)
> In the first variation, all robes are white with pale blue-green linings. In the second variation, all robes are white, but the blue-green linings deepen in hue from outer to innermost. In either case, the chemise is scarlet-pink.

Yanagi connotes early spring because it begins to bud around the second lunar month. Willow is one of the classic overlay colors found in the *Tale of Genji*. The æsthetic urge to provide color contrast calls for a pink chemise.

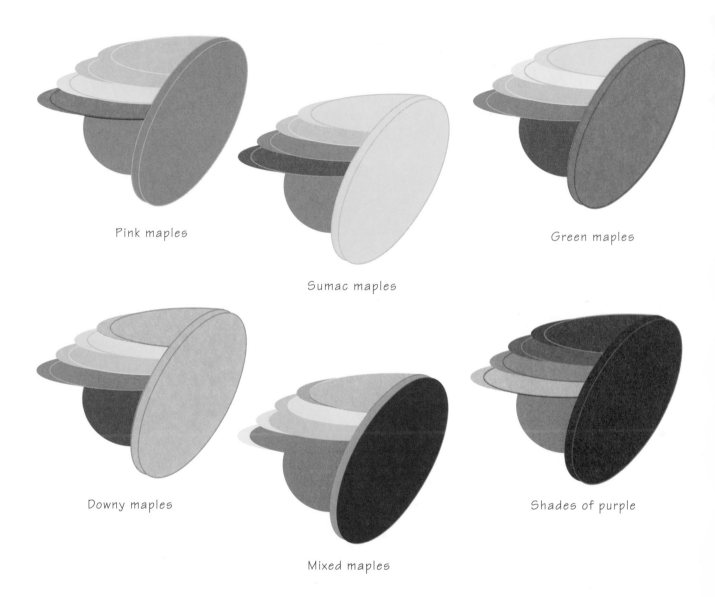

Pink maples

Sumac maples

Green maples

Downy maples

Mixed maples

Shades of purple

Purple layers on white

Shades of golden yellow

Golden yellow linings

Flowering kerria rose

Plum dyeing

Plum layers

From this point, all sections are defined by time of year and robe material. The tenth lunar month, modern November, marked the official beginning of winter. Glossed silk (*neriginu*) garments were made of silk cloth treated with lye and pounded to remove natural sericin. This process rendered the cloth soft and pliant. These robes were also made warmer by inserting padding of silk floss between the face and lining. Such robes were worn for precisely half the year, from the start of winter through spring right up to the official beginning of summer, corresponding to modern May. At that point they were replaced again by lighter robes.

If clusters of kasane marked by similar colors were themes with variations, the type and weight of silk might be considered their key or mode. For example, the maple and chrysanthemum kasanes of autumn are themes done in the mode of unpadded and raw silks. When they played in early winter, however, the mode changed to padded, glossed silk. Seasons are cyclical, but text is linear. Masasuke began his list with winter, so we see the hivernal mode of chrysanthemums and maples before the autumn ones that would have been their proper prelude.

> Diverse chrysanthemums (*kiku no yōyō*)
> The robes are composed in *suo no nioi* [shades of maroon going from dark to light], with white linings. The chemise is blue-green.
>
> Yellow chrysanthemums (*kigiku*)
> The top three robes are three shades of maroons, and the two under-robes are pale yellow. The chemise is either a variegated scarlet-pink or blue-green.

Curiously, this combination (among others in the winter-spring section) does not mention linings, although we must assume, since it was the season for padded robes, that linings were necessary. Perhaps the linings were of the same color as the robes?

The chrysanthemums have the same dominant theme of maroon and minor theme of green that characterized the first cluster of kasanes. Surely this color harmonic sang of early winter to the Heian Japanese. The chemise in Yellow chrysanthemums seems to be transitional. If it is green, the ensemble recalls its predecessors—if pink, it is linked to the succeeding cluster of maple kasanes. The yellow note introduced in its middle layers will also crescendo in the maples that follow.

Maple leaves are the seasonal reverse of spring blossoms, but in the clothing cycle, spring flora (plum, willow, and kerria rose) are confined to spring, whereas the maples and chrysanthemums can ramble over the border to winter. Five distinct yet related combinations of colors are expressed by the maple motif in the following group called 'Diverse maple leaves.' The changing colors of the two outer gowns—pink, yellow, or green—give a staccato effect to each ensemble, but the continuo of the rouge minor tone of the chemise gives them unity.

Pink maples (*kurenai momiji*)
 The top robe is scarlet-pink, followed by golden yellow, pure yellow, and blue-green. The chemise is scarlet-pink.

"I believe the chemise should be maroon."

Sumac maples (*haji momiji*)
 The top two layers are pure yellow. They are followed by a third layer of golden yellow and a fourth of scarlet-pink, and the innermost robe is maroon. The chemise is scarlet-pink.

"One layer of yellow, two of golden, the rest maroon."

Haji is the name of a tree in the sumac family, the sap of which was used to make a pumpkinish, yellowed orange dye. This kasane probably appeared as gaudy to Heian Japanese as it seems to us. The combination of reds, pinks, and yellows was seen as rather *à la mode chinoise*, hence exotic. It also projects a different feeling from the graduated nioi combinations and the 'pale-style' usuyō kasane regarded as being more essentially Japanese in sensibility.

Green maples (*ao momiji*)
> The top layer is blue-green. This is followed by a layer of deep yellow, one of pale yellow, one of golden yellow, and then a last layer of scarlet-pink. The chemise is maroon.

Downy maples (*kaede momiji*)
> The top two layers are light blue-green, the third layer is pure yellow, the fourth is golden yellow, and the innermost is scarlet-pink. The chemise is either scarlet-pink or maroon.

Mixed maples (*mojiri momiji*)
> The top robe is deep blue-green with a light scarlet-pink lining. The second robe is pale blue-green with a lining of scarlet-pink. The third robe is pure yellow with a golden yellow lining. The fourth robe is golden yellow with a pure yellow lining. The last robe is scarlet-pink with a pale yellow lining. The chemise is scarlet-pink.

While the maple combinations in general are among the most flamboyant, this last, Mixed maples, must have been spectacular. Yet no matter how riotous the above combination may appear today, it was not random. Was randomness possible? Yes, and its effect was odious. In "The Shell Matching Contest," a piece of late Heian fiction, we find an instance of random colors in this description of a disagreeable young lady: "She entered—this person bundled up in ill-assorted colors of yamabuki, kōbai, and usu kuchiba."[19]

The yamabuki color pair was a golden yellow robe with a yellow lining, kōbai a scarlet-pink robe lined in maroon, and pale kuchiba a light tan robe with the same color lining. The story is set in early winter, but the seasonal significances of the color duos bespeak a hodgepodge of summer, spring, and autumn. No wonder the girl was disagreeable.

The Gosechi Festival was celebrated around the middle of the eleventh lunar month. The sixteen color combinations described below run from the height of winter through the end of spring. The nonfloral kasane names cluster at the beginning, dead winter, perhaps a reflection of the lack of bloom at that time of year.

In a famous scene in the *Tale of Genji*, the hero chooses New Year's gifts of clothing for his wives and paramours.[20] Genji is advised by the heroine Murasaki that the ensembles should be composed with a mind to each lady's character and looks. It went without saying that the colors also had to be appropriate to rank. Less obviously, Genji was limited by the season—winter. Given these constraints, Genji exhausted most of the available color possibilities in dressing all of his ladies.

> Shades of purple (*murasaki no nioi*)
> All five robes are in shades of purple. They begin at deep purple for the top, shading successively down to pale laven-der. The chemise is scarlet-pink.

Deep purple was rarely used as an accessory color in Tashi's wardrobe. When it appears, murasaki tends to be the whole show, its superiority undiluted or highlighted with white. This kasane is the only one in which purple is accented by red. Purple never occurs with the yellows.

> Purple layers on white (*murasaki no usuyō*)
> The top three robes are dark, medium, and pale pur-ple. They are worn over two layers of plain white robes. The chemise is also white.

This combination must have been stunning in its severe hauteur. Deep purple, like the reds and scarlet-pinks, was a forbidden color. As an empress, Tashi could wear any color or weave of silk. At any one time in the Heian court, no more than thirty women would have been eligible to wear the colors of this combination.[21]

Shades of golden yellow (*yamabuki no nioi*)
> All five robes are in shades of golden yellow. The deepest shade goes on top. They become successively paler and the last robe is pure yellow. The chemise is blue-green.

Golden yellow linings (*ura yamabuki*)
> All five robes are pure yellow with linings of deep golden yellow. The chemise is blue-green.

Flowering kerria rose (*hana yamabuki*)
> All five robes are a medium golden yellow. The chemise is blue-green.

Here is another case in which the natural object (the kerria rose), the color name, and the layered combination all of the same name, yamabuki, blend together. The classic Genji yamabuki combination was old-leaf tan (kuchiba) over pure yellow (ki). These three variations on the yamabuki theme play with the possibilities of yellows on yellow, yet by preserving the same green chemise they maintain the kerria rose image.

The following three kasanes abruptly switch to a plum theme that can be characterized as a major tone of pink-accented white with a minor tone of green.

Plum dyeing (*umezome*)
> All five robes are white, lined with deep maroon. The chemise is blue-green.

Perhaps this plum combination (plum = spring) was regarded as an inverse echo of the chrysanthemum kasane (chrysanthemum = fall). Chrysanthemum consisted of maroon robes lined in white, whereas the plum set contains white robes lined in maroon. Both maintain a blue-green chemise. The plum combination is similar to the classic *sakura* (cherry blossom), the color overlay appearing most frequently in the

Tale of Genji. Sakura was a top layer of white with an underlayer of red or purple glimmering through. Interestingly, Masasuke does not include a sakura combination. Perhaps by his time even the gentlefolk of Heian had become jaded to the cherry blossom reference?

> Plum layers (*umegasane*)
> The top robe is white with a very pale tinge of plum-pink. The second robe is light plum-pink. The third robe is plum-pink. The fourth robe is scarlet-pink. The fifth robe is maroon. The chemise is either deep purple or blue-green.

"For umegasane, the top three robes may all be plum-pink, or they may all be scarlet."

This is the only kasane that employed a deep purple chemise.

> Beneath the snow (*yuki no shita*)
> The top two layers are white, followed by three shades of plum-pink in the order dark, medium, light. The chemise is blue-green.

"The chemise ought to be scarlet-pink. Blue-green is in bad taste."

Japanese scholars point to this combination as an example of straightforward *imitatio naturæ*.[22] In this view, the top two layers represent white snow, the next three are the opening buds of plum flowers, and the green underlayer is the stem. Tashi's comment (*aoki wa waroshi*), her strongest by far, suggests that if color references were merely a one-to-one matching game with nature, then the whole pursuit becomes trivial. The fine line between trivial pursuits and the creation of something with æsthetic integrity is definitely crossed when the effect becomes too literal. To suggest that a green chemise represented a stem risks tipping the sublime to the ridiculous.

As an æsthetic principle, a blue-green chemise is worn only when the colors of the rest of the ensemble are warm tones—reds, pinks, and yellows. Green chemises cannot have been meant as flower stems, but because they often occurred with flower-named kasanes, literal-minded

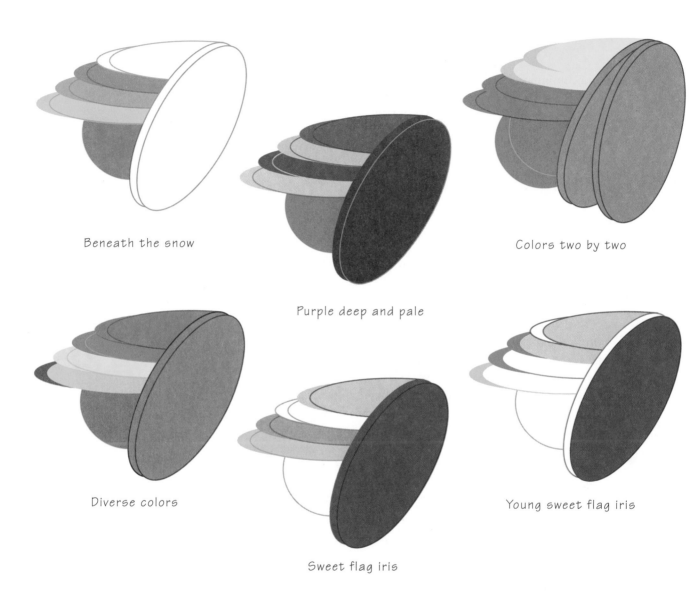

Beneath the snow

Purple deep and pale

Colors two by two

Diverse colors

Sweet flag iris

Young sweet flag iris

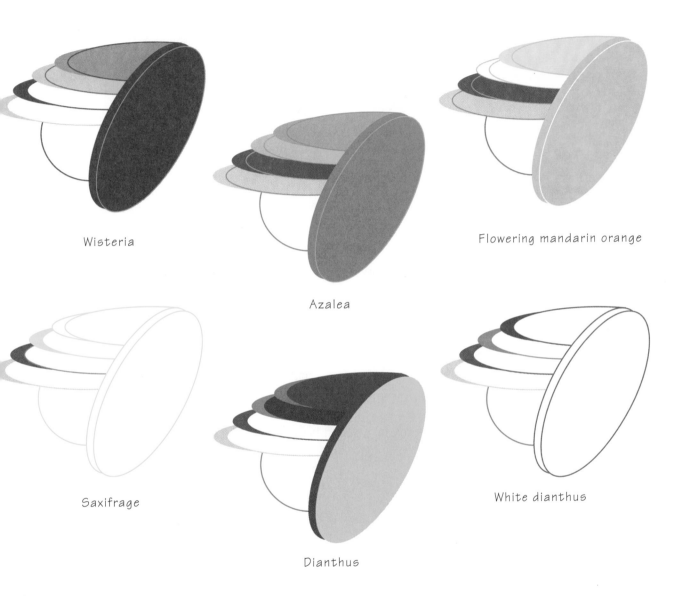

Wisteria

Azalea

Flowering mandarin orange

Saxifrage

Dianthus

White dianthus

Heian persons may also have made the analogy to a flower's calyx. Nevertheless, when the effect was liable to be read too closely, as in 'plums under snow,' a person of taste would probably have considered it unsubtle.

Yuki no shita was also the name of the small perennial evergreen we call strawberry begonia, which bears tiny white flowers and has round fuzzy green leaves that are red underneath.

> Purple deep and pale (*murasaki murago*)
> The top three layers are dark, medium, and pale purple. The next two layers are dark blue-green followed by pale blue-green. The chemise is scarlet-pink.

Murago refers to a pattern applied to a finished garment in which random spots of deeper hue are dyed onto a lighter ground. It is not clear whether this is what is meant for the purples in this kasane. If it is, murasaki murago comprises the only example of patterned robes in the entire set. It is also the only kasane in which deep purple appears with another color in the robes.

This and the following two kasanes refer to colors per se rather than to flowering plants. The dominant tone of late spring is a lavender-purple with a minor voice of pink. The accents range from yellow to green to pink. The nonfloral names of this cluster highlight the upcoming major division between spring and the completely florid names of early summer.

> Colors two by two (*futatsu no iro ni*)
> The first two robes are lavender. The next two are pure yellow with linings of golden yellow. These are followed by a double layer of sprout-green. The double chemise is scarlet-pink.

"According to rule, lavender is layered on top, but there are occasions when sprout-green may be on top. If the layers are increased, plum-pink may be added to good effect."

This combination is unusual because of the number of layers. During Tashi's time, the number of robes any court lady, even an empress, could wear was regulated by sumptuary law. Five was the accepted number, a limit set in 1074 in reaction to an earlier period of extravagance when ladies wore as many as twenty layers. A scene from the *Eiga monogatari*, in which ladies prepared for Grand Empress Kenshi's banquet in 1025, gives an idea of the situation: "[The ladies] walked toward the Grand Empress with attendants carrying their skirts. They were graceless figures, their robes too numerous and thick to let them raise their fans to their faces. The seams of their jackets, it appeared, had split open because of their bulky garments."[23]

> Diverse colors (*iro iro*)
> The uppermost robe is lavender. It is followed in order by one each of sprout-green, plum-pink, pale golden yellow, and one in light maroon with a dark lining. The chemise is scarlet-pink.

"There are various ways to layer the Diverse colors and they are not always identical."

Heian nobility responded to warming temperatures by wearing thinner silk and fewer layers for summer wear. The custom of changing robes by season was not simply a functional response to nature, however, since the seasons themselves were culturally defined. Winter began on the first day of the tenth month, no matter what the temperature. And although it was fashionable to rush each season slightly in terms of kasane colors, it is doubtful that even perspiring ladies would have changed to thin silks before the prescribed date.

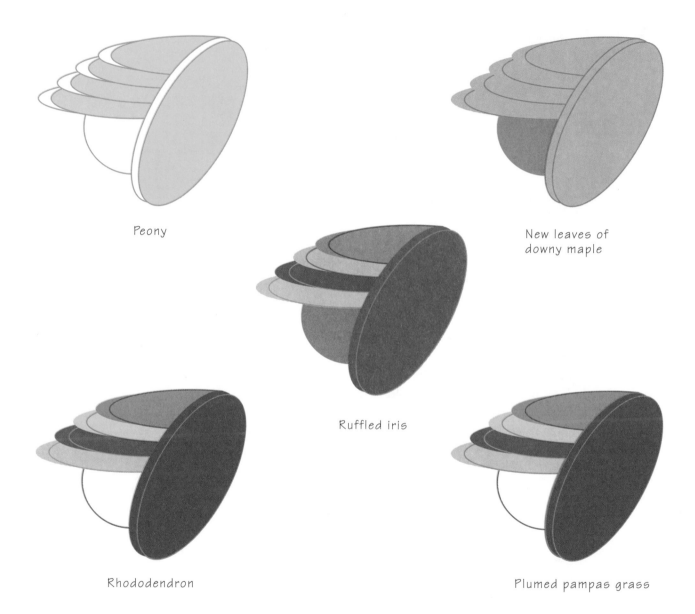

Peony

New leaves of
downy maple

Ruffled iris

Rhododendron

Plumed pampas grass

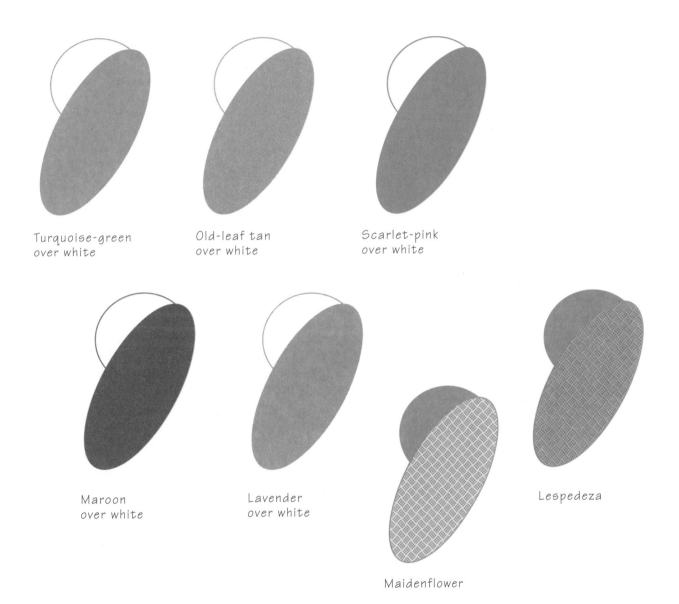

Turquoise-green
over white

Old-leaf tan
over white

Scarlet-pink
over white

Maroon
over white

Lavender
over white

Maidenflower

Lespedeza

IV THE FOURTH LUNAR
MONTH: COLORS FOR
THIN ROBES

Summer officially began with the fourth lunar month, May in the modern calendar—the time to put away lined robes of glossed silk and take out translucent gauze-woven silk called *ra*. Ra is light and airy, a weave created by twisting the weft thread on each pass through the warp. Since lining colors are often specified, we must assume that many of the robes in this section were still composed of two layers. The early summer robes were designed not so much to be cool as to look cool. Summer begins with two variations on a set of colors named Iris.

> Sweet flag iris (*shobu*)
> The robes are arranged in this order:
> deep blue-green
> pale blue-green
> white
> deep plum-pink
> pale plum-pink.
> The chemise is white, raw silk [*susushi*].

The summer robes and chemise break with spring in their materials. The chemise changes to a different silk, called susushi, which was less pliant than glossed silk because of the waxy sericin that remained on the threads. It stood slightly away from the skin, thus rendering it cooler. Color bridges the seasons. The Iris colors—blue-greens, pinks, and lavenders—cluster across the seasonal border, playing out on six ensembles before a note of yellow at last replaces pink and a new theme amplifying yellow begins.

> Young sweet flag iris (*waka shobu*)
> The set of robes is composed as follows:
> deep blue-green with a white lining
> pale blue-green with a white lining
> pale blue-green with a deep plum-pink lining

white with a plum-pink lining
white with a pale plum-pink lining.
The chemise is white raw silk.

Wisteria (*fuji*)
This is the order of robes:
deep purple with a deep purple lining
medium purple with a medium purple lining
lavender with a lavender lining
white with a deep purple lining
white with a lavender lining.
The chemise is raw silk, either white or scarlet-pink.

The Kamo Festival was celebrated on a date falling sometime between the end of April and the ninth of June in the modern calendar, marking the beginning of hot weather in Kyoto. Tashi remarks that raw silk robes would be worn then, although the text doesn't specify them until mid-September. Tashi shows a tendency to rush the season, as we shall see again further on.

Azalea (*tsutsuji*)
The top three robes are graduated shades of scarlet-pink in the order dark, medium, light. The remaining two robes are deep blue-green and pale blue-green. The chemise is either white or scarlet-pink.

"With lined garments in the fourth lunar month, it is always preferable to wear a chemise of white raw silk. After the Kamo Festival, when one wears robes of raw silk, then it is fine to wear a pink chemise. I think that when the lined garments are colored, the chemise ought to be white. Am I mistaken?"

Azalea uses the same color spectrum as Iris—pinks, white, and blue-greens. In the next ensemble, the pink tone is replaced with yellow and we see a new theme.

Flowering mandarin orange (*hana tachibana*)
> The top two robes are golden yellow, first a deep shade, then a pale. The third robe is white. The fourth and fifth robes are blue-green, deep and pale. The chemise is either white or blue-green.

This combination echoes the color pair of the same name consisting of old-leaf tan over blue-green in most sources. The tachibana tree, a citrus with a white flower, is assigned to the summer cultural season, so it makes sense for it to appear at this point. The colors may refer to the botanical fact that the golden yellow fruit and white blossom may occur simultaneously on the tachibana. Reference to fruit is rare in Japanese colors. In contrast, English is disposed to name hues after fruits rather than flowers. This accounts for the ladies dressed in fruit salads of grape, cherry, and apricot robes in English translations of Heian literature.

Saxifrage (*u no hana*)
> All five robes are white. The first two are also white-lined. The remaining three linings are yellow, deep blue-green, and pale blue-green. The chemise is white.

The classic saxifrage duo was white over green. This combination of robes clearly reflects this common understanding of u no hana, but with a twist of lemon in the least conspicuous place. The Saxifrage layered set uses the same yellow-white-green scheme as Flowering mandarin orange, constituting again a short theme with variation.

Dianthus (*nadeshiko*)
> The first robe is pale maroon lined in maroon; the second is maroon lined in scarlet-pink. The third robe is deep maroon lined in plum-pink. Robes four and five are both white, one lined in deep and the other in pale blue-green. The chemise is either white or scarlet-pink.

Except for the excruciatingly muggy month of July, at least two layers of gowns were worn—a chemise with something on top of it. Any color other than white, scarlet-pink, or blue-green for a chemise is rare. A white chemise, worn under the thin and raw silks, occurs most frequently in summer. The scarlet-pink chemise occurs most often with the padded glossed silk robes of winter and spring. The blue-green chemise occurs throughout the year.

A white chemise had a clear summer connotation for Heian Japanese. In one of her *Pillow Book* lists of 'depressing things,' Sei Shōnagon includes the sight of a woman wearing a white chemise in the eighth month, September. Imagine a modern New Yorker wearing white linen to a luncheon of fashion mavens in September. The reaction would be close to Shōnagon's.

> White dianthus (*shiro nadeshiko*)
> All five robes are white. The linings should be white, maroon, plum-pink, deep blue-green, and pale blue-green. The chemise can be white or scarlet-pink, as one pleases.

> Peony (*botan*)
> All five robes are pale maroon lined in white. The chemise is white raw silk.

> New leaves of downy maple (*waka kaede*)
> All five robes and linings are in a light sprout-green. The chemise can be white or scarlet-pink, as one likes.

The monochromaticity of this combination is unusual, breaking the rhythm of maroons and whites before it becomes boring. Although this is the plainest kasane, New leaves would have stood out in its simplicity because of its placement here. The next kasane finishes off the maroon-white phrase.

Rhododendron (*mochi tsutsuji*)
> The top three robes are shades of maroon in the order dark, medium, light. The succeeding two robes are deep blue-green and pale blue-green. The chemise must be white.

V THE FIFTH LUNAR MONTH: STIFF EDGES

Stiff-edged robes (*hineri-gasane*) were created by folding back the sleeve edges into heavily starched hems, giving a crisp effect. Hineri-gasane is specified for the fifth lunar month (modern June), the height of the rainy season. Each set in this section is a replay of an earlier ensemble. Clothing historian Maeda Ujō suggests that because of the rain, ladies would have been confined to their quarters and therefore less interested in displaying new combinations.[24] But hineri-gasane is also specified for another period, the dry days of autumn. Perhaps the heat of early September kept women in as well? This interpretation seems wrong in any case, since being kept in was the primary mode of existence for Heian noblewomen. Both hineri sets are replays of kasanes of other seasons. It is conceivable that the very same robes were worn with starch applied, giving them the proper aspect for the fortnights of hineri.

Five of the six kasane in this section are names we have already seen and the last is a variation on the familiar iris theme. The text lists them with the note that the color arrangement is to be the same as previously specified. In effect, here is an echo of early summer themes in a starched mode.[25]

"The thin silks can have linings of various colors, so how is it possible to follow the same rules in arranging the unlined stiff-edged garments? Do the rules concern only the robes' face and not the linings?"

Ruffled iris (*kakitsubata*)
> The top three robes are shades of lavender, successively paler. The remaining two layers are deep blue-green and pale. As is customary, the chemise is scarlet-pink.

Good question, Tashi.

It is the equivalent of modern July, the hottest time of the year.

> The chemise must always be white. Over it one wears a single
> unlined robe in one of the following colors: maroon, old-leaf
> tan, scarlet-pink, lavender, or turquoise-green.
>
> Or one may wear a *karakami* [stencil-painted silk] robe, which
> may be in various colors, over a blue-green or a white
> chemise.
>
> Or one may wear *kemonsa* [silk gauze with a woven pattern] or
> *fusenryō* [a floating warp pattern gauze.]

During this hot summer month, these patterned weaves would presumably have been worn by themselves. In fact, the July combinations
were probably completely transparent. In Kyoto's sweltering summer
heat, the palace ladies still wore their indispensable long trousers as basic
underclothing, but the stiff gauze layers of the unlined gown, standing
away from the skin of their upper bodies, were probably quite revealing.
We usually think of Heian ladies as veritable cocoons of cloth, but in the
summer they were visibly bare-breasted under a single sheer silk enve-
lope. Whether the glimpse of a nipple was erotic to the Heian male,
however, can only be conjectured. Voyeurism in the *Tale of Genji*, for
example, focused on stolen peeks of a different forbidden part of the
anatomy—the face.[26]

"There are several kinds of Chinese paper silks. We mostly see
yellow or blue. The maroon
and pale old-leaf tan varieties
usually have the same color
above and below."

"A combination like Maidenflower is usually worn after the
Gion Festival in the sixth
month."

Only two combinations are given for this approximately three-week period of miserably hot weather. Both kasanes denote woven colors. The cultural, as opposed to functional, importance of this section is to denote the technical beginning of fall. The shift from summer is played down, just as the shift from winter to spring was very low-key. It is accomplished with color—the white chemise is abandoned in favor of blue-green—and by the introduction of autumnally significant floral names.

> Lespedeza (*hagi*)
> A gown woven of lavender and blue-green thread, worn over blue-green.

> Maidenflower (*ominaeshi*)
> A gown woven of yellow and blue-green thread, worn over blue-green.

Tashi clearly approves of rushing the season. The maidenflower, a lacy yarrow-like perennial with yellow umbels, was one of the classic seven autumn herbs. Kyoto-ites have a tendency to feel that after the Gion Festival, the highlight of summer is past, it is as good as autumn.

VIII FROM THE FIRST DAY
OF THE EIGHTH LUNAR
MONTH TO THE FIF-
TEENTH:
STIFF EDGES

At this point we return to a full set of five robes. Like the hineri sets in June, the September kasanes repeat color schemes we have seen before. There is only one novel entry:

> Plumed pampas grass (*susuki*)
> The top three robes are shades of maroon: deep, medium, and pale. The last two robes are deep blue-green and pale blue-green. The chemise is white.

Although most of Masasuke's kasane names can also be found in other sources, this one, Susuki, occurs only in this text. Tashi's comment, however, indicates that she has seen it, done differently, elsewhere.

The next eighth-month ensemble is called Gentian (*rindō*), a new name, but the text notes that its colors are the same as the Ruffled iris of June. Chrysanthemum and Maple then make their debut in unlined robes with starch-stiffened edges, as a prelude to autumn.

"I think the blue-green should come on top. In the middle is [text missing]. The maroon layers should be underneath and finally there should be a maroon chemise. I might be wrong."

Centering on the autumnal equinox, this three-week period constitutes the height of autumn. The colors continue in the same vein as above, although the robes have changed into a different silk.

> Maroon, lavender, and white are appropriate colors for robes. Also, the Chrysanthemum and Maple combinations (which are the same as in the glossed silk versions), and the Maiden-flower ensemble. For Maidenflower, all five robes are of the woven color *ominaeshi* [yellow and blue-green] with blue-green linings. The chemise is scarlet-pink.

This is Masasuke's last category. The ninth day of the ninth month was marked by the ceremony *Chōyō no en*, one of the five big seasonal festivals. This one, autumn, was celebrated with chrysanthemums. We are now but three weeks from the semi-annual wardrobe change that marks the beginning of the winter-spring season. The text establishes the change to padded robes but lists no new ensembles. It simply notes that "the following colors are appropriate: scarlet-pink, purple, lavender, and white."

IX FROM THE FIFTEENTH DAY OF THE EIGHTH LUNAR MONTH TO THE NINTH DAY OF THE NINTH MONTH: UNPADDED RAW SILK

CULTURED NATURE

Three distinct orders of phenomena combine to create the object of the kasane ensembles: nature (the actual florid herbage), season (a cultural construct giving human order to cosmological process), and clothing (a purely human artifact). Nature in this case is not raw but has been filtered through a cultural process that has ascribed certain significances to it. The pine in its natural state, oblivious to the felicitous connotations bestowed upon it, is green throughout the year—yet it is culturally an early spring phenomenon. Likewise the flowering *prunus* varieties are assigned seasonal significance in approximately their blooming order, but irrespective of the time trees actually set forth blossoms. Tashi's commentary suggests that overly literal resemblance was considered slightly crass.

Seasons are seamless—blending into one another without break. The cultural construction of the seasons, in contrast, is necessarily discrete. The kasane cycle reflects both aspects. Winter and summer begin at specific points. The wardrobe oscillation between padded and light silks must have been as obvious as the modern change in school uniforms from winter blue serge to summer white cotton. At these junctures, however, the color themes of the previous season carry over. Conversely, the lower-key transition between summer and autumn, or between winter and spring, is marked not by a change in material but by a new color note. Expressions of continuity, phrases, are juxtaposed with pauses. An individual ensemble is isolated, lacking significance until we know the notes that surround it, the phrase of which it is a part. And the phrases, too, have an integrity best seen in relation to their surroundings—when the major tone of one phrase is picked up as the succeeding minor, for example.

The kasane cycle was a cultural composition of color played on instruments of silk. Its rhythms echoed nature and season, of course, but primarily they echoed each other. Color and fabric worked in counterpoint to express an æsthetic vision that adjusted a lady's being to an appropriate expression of cosmic time and place. Though attenuated by a thousand years of clothing evolution, the ideal still echoes faintly in the rules that govern the wearing of wafuku today. It remains impossible to be arbitrarily creative in kimono. Appended to Masasuke's text is the following anonymous and enigmatic remark:

> There are those who tried making displays of ladies' robe edges after having seen Masasuke's arrangements at an imperial lon-gevity celebration, but their attempts were unsightly. They really ought to consult this book.

And there, perhaps, is the final word on Heian creativity, as well as on the marvelous ensembles of color that transcended the women who wore them.

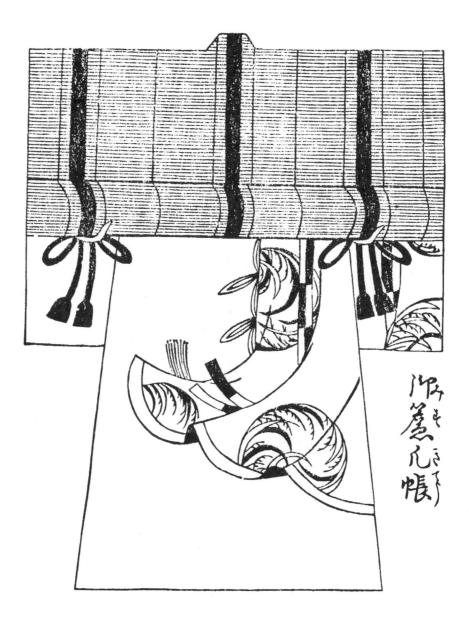

作り蓮兄帳

> Fashions have changed from the simplicity of the past to great ostentation. People today crave finery above their station and purse in everything they do and buy. Look at the way the wives and daughters of the townspeople dress—it is impossible to go to further extremes.
>
> —Ihara Saikaku, *The Japanese Family Storehouse*, 1688

THE DIRECT ANCESTOR OF MODERN KIMONO was the kosode as it was worn by urban Japanese in the seventeenth century. A critical mass of wealth, talent, and taste had converged in the early Tokugawa cities. The towndwellers, prime agents of this cultural concentration, expressed their *savoir vivre* partly through the extravagant beauty of their clothing. While color, pure and per se, had been the æsthetic focus of the classic Heian robes, striking patterns came to dominate kosode fashion during the Genroku era (1688-1704). The multifarious Genroku colors shone within the contours of design—dyed, embroidered, foil-impressed, painted, and appliquéd.

Unlike the aristocratic exclusivity of Heian, the luxury of Genroku was accessible to all who could afford it. The creators of the kosode fashions of the early feudal period were wealthy, upstart, urban commoners, not courtiers. The government's perceived need to regulate ebullient display of the growing wealth of the merchant class in itself testifies to the reality that anybodies, despite their low official status, could control the means to live like lords, even as some authentic lords were feeling pinched.

Earlier in the seventeenth century, the great *daimyō* autocrats had finally been brought under the central political control of the Tokugawa shogun. The economy benefited from the peace that settled on the country after a century and a half of internal warfare. Trade and the production of goods for consumption grew, and people were siphoned out of the countryside into town and city. Three major cities largely created the urban culture of Genroku. These were Kyoto, abode of the emperor and the city with the most venerable urban tradition; nearby Osaka, which became rich as Japan's central exchange market for goods; and the shogun's newly established capital, Edo.

It was to Edo that most people flocked. The shogun dwelt in Edo, and provincial lords were required to maintain households there. Although they were still the undisputed leaders within their own domains, in the shogun's capital these lords with their samurai retinues were required to subsidize public works, supply military details, and sustain elaborate residences. The expenses entailed in their high status grew all the more when a developing cash economy created inflation. The extensive retinues drew a population of merchants, artisans, and vendors to provide necessary services, and Edo became a vast congregation of consumers as agricultural wealth gathered from all corners of Japan was spent on luxuries there. Although unprepared for the ultimate consequences of mercantile development, the shogunate encouraged consumption. Daimyō squandering their resources in Edo were less likely to fund sedition in their home provinces. Meanwhile, as the warrior class stockpiled moral resources, commoners produced and spent the æsthetic currency of Genroku.

CLOTHING AND
COMMON CULTURE

The comfortable urban dweller of whatever class—samurai, merchant, or even craftsman—wore kosode for work and leisure. Tucking hem into obi enabled the wearer to walk briskly; untucking the skirt to cover the legs transformed kosode back into proper attire. Kosode was not suitable for the peasant farmer, but the mercantile labor of the cities was not the backbreaking physical labor of agriculture. Hitching the skirts or sleeves out of the way was all that was necessary to make kosode practical for city work. In addition, by varying fabric and colors, kosode served as both business suit and leisure wear. According to popular literature of the late seventeenth century, the fashion-mad wives and daughters of townsmen became kosode addicts.

The essence of fashion is change for the sake of change. In this sense, fashion seems to have moved much more slowly before the Edo era. In Heian times, the *Tale of Genji* describes pitiful Suetsumuhana, the Safflower Lady, as being hopelessly out of date in her clothing taste, indicating that an element of being au courant was important in Heian couture. Yet virtually all styles were dictated by tradition. Change for its own sake did not really arise in Japanese dress until the seventeenth century, when kosode shook off the trousers and over-robes of earlier modes and stood on its own.

Kosode was originally a part of the underwear of Heian nobility. Courtiers wore a little sleeve (*kosode*) underneath their many wide-sleeved (*hirosode*) outer robes. As ultra-refined court culture wilted and demurred to the age of the warrior after the fourteenth century, clothing became simpler. Noblewomen ceased to wear extravagant layers of colored robes except for high ceremony. Being dressed now consisted of wearing a plain white silk little-sleeved undergarment with scarlet hakama trousers. Women of the warrior class adopted this outfit and continued the process of simplification. Hakama for women gave way to a robe called a *koshimaki* that was gathered about the hips with the upper half left to drape. Eventually this, too, was left off and the kosode emerged on its own. Like the T-shirt, the kosode worked its way from underwear to respectability over time, metamorphosing from plain white to stripes, colors, and daring design. During the Edo period kosode in cotton, ramie, or silk became standard wear for men and women of every social stratum.

The shape of early Edo kosode was identical for both sexes. Seen with eyes accustomed to the proportions of the modern kimono, the body section appears wide but short, with smallish rounded sleeves sewn directly to the side seams. The sleeve opening for the wrist is surprisingly small. By the Genroku era, the body width had narrowed and sleeve widened to more familiar proportions. Women's sleeves also began to distinguish themselves from men's by their increasing length. In the 1670s, a sleeve bag of eighteen inches was considered a long 'fluttering sleeve.' Twenty years later, women's sleeves had doubled that length.

Kosode's move to center stage brought the obi, previously as unobtrusive as the kosode itself, into prominence. The early seventeenth-century obi was unisex. It originally consisted of a narrow woven cord. Soon cloth sashes three to four inches wide and approximately two yards long became standard. The men's obi has never gotten any wider. The obi for women gradually expanded to six or seven inches in the Genroku period. Eventually the woman's obi would grow to overwhelm the kosode, practically relegating it to the position of backdrop. By the turn of the nineteenth century the obi had reached an extreme of about eighteen inches wide and four yards long. The decline of the brilliant Genroku mode of kimono pattern is directly due to the influence of the expanding obi. Even the nine-inch-wide obi of the mid-1700s chopped the dramatic sweep of earlier designs in two.

MERCURIAL GENDER

Early Edo popular woodblock prints reveal how people lived, what they ate, what they wore, and—in distinct detail—how they made love. Yet the modern viewer is unsettled by a nagging tentativeness regarding the gender of some of these lively figures. For every other era of Japanese history the conventions of hair and clothing styles for men and women are quite distinct. One is unlikely to confuse a geisha with a gigolo. Of course, a figure wearing a sword can be definitively tagged as male, and there is no doubt in the explicitly erotic prints as to who is what, but that still leaves a large crowd of Genroku figures of mercurial gender who are not easily identified at a glance.

Ambiguous men and women can be distinguished by painstaking knowledge of the context of a particular work, but the idea that such a basic attribute as sex should require such effort to discern points to a fascinating facet of Genroku culture—the mixing of male and female in the world of fashion. A few unmistakable clothing cues signaled masculinity and femininity, but in the fashion arena, men borrowed styles from women just as women copied fads from men.

The premier style-setters of Genroku were the kabuki actors and professional ladies of the licensed quarters. After women were banned from the kabuki stage in 1629, women's roles were taken by young men known as *wakashū*. Their mode of dress was adapted from that of samurai youth. These young men wore their hair and sleeves long, as did women. The wakashū specialized in depicting women not only on stage but off as well and often led lives as glamorous homosexual companions to their patrons.

Because of their ardent pursuit of feminine personæ, wakashū served as showcases for original kosode patterns, hairstyles, and ways of tying the obi. These styles in turn inspired the wardrobes of townswomen. In effect, women strove to copy men who were mimicking women. Furthermore, certain female dancers (*odoriko*) and a specialized subset of prostitutes called *wakashū jorō* played on the popularity of the stylish young men by reproducing their mode as faithfully as possible. These creatures were women taken for men who wished to be taken as women. Certain subtle cues no doubt distinguished all of these male and female variants to the contemporary Genroku observer. We shall try to look at their fashions with Genroku eyes as well.

Bustling Edo suffered a devastating fire in 1657. Half of the city was destroyed and more than a hundred thousand citizens perished. Edo was soon rebuilt on a broader scale than before, and this second boom attracted even more fortune seekers to the city. One was Hishikawa Moronobu, a middle-aged artist from Chiba. Moronobu is usually credited as the consolidator of Japan's artistic tradition of *ukiyo-e*, woodblock prints and paintings depicting the fashionable ephemera of contemporary life. Moronobu's work was aimed at, appreciated, and paid for by townspeople—the new class of commoner that now was gaining the wealth, leisure, and culture to demand its own arts.

Moronobu's fame as a woodblock artist and premier practitioner of the developing genre of ukiyo-e is firmly established. It is less well known that he was the son and grandson of Kyoto fabric dyers and was versed in every aspect of his family's business. His background in textile design provided the springboard for his compositions, and his finesse as a painter clearly derives from the decorative arts he practiced on kosode. Even after achieving success as artist and illustrator in Edo, Moronobu continued to design kimono patterns for the kosode of wealthy patrons.[1]

A pair of six-fold painted screens now in the Freer Gallery, in Washington, D.C., gives an idea of Moronobu's textile background. One scene depicts cherry blossoms at Ueno, the other maples at Asakusa. Both screens are filled with multitudes of Edo people of every age and station enjoying a festival atmosphere. Nearly two hundred figures enliven each screen, yet each wears a kosode of unique design. In a painting of almost four hundred people, Moronobu was careful not to repeat a kimono pattern even once.

The silk of the kosode may have been the foremost canvas for artistic creativity in seventeenth- and eighteenth-century Japan. Besides being overwhelmingly important as the *subject* of popular graphic arts, kosode themselves were often works of art not inferior to paintings. The dress of the courtesans, dancing girls, and kabuki actors who were frequently depicted in woodblock prints is of far more interest than any face or figure per se. The line of the drapery, the pose of the sleeve, the arrangement and color of the pattern—these hold the primary interest in these works.

We shall examine kosode as an art form by looking at the texts called *hinagata-bon* that served as contemporary fashion magazines from the seventeenth century through the Meiji era.[2] A kosode hinagata book is immediately recognizable by the conventionalized kimono-shaped outline embellished with different designs from page to page.

Hinagata texts had a variety of purposes and audiences. Some were published by dyer's shops as prosaic buyers' guides. Others read like mail-order catalogues, listing various colors available to the customer. Yet others include pictures of models dressed in the kosode described on the facing page. The models are clearly an attempt to establish a mood or an image of the elegant person who would order such a kosode. In this way they anticipate the most sophisticated techniques of modern advertising. Hinagata texts with figures contain such extravagant designs that one may doubt that the people reading the booklets were actually preparing orders for their own clothing. It seems rather more likely that these were books for fantasy and daydreams, as *Vogue* is today. Few manage to wear what appears on those pages, but the fashion statements are nevertheless entertaining to look at.

First let us take up a hinagata-bon produced by Hishikawa Moronobu himself. In addition to its intrinsic charm, the *Kosode Full-length Mirror* represents a high level of design and an unequivocal vision. My guess is that Moronobu was not drawing here for the taste of an anonymous customer but rather designing according to his vision of what these masterpieces should look like. The following booklet reproduced here is the Mitsui Bunko xylograph of an original text.[3] The translation appears in quotation marks in the left margin.

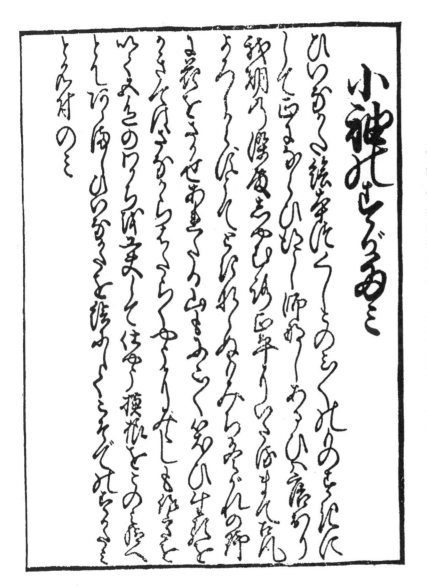

THE KOSODE
FULL-LENGTH MIRROR

"There are lots of kimono pattern books you can look at out of curiosity, but none of them sets a standard. They may show Chinese brocades, Japanese dyed work, even Siamese calico. But this tired old stuff is boring. You want to see maple leaves out of season! Flowers blooming in a winter landscape! Joyful living creatures in a barren mountain scene! That is what I labor to give you in this book, devising patterns and colors for your delight. I call these little models I have drawn the *Kosode Full-length Mirror*."

"A broken snowflake rondel pattern on a dark red background. Two rondels are dapple-dyed in old-leaf tan, one is pale blue. Another is reserved from the dye and done in saffron. The last rondel is white with embroidered cherry blossoms in pink, lavender, and red. The edges of the rondels are outlined in twisted gold thread. One rim is done in stamped gold foil, another in a zigzag honeycomb motif. The dapple-dyed areas are highlighted in gold thread."[4]

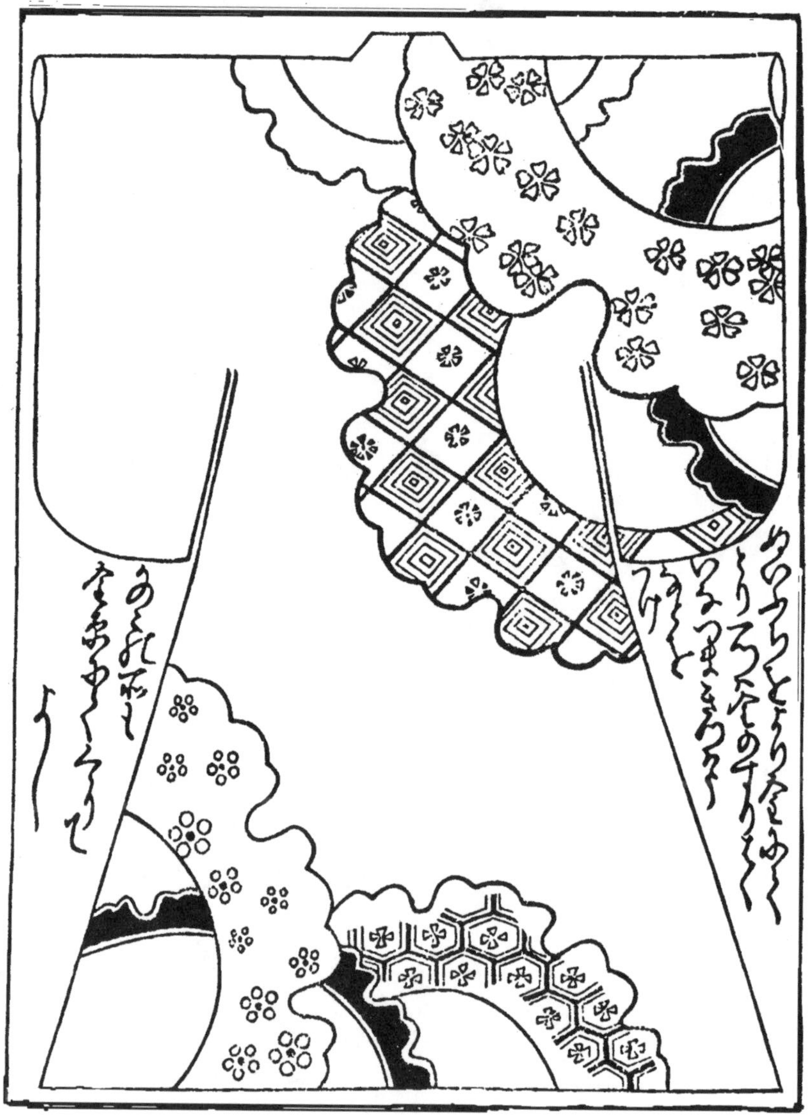

The text is almost entirely devoted to describing the colors and techniques to be applied to the kosode depicted on the left side of the page spread, and very little is

written about the figures on the right. The audience for this book was undoubtedly able to read nuances of hair, pose, and gesture that are opaque to us today. The right-hand figure here is an older, conservative, aristocratic lady. What appear to be *guillemets* on her forehead are the convention for representing wrinkles. Her hair is done in the palace style,[5] and she wears an unpatterned kosode over a double set of under-robes. Her uchikake over-robe is tame and conservative in design. She seems to be listening to her much more modish companion, who wears a weirdly dramatic kosode patterned in mossy seashells worn over what looks like a scarlet under-kimono. The companion's hair is done in a variant of the newly developed shimada style. Could this be conservative Kyoto confronting brash Edo? The old and boring next to the new and exciting? Perhaps it is a graphic reiteration of the aims Moronobu just stated in his introduction.

"When this young lady was a child, she didn't yet comprehend the allure of scarlet satin. As she matured and became more experienced in matters of the heart and body, she began to appreciate deeper colors. But deep red has a tendency to fade to the pink of this kimono with a scattered design of bouquets of raw cotton arranged from shoulder to hem. The bouquets should be done in dapple shibori in dark red, pale blue, and pea green. Some of them should be reserved from dye and filled with stamped foil and the Chinese vine motif. The edges are outlined in knots of gold thread. They would also be nice with the bent chrysanthemum branch motif embroidered upon them."

When the shy maiden pictured here began to grow up, states the text, she began to enjoy color (*iro o konomite*), which also means 'to be interested in sex.' The connection between color, *iro*, and

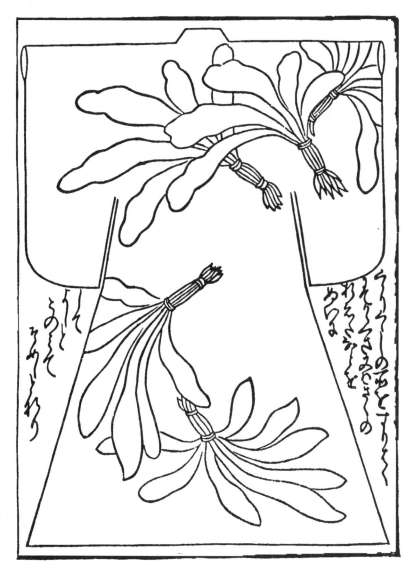

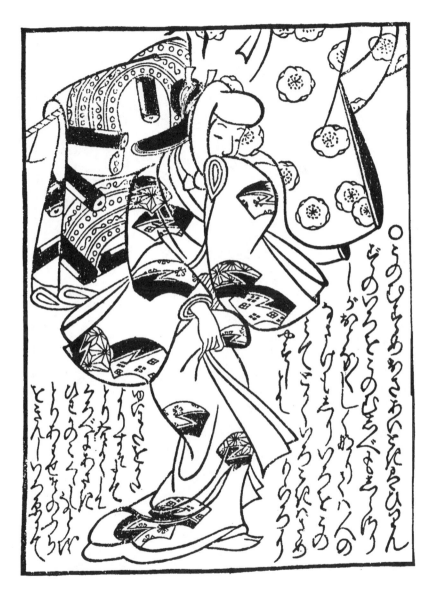

sex went beyond double entendre in Moronobu's day—it was a simple equation. Yet in the context of a kimono pattern book in which color in its original sense is explored on every page, the metaphorical extension to the sensual appears fresh. This paragraph begins like a contemporary pulp novel, then suddenly does a twist in mid-sentence to continue in the vein of fashion description.

The demure young lady's long sleeves classify her kosode as a *nagisode*, the precursor to the modern furisode kimono for girls and young women. Wrapped around her head is a *wata bōshi*, a fashionable headwrap made of silk floss popular in the early part of the Tokugawa era. The visual reference to wata relates to the pattern of fluffy bundles of raw cotton (also called *wata*) on the kosode. Moronobu's designs are outstanding in part because of the unorthodox subjects he chose to stylize. At this time the homely cotton plant was a relatively exotic specimen.

"A snowflake rondel pattern combined with pine branches on a patterned purple background. One rondel is crimson dapple shibori, one is pale blue, and one is reserved from the background dye. The edges are outlined in twisted gold thread. The areas reserved from dye are embroidered with pink thread with centers of stamped foil Genji cloud motifs. The pine needles are in muted chartreuse with the inner umbels defined in twisted gold thread around a mustard-colored center. The branches are light blue, embroidered at the edges. The design is especially suitable for a young girl's swinging-sleeved kimono."

There is a tendency for the design on early kosode to swell at shoulder and hem while diminishing at the center. This may be because the design composition would be interrupted by the obi there. By the mid-eighteenth

century, the width of the obi increased to such an extent that design often disappeared from the mid-region of kosode altogether. Instead of the dramatic, asymmetrical wholes that we see in Moronobu's designs, pattern tended to separate into two chunks, above and below.

Two figures together on a page always imply some contrast. If one has long sleeves open at one edge, the other invariably has shorter sleeves with sewn edges. Then as now, long sleeves indicated youth. The woman on the left seems to be an older sister, more knowledgeable in the ways of the world. She wears the elaborate *katsuyama* hairstyle popularized by a courtesan of that name in the 1650s;[6] the woman on the right wears the less flashy palace style. The 'older' (meaning perhaps twenty instead of seventeen) woman is casually barefoot and her kosode is worn somewhat negligé; her younger sister wears socks and her collars are more properly aligned.

"A hem-to-shoulder pattern of
pampas grass and agueweed
(*fujibakama*) on a tea green background. The flowers are embroidered in lavender thread, the stems
in deep purple, the leaves in
sprout-green. The design is outlined in knots of gold thread, as
are the flower stamens. The blades
of grass are done in deep blue
dapple shibori with veins of gold
thread. The tips of the buds are
embroidered in red and gold satin
stitch."

The dapple effect that occurs
frequently in this booklet is a dyeing technique called *kanoko shibori* (fawn dapple), which produces a pattern of small spots.
Tiny pinches of the fabric are
twisted up and tightly bound with
thread before the whole is dyed.
After dyeing, these are un-
wrapped, leaving tiny dye-reserved rings of white around spots

of color. The process is extremely time-consuming and painstaking. Usually dapple shibori occurs in limited areas, although an entire kosode could be done in dapple. Such a garment would have taken a skilled dyer more than a year to create and represented the ne plus ultra of Genroku extravagance. In fact, so outrageously luxurious was total dapple that it was banned by the sumptuary laws of 1686.[7]

The model is a young woman wearing the modish katsuyama hairstyle. She obligingly assumes a pose that will show off her long sleeves. Notice the small size of the opening where her hand emerges. This *koiguchi* (carp mouth) sleeve is a distinctive feature of early Edo period kosode. The opening is also encircled with a band of cloth (*sodeberi*) in a contrasting color, probably scarlet, and slightly puffed with padding. This sleeve edging was a fashionable accent that also preserved the sleeve opening from wear and tear.

"The Chinese vine motif is here dyed on a background of pale blue crepe. The flowers are done in finch green, purple, and crimson dapple shibori. Two are reserved from the background dye and done in white or saffron. The inner rondels are stamped gold foil with repeat designs or the Chinese vine motif embroidered in gold and colored thread. The leaves are done in sprout-green satin stitch. This is a sweetly feminine design suitable for both young women and older ones."

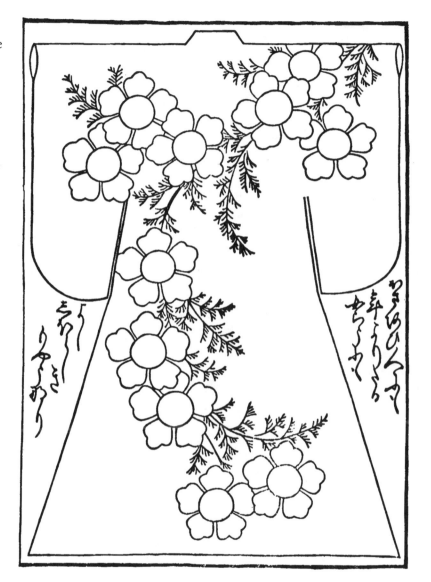

The seated figure is a young man. Either he has not yet come of age to shave his forelock or he is a *wakashū*, a companion to older men who has chosen to leave it unshaven as a mark of his sexual proclivities. The standing figure is clearly female in hairstyle and dress. The wider obi suggests a style found among professional women of pleasure. Yet 'her' face has the longish chin often found in Moronobu's depictions of men. Could this be a kabuki actor specializing in female impersonations? Perhaps Moronobu's comment on the femininity of the design was meant as a little joke. Note the erect toe—a medieval Japanese convention for indicating an erotic nature.

"A scattered pattern of round fans on a purple background. The fans measure about six inches across. Above and below are areas reserved from the purple dye, done with stripes in light blue dapple shibori and outlined in gold thread. One fan is striped in crimson and pale blue dapple shibori, one is reserved from the dye and done in a pattern of cut flowers in gold. Others are appliquéd satin outlined in colored silk floss. Others may be stamped foil or embroidered in colored thread. The fans themselves should be outlined in knots of gold thread."

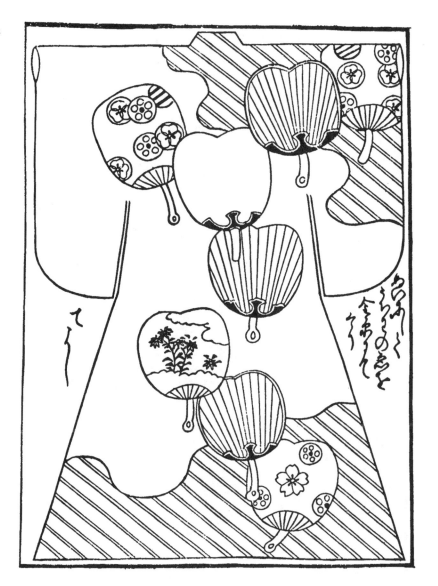

This model displays a negligently stylish pose that tempts me to label her a lady of pleasure. The wide obi reinforces this impression. She wears a plain unpatterned kosode that sets off the flamboyant uchikake and highlights the scarlet juban peeking out prominently under its edges. The fashion of scarlet under-kimono originated with courtesans and is another indication of her status. The hollyhock motif on the garment in the background was considered to be very elegant—the sort of thing appropriate for a daimyō but appropriated by his mistress in Genroku times. A robe draped over a stand made for the purpose of displaying it was by this time a standard artistic convention. Known as *tagasode*, 'whose sleeves,' it had romantic connotations, too, evoking the existence of the person who casually (but intentionally) arrayed it there.

"A pattern of scattered scallop shells on a dark olive crepe background. One shell is crimson dapple shibori. One is pale blue. One is reserved from the background olive dye and done in white and saffron with a diamond lozenge pattern. Another shell has a scattered cherry blossom motif of stamped foil. The edges are outlined in knots of pink thread, and the dappled areas are defined by twisted gold thread. The trailing sea grass may be done with saffron and twisted gold satin-stitch embroidery."

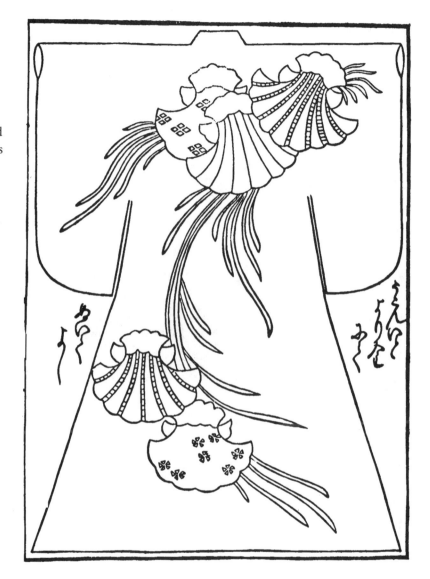

The hairstyle identifies the smaller figure as a young man. The middle section of hair is bound into a ponytail, and the ends are tucked upward toward the forelock. This is the distinguishing characteristic of the *shimada-mage* hairstyle, which by most accounts was originated by the stylish wakashū. At this time, long flowing sleeves were worn by young men as well as women, and they were especially favored by wakashū in their overall effeminate dress. The taller figure is female in hair, dress, and pose, but the she could be a he underneath. The front-tied obi was beginning to be fashionable at this time—another fad started by professional women in the licensed quarters.

"Chestnuts on a dark gray-brown background. The burrs are done in light blue, crimson, and finch-green dapple shibori. The nuts are embroidered in twisted gold, dark yellow, and persimmon colored thread. The leaves are reserved from the dye and outlined in sprout-green thread. The tops of the chestnuts should match the color of the burrs. All dappled areas may be outlined in knots of gold thread."

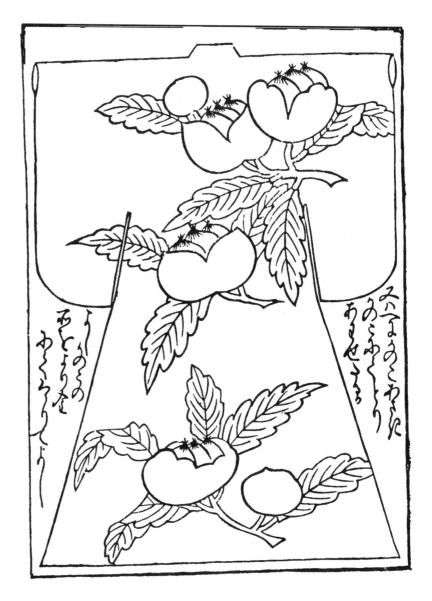

The person depicted here gathers up the material of her full skirt as she prepares to walk. In the late seventeenth century the kosode was worn much more flowingly than kimono is now. Women did not yet have to pigeon their toes in a strangulating tube of a skirt. The hair, scarlet underkimono, and hollyhock-patterned kosode are quite similar to an earlier figure whom we labeled a high-ranked courtesan. Yet there is something about this person—the large-ish hand, the slightly beefy neck—that gives us pause. The form is undeniably female, but the content could plausibly be male. It is just possible also to see a salacious significance to chestnuts. I recall being told that to Japanese the smell of chestnut trees in bloom is reminiscent of semen. Whether man or woman, this person is no naive innocent.

"Large pinwheel rondels arranged on shoulder and hem over a dark purple ground. The larger pinwheels are done in pale blue dapple shibori, outlined in colored silk floss. Another one is done in crimson dapple shibori, outlined in gold thread. Another is reserved from the dye and done in saffron with edges defined in pink thread. Two of the smaller pinwheels should be composed entirely of gold thread embroidery."

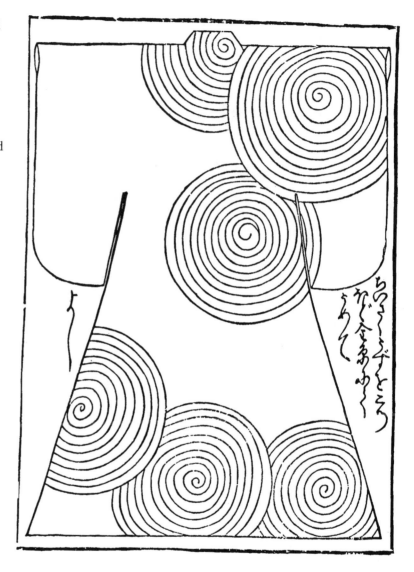

The figure here is clearly male—the sword, the shaved pate, and the simple obi declare masculinity. It is the figure of a charming young man, a wakashū with long swinging sleeves and the exaggerated hairstyle that was the precursor to the shimada variations later adopted by women. Yet the face is very sweet. It is not utterly impossible that this male figure might be an *odoriko*, a girl dancer dressed in wakashū style for a performance. The kosode design illustrated in this set certainly seems more masculine in sensibility, but by now pinpointing gender has come to seem as slippery a task as trying to catch a catfish with a gourd.

"Chrysanthemums on a background of deep chartreuse. The petals surrounding each bloom are done variously in crimson, finch green, purple, and pale blue dapple shibori. One is dyed dark red, one is reserved from the dye altogether. The centers may be either satin-stitch embroidery in different colors or appliquéd with damask. The edges are outlined in knots of gold thread or stamped foil suitably applied and edged with gold thread."

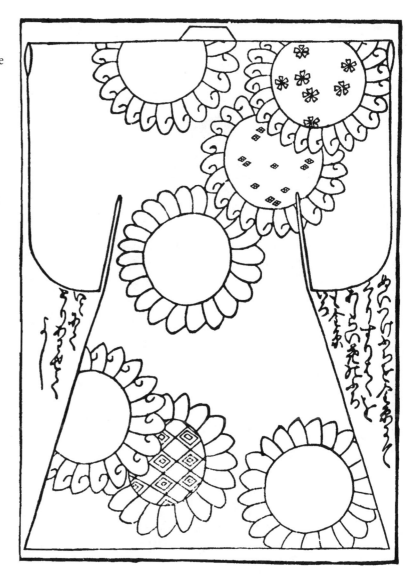

Moronobu varies the poses of his models, here giving us a full back view. The girl's hair is tied in a simple *tamamusubi* looped ponytail, and her bangs have been left wispy, rather than being tied up in the little front loop depicted in all the other figures. The bangs recall the simpler hairstyles of an earlier era. This young lady also has interesting ears. In Ihara Saikaku's *Life of an Amorous Woman*, "ears which stand out a little from the head" are included in a list of desirable features of feminine beauty.[8]

"Dark red lattices dyed sparingly on a saffron background with a scattering of flowers over the entire garment. Approximately half of the flowers are done in purple dapple shibori, three are light blue, three are crimson, and five are left reserved from dye. The edges are outlined in knots of sprout-green, pink, violet, pale green, and so on. The centers of the flowers are embroidered in twisted gold thread. The edges of the lattices may be done in stamped foil."

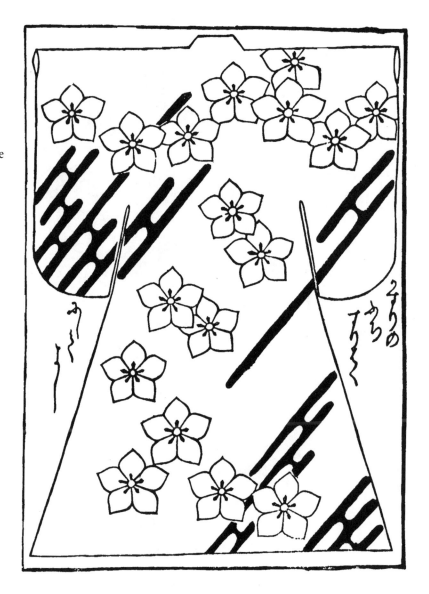

Two young women display subtle contrasts. One wears socks, the other is barefoot. One has short sleeves, the other has long. One's hair is done up, the other's is unbound. They have neither the pose and accoutrements of high courtesans nor the shy demeanor of maidens. Perhaps these are simply city girls, daughters of the merchant class that supported Moronobu's work.

"A hem-and-shoulder pattern of intaglio chrysanthemums in dark red dapple shibori on a white background. The edges are defined in stamped gold foil. The rondels carry a wood sorrel motif about two-and-a-half inches across, either appliquéd in gold brocade satin or done in blue or crimson dapple shibori. The edges are embroidered with knots of purple and other colors and filled in with gold embroidery."

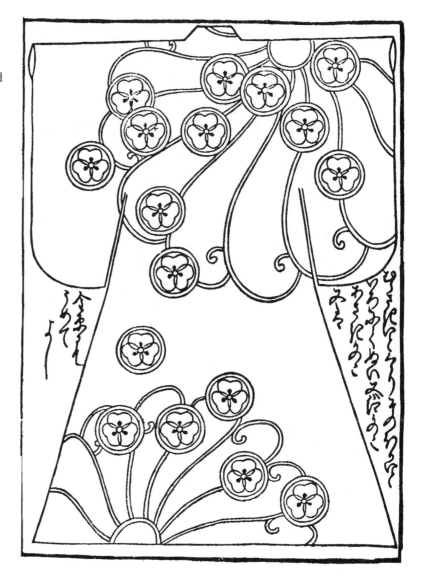

A feminine figure wears the crimson under-robe of a lady of pleasure. The soft, narrow obi is tied simply and left to hang in back. Something about the face of this jaded beauty hints that she might not be a she under her silks. Only Moronobu knew for sure.

Hishikawa Moronobu became the most popular graphic illustrator of his lifetime. He founded a school of followers who worked in his style after his own long and prolific life ended. (He was born around 1618 and lived until 1694.) Moronobu's sons were among his artistic successors, although his eldest, Morofusa, the one expected to inherit his father's mantle, never gained the fame and recognition that Moronobu had. In fact, Morofusa finally gave up the art of painting and ukiyo-e and went back to the original family business, painting kosode in the dye shops of Kyoto.

We now turn to a somewhat later example of a hinagata text to show the variety of audiences and interests at which this genre of fashion magazine was aimed.

Toshi no hana (Flowers of youth, 1691) is essentially a fan magazine. It uses the hinagata format of a kosode design facing a page with a model, but the models are not anonymous—they are clearly labeled as popular kabuki actors of Kyoto and Osaka. The kosode descriptions, unlike those in Moronobu's work, are vague and rather perfunctory. They seem secondary to the depiction of the actors. If *Kosode no sugatami* was *Vogue, Toshi no hana* was more like *Hollywood* or *GQ*.

Kabuki had undergone a momentous change between the time of Moronobu's hinagata and this one. In 1652 the shogunate, concerned with public morals, ordered kabuki's alluring female impersonators to shave their forelocks to appear like the men they really were. The wakashū were distraught. An unshaven forelock was one of the prime attributes of their beauty and marks of their identity. By shaving it, they became adult men, *yarō*, and henceforward their art became known as *yarō kabuki*, the form it has maintained until the present day. Forced to comply with the regulation, the newly shaved actors covered their naked pates with little silken caps. Needless to say, these caps were regarded as quite becoming, and townswomen proceeded to adopt them into their own fashions.

Each actor is named, preceded by his city and/or the theater where he was affiliated. The kosode is laid out on the facing page, identified by the actor's professional crest and a bouquet of flowers (translated in italics).

Kyoto, Murayama-za: Tamagawa Handayū

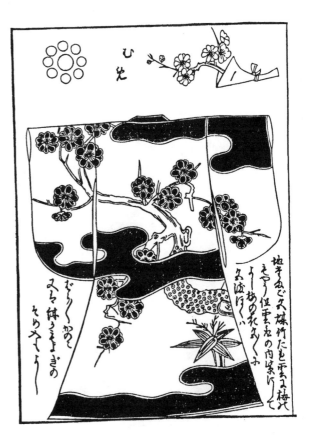

Plum blossom

"Clouds of smoky bamboo color drift over an egg-shell-colored background with a pattern of plums. The linings of the clouds are in purple. The plum blossoms are in various colors, and some are executed in dapple shibori. Touches of dark blue and chartreuse are over-dyed as well."

Murayama-za: Matsumoto Heizō

Chrysanthemum

"Waves rise up from the hem of this purple robe with a design of ship in full sail. The hull of the boat is scarlet dapple shibori. The crest is embroidered. The sail is dyed a shade of light smoky bamboo. The clouds are outlined in white thread. The waves are crimson, or yellow fading to brown. The ropes to the sail are embroidered."

Osaka, Ishikawa Kaoru

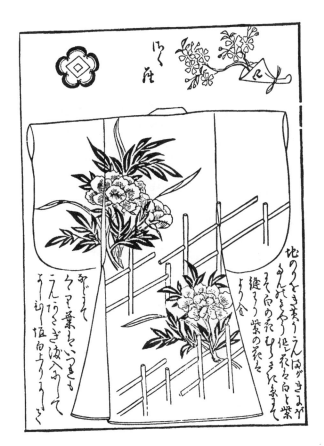

Cherry blossom

"Trellised peonies on a background of deep yellow.
The flowers are white and purple. The white ones are
etched in purple embroidery, the purple ones are
done in gold. The dye-reserved leaves are colored
light and dark blue. The trellises are white."

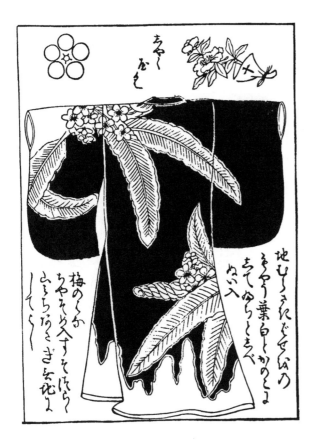

Mandayū-za: Fujiyama Sennojō

Peony
"Banana leaves on a deep purple background. The leaves are white and dapple shibori, embroidered. The plum blossom clusters are dyed brown. The icicle pattern on the hem is pale blue without pattern."

This hinagata is probably of the same vintage as *Flowers of youth*. The title, *Man'nyōshū*, 'Anthology of ten thousand women,' is a pun on Japan's earliest poetry anthology, the *Manyōshū* (Anthology of ten thousand leaves). The booklet depicts altogether thirty-two poses of women in kosode of fashionable pattern. Five are sampled here. These designs are less inspired than Moronobu's but possibly more wearable. Except for an ultra-elite who wear designer originals, most people prefer to wear fashionable clichés. The tone of the book suggests that these designs may have been used by women actually planning to order kosode from their dyers. The soignée poses and elegant surroundings of the models call to mind the fashion layouts in *Cosmopolitan*.

"Cranes, turtles, pines, and bamboo on a white background. Sections of pale blue and scarlet dapple shibori decorate the top portions. The pine is embroidered in chartreuse, the turtle in twisted gold thread. The crane's wings are embroidered in dark brown and purple. Bright green bamboo is outlined in gold thread; available in white, purple, iron gray, saffron, dark red, khaki, and pumpkin, or any combination of the above. Have thread dyed to match whichever background color you choose."

This girl's hair is done up in the high-class *sagegami* style. The turtles, cranes, pine, and bamboo are all felicitous objects that are appropriate to a kosode for New Year's day. The illustrator has taken care to place his models in the most elegant atmosphere. The screens, sliding doors, and brocade-edged tatami mats that appear throughout the book would be found in the house of a person of wealth and taste.

"On a pale blue background we have a design of strips of pale green and crimson dapple shibori outlined in white and purple thread, and chartreuse and saffron strips edged in scarlet thread and twisted gold. If the background color is to be olive green, the strips can be in crimson and pale blue dapple shibori and in stamped foil. Or, on a white ground, sky blue and dusty pink dapple shibori is recommended."

The lines of this figure are clumsy in comparison with Moronobu's work. She is as relaxed as a jellyfish. The landscape screen and crested mats of her room are indications of refinement. Lost in a reverie inspired by her book, she is meant to be an appealing model of a fashionable young woman.

"A crepe kimono with sections reserved and dyed in iron gray and purple dapple shibori, outlined in gold thread. The hem alone may be dyed. The background is purple with sections of pale blue dapple shibori. A pattern of deer antlers outlined in knots of gold thread also works well."

This young girl could be the daughter of a wealthy merchant or a samurai. Her kosode has the autumn motif of maple leaves (the deer antlers mentioned above are also a fall theme), and she gazes on a sliding door painted with bamboo bending under snow.

"Oak leaves on a scarlet background. The upper ones are in pale blue dapple shibori, the lower ones in purple. Large grass motifs are painted on the unpatterned sections. Or you may prefer the background in pale blue with scarlet and light green dapple shibori in the leaves, and swaths of scarlet grass outlined in gold. Or again, you might like the same design on an olive green background. The leaves are spaced approximately one foot apart."

The casual elegance of this figure could belong to a sophisticated woman in her twenties. Whereas Moronobu's models posed in a vacuum, the 'ten thousand women' of this collection strike a variety of attitudes in evocative settings. The message is as sophisticated as anything in modern advertising—these sorts of elegant women in these kinds of settings wear these kinds of kosode. Projecting herself into the scene, the reader would dream about the kosode she might order for herself.

"Waves and chrysanthemums on a pale blue background. Scarlet and light green dapple shibori waves with ripples painted upon them. The mums are filled with colored embroidery and outlined in gold stitches. Or, you might prefer the whole thing done on a purple ground with touches of light blue dapple shibori."

This relaxed and sensuous figure would have been the height of Genroku sex appeal. It is possible that these depictions of idealized beauties were the way townswomen picked up fashion from the licensed quarters.

The final hinagata text we will peruse is a pattern book dated 1688, from the House of Yūzen, the most famous dye workshop in Japan. There are no models in this four-volume text, and the descriptions are terse. These designs were clearly meant to help the customer decide generally what he or she wanted, with the details to be worked out directly with the dyer. This was more a catalog for orders than a magazine for fantasy.

The preface to these volumes introduces the customer to the fame of Yūzen by claiming expertise in every technique of dyeing, dapple, embroidery, and foil stamping in the most modern and up-to-date fashion. "We aim to please," stated the Yūzen craftsmen, boasting of their versatility to dye to anyone's specifications, be she innocent maiden or grand doyenne.

The techniques of Yūzen are explained as follows: The dyers sketch an underdrawing of the chosen design on the fabric. The design is then covered with paste or sewed into a section to be reserved from the overall dye. Details are later hand-painted on this reserved section. The various sections may be re-dyed, stamped with foil, embroidered, or dapple-dyed and pictures painted on these areas.

Customers were invited to commission fabrics for their kosode, of course, but also for unlined bast-fiber summer robes, bedding, obi, carrying cloths, towels, scent bags, and tea ceremony cloths. The following selections give an idea of the kinds of designs that townspeople actually ordered.

みな白く ちゃ*の とれ** 岩や 色にして **き *け 瀧ハ白 さいき

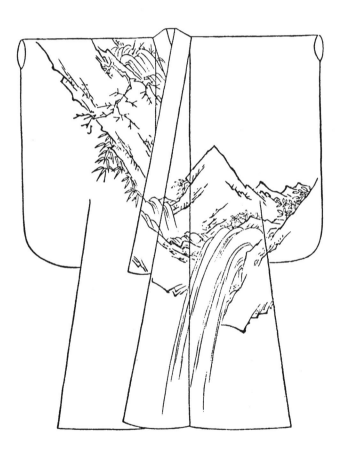

Waterfall with Pine (front and back)

"Background of brownish purple. Design of mountain crags reserved from dye. Waterfall is white."

Warbler with Plums

"Gray background. Plums and warbler in colors painted freehand over gray."

A bedding coverlet—Pine, Bamboo, Plum Rondels

"Background color in whatever hue you like. Rondels reserved with paste, designs painted in freehand."

Design for a summer bast-fiber katabira

"Gray background with the water motif reserved by paste. Iris painted in colors."

Design for a cotton summer yukata

"Pale blue background with water motif paste-reserved. Wisteria pattern on shoulder painted in colors."

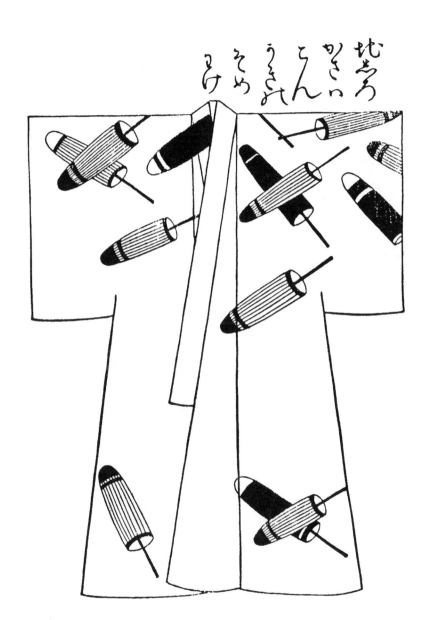

Yukata

"Indigo umbrellas dyed on
a plain white background."

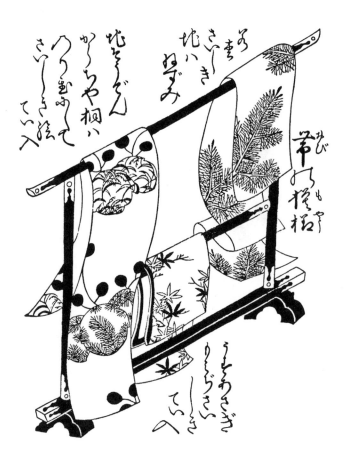

さ
き
地
八
ぬ
ず
み

さ
き
地
八
ぬ
ず
み

そ
き
ば
か
ら
ち
や
桐
ハ
く
ろ
鼠
ゆ
て
さ
い
し
き
ゑ
入
に

う
と
う
さ
ぎ
り
も
ぢ
さ
い
し
き
て
い
へ

Obi Patterns

"Young pine branches painted in colors on a gray background.
Maples painted in colors on a light blue background.
Paulownia motif paste-resist dyed in brown on a blue background."

Informal (kakae) *obi and hand cloths*

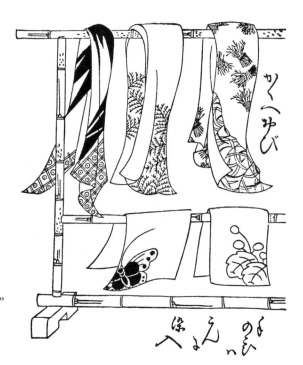

In their prefaces, many seven-teenth- and eighteenth-century hinagata texts refer to Heian can-ons of beauty, and some feature drawings of Heian ladies at the beginning of the text. But just as modern movie producers make period dramas in the æsthetic style of their own era, so did Genroku artists represent the plump-faced Heian beauties in a seventeenth-century mode. Not only do diamonds, clouds, loz-enges, curling vines, stars, flow-ers, and checks adorn this lady's layered robes, but the background is busily filled in with painted blinds and a row of patterned bolts of cloth. Nowhere are Gen-roku æsthetic obsessions more clearly depicted than in this charming anachronism.

船遊び

NINE   GEISHA AND KIMONO

A FTER RENTING A ROOM near the Pontochō geisha quarters in Kyoto in 1974, I spent my first months interviewing geisha during their daytime off-hours. When they had gotten used to me and had decided I wouldn't embarrass them, I was invited to sit on the sidelines of a formal party to observe their evening work.

At the time I owned one kimono, a handsome persimmon-colored antique with a willow branch woven in brown and gold.[1] The obi and other accessories I had to borrow from the geisha who helped me get dressed. Although I didn't realize it then, the way she tied the pale green obi and tucked in the ends of the obi scarf were not exactly the way a proper middle-class lady would have done them.

After the party, I ventured out to a local bar and restaurant, where I struck up a conversation with a pair of professors sitting at the counter. As we talked and I mentioned my reasons for coming to Kyoto, the bartender, who had been listening with half an ear, suddenly interrupted.

"Now it makes sense," he said. "I've been trying to figure it out since you walked in the door. Your kimono is that of an *ojōsan*, but there's something more professional about your obi—something almost geisha-like about it."

The man's eye was acute. My kimono had been given to me by a friend in her forties who, as the daughter of a prosperous doctor, had worn it in her youth. So it was definitely the kimono of a bourgeois young lady, an ojōsan, while my obi, of course, had been tied by geisha hands. This experience gave me my first insight into the way kimono is governed by rules that express a code, and the first impetus toward this book.

Kimono are one of geishas' major preoccupations. When I wrote the book *Geisha* in 1983 I included a chapter entitled "Kimono" because so much of a geisha's self-image, interest, and money is tied up in her clothing. Now, in *Kimono*, it seems fitting to reciprocate this influence with a chapter on geisha. If kimono are important to geisha, geisha have also been pre-eminent in the development of kimono.

The first time I was allowed to join the geisha ranks at a banquet, my geisha sister gave me one of her kimono to wear. It was light pink satin, with sprays of cherry blossom artist-dyed on hem and shoulder. My obi was gold brocade—a hand-me-down from my geisha mother.

Pale colors were popular in the mid-seventies, and so of course geisha were wearing the most pastel of kimono. I wasn't yet aware that geisha have always been the first to pick up the latest vogue in kimono colors and accessories. Geisha inject these fads into mainstream kimono fashion, from whence their geisha origins are often forgotten by the proper ladies who adopt them.

Geisha have a distinctive formal trailing kimono (known as *de*, 'going out') the neckline of which dips deeply in back to show off a shapely nape. No one but a geisha dresses this way. The style demands full white makeup and wig oiled in the heavy traditional manner of a century past. The *de* costume is not a geisha's normal working outfit, however. Unless she is requested to come in full formal attire (for which there is an extra charge), a geisha wears a regular, nontrailing kimono with a taiko-tied obi—like the pale pink one I wore on the night of my debut as Ichigiku, younger sister of Ichiume. A geisha's usual kimono does not differ greatly from what any other Japanese woman might wear—if anything, it may be more subdued. The telling differences emerge in the geisha's manner of wearing it.

In the nineteenth century, geisha fashioned the æsthetic mode of cool chic called iki. They continue to exhibit it in their dress today. Instead of wrapping the obi high with a straight, square taiko fold in back, for example, geisha wear the obi low on the waist and fold the taiko with a little tilt. Geisha set the collar back from the nape a hair more than do wives, allowing slightly more of the right-hand side of the white collar of their underkimono to show in front. These subtle asymmetries, hardly noticeable to a foreign eye, along with the smooth bouffant hair and pointedly pale complexions favored by geisha, set them apart in Japan as professionals—a traditional category meaning geisha, actresses, and dancers, as opposed to 'amateur' wives and daughters.[2]

In clothing, the main distinction between geisha and kimono-wearing amateurs derives from a geisha's sheer familiarity with the garment. Geisha are among the few women in Japan who still wear kimono every day. Among geisha it is possible to see kimono worn with ease, panache, and even comfort. A hundred years ago, all Japanese women were comfortable in kimono because they were used to it. Today a Japanese woman may put on kimono, usually its most stiffly formal version, only once or twice a year. The unaccustomed effort invites mental and physical fatigue. Modern women are only too happy to revert to more familiar skirts and shirts.

When I first began to wear kimono I never questioned the obvious fact that it was less comfortable than Western dress. How could anyone think otherwise? I lost weight simply because the wide obi tied about my middle made it impossible to fill my stomach. Half a meal left me feeling stuffed. Walking rendered me breathless, and moving around seemed an unnatural activity. My regular step caused the hem of the kimono to flap, so I had to learn a different way of walking. When I sat in a chair, the obi rode up—I had to perch at the edge. Yet one evening I was surprised to hear a plump older geisha say that whenever she was invited out to dinner, she always wore kimono because it was more comfortable than a dress. And, she said, she could eat more wearing a nice wide obi than she could if her waist were constricted in a Western-style belted skirt. This was the first time it occurred to me to question the truism that kimono are inherently uncomfortable.

The human body is almost infinitely malleable where clothing is concerned. Given enough time and experience with a garment, our bodies adapt themselves to its contours and familiar pressures. My great-grandmother grew accustomed to corsets, my grandmother became familiar with brassieres, my mother got used to girdles. Eventually our bodies come to expect the feel of our clothes, shoes, or hats, and to miss that constriction if it is absent. After a childhood summer of sandals, I felt the start of the school year through the immediacy of my feet stuffed back into Oxfords. It probably would have been difficult to get serious without that little pinch—not painful, merely present. A businessman knows through his skin that the weekend is over when he pries open a freshly starched shirt on Monday morning. Kimono has a similar effect.

We do not wear our clothes in a vacuum. Abstractly, clothing shapes our bodies according to the current notion of what a fashionable body should look like. Concretely, it does this within an architectural framework of buildings, rooms, and furniture, and a social framework regulating activity, modesty, and behavior. The height of tables, the shape of chairs, the cleanliness of floors all influence the parameters of clothing. So do ideas regarding which parts of the body may or may not be exposed, as well as how people are expected to move. Kimono evolved in a chairless environment with low tables, where a clean matted floor was the primary location for social interaction. Kimono appears to its best advantage under these conditions, and can even be comfortable.

Living with the geisha, I started wearing kimono in a mostly chairless, tatami-matted environment, sitting on my feet in Japanese fashion, speaking Japanese. After a while, it felt odd to speak English in kimono. The kimono requires its own dialect of Japanese body language, a lingo ill-suited to the gestures and postures natural to American English. Gradually pressed into the kimono mold, my shoulders began to slope slightly and my feet to turn in. I began to feel, if not yet comfortable, at least less self-conscious. Sitting for hours on the floor was hard on my knees, but I came to appreciate that it would have been even harder on my back without the stiff obi to provide support. I learned the technique of anchoring the kimono securely with hidden silk strips so that its neat lapover was not dependent on the obi. I was taught the trick of tying a slipknot in the obi scarf, threading the other half through in order to prevent an awkward square knot from pressing into my sternum. Unlike my older geisha companions, I would never change into kimono for ease, but I did become accustomed to its demands on the body within the context of everyday geisha life.

Our physical surroundings also affect the visual balance of clothing. Not surprisingly, kimono appears most beautiful in the environment in which it evolved. Driving a car or just sitting in a soft armchair are among the most awkward things a woman in kimono can do. Western women feel strange when required to take off shoes and pad stocking-footed into a Japanese restaurant. Our shoes, the height of the heel related to the length of the skirt, complete the balance and effect of the outfit. It's as if being perfectly made up, we then need to remove our mascara at the last minute. Shoeless, we can't help feeling slightly unfinished.

Kimono is likewise disadvantaged in a roomful of tables and chairs where its best points are hidden. A formal kimono sports most of its design interest on its skirts, and the obi on its taiko-fold. By far the major æsthetic focus of kimono is in the back, so even a chair destroys its proportions. The allure of the back view of a feminine figure, the *ushiro sugata*, has been recognized in Japanese culture for a thousand years. Kimono styles evolved with this in mind. Even the modern, somewhat flat version of Japanese dress is more striking viewed from behind.

I first became aware of this aspect of kimono beauty when invited to view a banquet attended by geisha. Sitting at the outer edge of a ring of low tables, I watched the geisha move about the inner edge talking with other guests. Their backs were always turned to the opposite side of the room, offering perfect tableaux of rearview poses. It cannot be an accident that this particular arrangement of tables should set off kimono to such advantage. When seated Japanese-style on the floor, the kimono figure becomes a compact, almost sculptural shape, the robe framing the square of the obi by its contrasting color.

GEISHA INFLUENCES
ON KIMONO

Geisha were the women most central to Japanese social life from the late nineteenth century through the 1920s. Politicians, businessmen, entrepreneurs, actors, and military men all sought their company. Any social gathering, daytime or evening, was felt to be insipid without the presence of a corps of geisha. As photography spread in Japan, pinups of geisha replaced the woodblock print beauties of an earlier generation. A number of Meiji leaders' wives had risen from the geisha ranks, and most prominent politicians kept geisha mistresses. These relationships also kept geisha in the social limelight.

During this period geisha were without question the prime arbiters of kimono fashion. They initiated the new trends in colors and patterns that made this year's kimono up-to-date, last year's obsolete. In addition to the fashions of the season, geisha also affected quite basic aspects of wearing kimono. Among the modern components of kimono having geisha origins, the taiko style of obi fold, the convenient Nagoya cut of obi, and the wearing of a haori overjacket stand out.

A taiko is a kind of hand drum. If you ask a modern Japanese why the obi fold should be called a drum, she or he will probably mumble something about its square shape. In fact, taiko refers to the name of a bridge in Tokyo, the Taikobashi, opened with fanfare in 1823. Some of the numerous geisha who attended this event created a stir by a new way of tying their obis. Described as the 'shape of a playing card' (*ichimae karuta*), the style was a puffed-out variation on a simple masculine style of obi fold. The taiko style also originated the use of the obi-scarf, cord, and stiffener slipped into the front fold—all of which remain part of standard obi equipment today.

Geisha were the first women to wear haori over kimono. During the late seventeenth century, geisha from the area of Fukagawa in Edo adopted the haori, until then an item of male formalwear, as a bit of daring masculine chic. Much later, the haori was taken up as fashion for ordinary women, and during the nineteen-teens and -twenties, three-quarter-length haoris were an important accessory to a kimono ensemble. By then, of course, women's haori made no statement other than bourgeois fashionability. Geisha had long since ceased wearing it.

The Nagoya obi is cut so that the torso-wrapping section is half the width of the part that remains to be tied in the wide taiko square. Less bulky, easier to put on, the Nagoya obi was created in the 1920s by geisha as a relatively relaxed yet stylish garment they could wear in the afternoons before going out to work in their more formal kimono outfits. Ordinary women soon saw its advantages, however. The Nagoya cut is now the most common form of obi worn with every kimono except the most formal. Thus even though modern women evince little awareness of geisha, women who wear kimono are still affected by trends taken up by the professional kimono wearers of the flower and willow world. The revival of embroidered and patterned undercollars in the early 1980s, for example, was first seen on young geisha in the Kyoto districts of Gion and Pontochō.

Geisha clothing in the Meiji and Taishō eras, before Western dress was adopted by most Japanese women, consisted of three major categories. Just as for everyone else, geisha dress was first classified by status. Formal party kimono (*zashiki-gi*) were appropriate for banquet attendance, as opposed to off-duty, everyday clothes (*fudangi*). Party kimono were further divided into formal (*de*) and regular (*futsū*) categories. Regular party kimono were subspecialized for either daytime or evening wear. In addition, these three basic types of a geisha's working wardrobe—*de*, regular daytime, and evening wear—each had seasonal variants, not to mention patterns appropriate to different ages, regional preferences, and passing fads.

Looked at from another perspective, a geisha's formal party gear constitutes her working outfit. Not surprisingly, the nature of her work creates wear and tear in specific places. Because geisha spend their working hours sitting on bent knees directly on tatami mats while they banter with customers, a kimono soon shows wear at the front skirts. Sleeves are always imperilled by soy sauce or other foods at banquets. Makeup smudges collars. Hems and tabi get dirty on the floors, and dirt from the soles of tabi in turn rubs onto the back of a geisha's kimono as she sits with her feet tucked under her. Pastel kimono are even more vulnerable to soil. Yet frugality has never been a geisha virtue. Geisha don't believe in mending and remaking—so they invest in new kimono at the least hint of wear.

A wardrobe remains a geisha's single biggest business expense. The formal black *de* outfit is worn when a geisha makes her public debut, and at the New Year season. However, *de* is the most theatrical kimono a geisha wears, as well as the outfit popularly associated with the image of the profession. This is undoubtedly why it continues to be worn practically unchanged today, whereas a geisha's other kimono ensembles have changed with the currents of fashion. A customer can always give prior notice that he wishes the geisha to appear in full *de* regalia at any time of year.

The complete set of *de* kimono once consisted of three layers, each patterned on the hem, the topmost also having crests. Now that kimono are no longer layered, even *de* have been reduced to a single robe. The *de* style is worn trailing rather than bloused at the hip. The obi is a wide brocade *maru obi*, tied in the taiko or in one of a few other simple classic styles. The underkimono is plain scarlet silk with attached white collar. Tabi are white calico cotton, the obi-scarf is scarlet crepe or satin, and the obi-clasp is an ornament of silver or gold. The final effect is a striking composition of the primal colors black, white, and red.

A modern geisha has both winter and summer versions of her *de* outfit. In the 1880s, her great-grandmother would have had nine versions marking even finer divisions of the seasons.

Whether in poetry, tea ceremony, or dress, Japanese have traditionally preferred subtle variation to outright novelty. Like so many things in Japan that are regulated into a uniform mode, the *de* costume also preserves room for nuances savored by the connoisseur. Even if every geisha wears her hair in the shimada-mage style, the length of the back loop, width of the side wings, and nature of the hairpins and combs all are opportunities to introduce variety into the final effect.

Before World War II, geisha parties might last all day and into the night. Geisha used to change their outfits during the course of a long engagement. A geisha initially appearing in her *de* kimono could later change into something more relaxed, such as a two-layer set of striped crepe, worn with a soft satin obi. This would presumably reflect the social rhythm of the party as it progressed from the decorous to the disheveled. Modern geisha parties are not the lengthy affairs they once were, so the custom of *kigae*, 'changing outfits,' has disappeared.

Clothing also provides metaphors for the progression of geisha life. When a woman graduates from apprentice to full geisha status, she is said to have 'turned her collar' (*erikae o suru*). The phrase refers to the fact that apprentices used to wear red collars on their underkimono, contrasting with white collars worn in the standard adult version of geisha dress. Similarly, 'to pick up one's hems' (*tsuma o toru*) came to mean joining the profession of geisha.

Hidarizuma (left-held hem) is another common sobriquet for geisha derived from dress. During the Edo period, when all women of means wore their kimono trailing about their feet indoors, there were three ways to handle the hem when walking outside. Skirts could be tucked up into the obi (the solution favored by the peasant class); tied with a separate cord about the hips, blousing the fabric over it (a more genteel method); or simply held up as their owners walked—the simplest expedient for short periods. By the mid-nineteenth century, ordinary women had stopped wearing trailing kimono except for high ceremonial dress. This trend left geisha as the most conspicuous hem-holders. Originally there was no preference in handedness. Geisha used the left hand, probably arising from a natural tendency of right-handed people. In time this was codified into the pose and the epithet.

Even a century ago, geisha were distinguished from amateurs not so much by the nature of their kimono as by how they wore it. The fact that a geisha had a professional attendant (*hakoya*) to help secure her skirts and tie her obi gave her an advantage in wearing kimono stylishly, but so did her training as a dancer, her more acute awareness of her body, and her interest in wearing clothes in the most flattering way. A practiced eye could distinguish geisha from amateur even if each wore the same outfit. The same holds true today.

The major late-Meiji fashion trend affecting geisha (and through their influence, all women) was an inclination toward brighter colors and more opulent fabrics. Even ordinary geishawear became fancier. Whereas in the 1870s striped *meisen* (a flat hard-finish silk) or, in summer, thin ikat kasuri had been acceptable for a geisha to wear to an informal afternoon gathering, by 1900 such fabrics had become déclassé. A set of two gowns in striped crepe was preferable, or for summer a transparent Akashi silk or fine linen *jōfu*. Similarly, formal became more formal. Originally triple-crested, ceremonial kimono began to carry five crests. The iki Edo geisha abandoned her celebrated custom of slipping sexy bare feet into sandals without socks, proudly disdainful of the winter cold. In the trend toward greater formality, even she donned tabi.

The drift toward luxury became more pronounced in the last years of Meiji, culminating in prodigious extravagance in the prosperous years around World War I. Whereas people, out of native frugality, had previously re-dyed old kimono in seasonally fresh colors, department stores at the turn of the century encouraged women to buy new garments rather than recycle the old. These stores used geisha as models to promote the bold Genroku revival styles that became popular around 1906. The latest high-fashion obi was selling for as much as five thousand yen in 1915; a Shimbashi geisha would have been the likely purchaser.[3] Such lavish display gave geisha the kind of cachet now attached to Hollywood stars in designer gowns.

It is somewhat surprising that more regional differences did not appear among the styles promulgated by geisha. However, by the beginning of the twentieth century Japan was already experiencing the effects of a homogenizing urban culture. If you were urban and fashionable, you had more in common with your sisters in Kyoto, Osaka, and Tokyo than ever before. For example, Edo women had traditionally favored lighter makeup than women in the Kyoto and Osaka area—a tendency also observable among geisha of the two regions—yet by the Taishō era

Western products had begun to reduce the difference, displacing the rice powder and matte white *o-shiroi* that women had previously used for cosmetic foundation.

Geisha were ambivalent concerning the challenge to kimono posed by the coming of Western clothing. As fashion trendsetters, they were among the first to try yōfuku—a young Nihonbashi apprentice made news when she wore a dress in 1873. Even provincial geisha appeared in Western clothes during the 1880s, the high Westernization era of the Rokumeikan. But although geisha widely adopted the new unpomaded sokugami hairstyle and its variants, they eventually let Western dress drop from their wardrobes.

Geisha reverted to kimono both because of their need to define their social raison d'etre and by the nature of their work as geisha. Unlike café girls (*jokyū*), who served guests at tables, geisha still worked in Japanese-style rooms, where even today Western clothing appears graceless. Once the jokyū and her descendant, the bar hostess, appropriated Western dress, geisha could not then adopt it without compromising their image as geisha. By the end of World War II, like most Japanese women, geisha had fully adjusted to wearing Western clothes for ordinary everyday wear, but awkward yōfuku has been firmly banished from the geisha workplace.

Kimono may be the most difficult of Asian women's ethnic dress today. Indonesian and Thai women often prefer to wear their comfortable sarongs rather than skirts or pants, Indians continue to wear saris in whatever country they dwell, Chinese bar girls perch on stools in their *cheongsam*, Koreans can easily wear the modern version of their billowy *hanbok*. Only Japanese seem to have such unrelaxed feelings about their native dress. It is clearly a bother to wear kimono in the current Westernized physical surroundings of modern Japan. Yet, like geisha, kimono's attachment to Japanese culture remains curiously deep.

In the modern world, geisha and kimono share remarkably parallel fates. Both experimented by incorporating aspects of Western style early on, but both rejected the novelty of the foreign in favor of familiarity and heritage. Geisha exist today because they made the conscious decision to be curators of tradition rather than fashion innovators. Their position in Japanese society is odd, but not tenuous. Whether or not a Japanese has ever met a geisha or used her specialized service (and most have not), a feeling remains that Japan would be losing something unique and precious by allowing geisha to disappear. Kimono has a similar hold on the Japanese imagination. Although most people seldom wear it, they take ineffable pride in the appearance and form of traditional wafuku. Perhaps it is no accident that geisha dress professionally in kimono. Their history, fate, and current status have much in common with the kimono they wear.

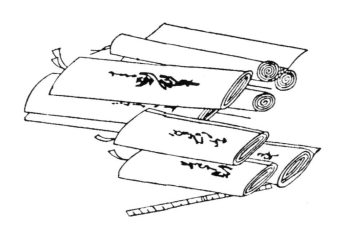

NOTES TO THE TEXT

| TWO | THE NATURAL HISTORY OF KIMONO |

1　From the *Weizhi* (=*Wei chih*, Records of the Kingdom of Wei, A.D. 221–265), section on "The Eastern Barbarians: The Wa People," in Tsunoda and Goodrich, *Japan in the Chinese Dynastic Histories*, 8–16. My translation of clothing terms varies from theirs.

2　This interpretation of the form of indigenous poncho-style garments (Japanese *kanto-i*) is from Inokuma, *Kodai no fukushoku*.

3　Takeda Sachiko has constructed an ingenious theory regarding the politics of clothing and cultural identity in *Kodai kokka no keisei to ifukusei* (Clothing regulations and the formation of the ancient state). Briefly, her thesis is that early poncho-wearing tribes adopted the pants and jackets of the more technologically advanced continental culture but that the Japanese continued to wear a native skirt (*hirami*) derived from the ancient pre-trouser culture—especially during periods when they wished to stress their independence and difference from China. Though well argued, her theory is not widely accepted by scholars.

4　From the *Sui History*, section on "Eastern Barbarians: The Country of Wa," in Tsunoda and Goodrich, *Japan in the Chinese Dynastic Histories*, 31–33.

5　This style was most notable in the many layers of *uchigi* women wore. It was possible to wear anywhere from three layers to as many as twenty, although five was standard. Even today the official ceremonial outfit for women of the Japanese royal family remains based on this Heian form of *itsutsuginu* (five robes), karaginu, and mo. In everyday Japanese, this distinctive Heian style of dress is known as *jūni hitoe*, 'the twelve robes,' a popular term that came into use in the Edo period. In this sense, the number twelve probably simply meant 'many' and was used to indicate the extravagant opulence of this form of palace dress.

6   For a beautifully explained and clearly illustrated exposition of Edo period kosode, see Stinchecum, *Kosode*.

7   From the *Fūryū tsurezuregusa*, quoted in Kanezawa, *Edo fuku-shokushi*, 194–95.

8   For some perverse reason, *asagi* is written with two characters meaning 'pale' and 'yellow,' although there is no question that the color to which it refers is light blue.

THREE   THE KIMONO DISCOVERS ITSELF

1   The precedent for defining 'Japaneseness' as *Wa-*, as distinct from something else, was historically set by Japan's relationship to China. The mode of *Kan-* (Chinese) versus *Wa-* was easily modified to *yō-* versus *wa-* in the nineteenth century.

2   Quite likely *kimono* is related to the ancient word *koromo* (gown) found in the *Nihonshōki* and other early Japanese texts. It would also have been understood as a gloss for the general term *yosoi* (clothing) throughout the ages. Nevertheless, 'kimono' did not become a standard term until the Meiji era.

3   The *senryū* quoted just above is a humorous, often scatalogical one-phrase verse form. This one comes from a selection of early Meiji senryū published by authors using jokey pennames.

4   Endō, *Fukushoku kindaishi*, 65–88.

5   *Shimbun zasshi* (News magazine), 1872, quoted in *Kindai Nihon fuku-sōshi* (hereafter abbreviated *KNF*), 22.

6   Fukuzawa, *Seiyō i shoku jū*. For a complete translation, see Meech-Pekarik, *World of the Meiji Print*, 65–71.

7   *Nichiyō shimbun* (Everyday news), December 1867, quoted in *KNF*, 45.

8   *Meiji no omoide miyazome banashi* (Talk of remembrances of the Meiji capital), quoted in *KNF*, 22.

9   *Nichiyō shimbun*, January 1872, "Yōfuku no oshaku" (The Geisha in a dress), quoted in *KNF*, 155.

10   Ishii, *Meiji jibutsu kigen*, 688.

11   *Haguro* began as a purely cosmetic fashion practiced by male and female courtiers in the Heian period. It later became part of the puberty rite for girls and eventually denoted married status for women. Men, especially samurai, blackened their teeth up through the Ashikaga period, but by the sixteenth century, except for the powerless and obsolete imperial courtiers, they had ceased the practice.

12   Wool first appeared as an exotic import from the West as early as the fifteenth century for the exclusive use of high-level samurai and the shogun. In the 1850s, just before the Meiji restoration, lightweight and expensive wool mousseline (*muslin de laine*, muslin) in purple, lavender, and various pinks was used in little girls' kimono and in women's obi and haori coats. By the 1860s, Japan was flooded with cheap import cotton, which all but wiped out the native cottage industry in that fabric, and with wools—rasha, serge, flannel, camlet (Japanese *goro*, a wool-silk blend), and muslins. The heavier wools were made into a new breed of overcoat: *tombi* and *nijūmawashi* for men, the Azuma coat for women. These types of outerwear were not old forms recreated in sheep's clothing but original yōfuku-inspired additions to the wafuku wardrobe.

13   Kondō, *Yosoi no onnagokoro*, 141. Iwakura Sakurako was the daughter of Saigō Tsugumichi, brother of Saigō Takamori and a minister in Itō Hirobumi's first cabinet, which explains his daughter's presence at the Rokumeikan.

14   Empress Haruko, "Opinion on Western Clothing," reproduced in *KNF*, 159–60.

15   *Yūbin hōchi shimbun* (Post information news), April 13, 1887, reproduced in *KNF*, 161.

16   *Yomiuri shimbun*, 1888, quoted in *KNF*, 182.

17 Inouye, *Home Life in Tokyo*, 83.

18 *Fūzoku gahō* (Customs pictorial), 1890, quoted in *KNF*, 165.

19 *Jogaku sekai* (Coed world), July 1906, quoted in *KNF*, 250.

20 *Fujin gahō* (Women's pictorial), January 1925, quoted in *KNF*, 248.

21 Hasegawa, *Zuihitsu kimono*, 36–38.

22 Woven silks (*kinu orimono*) were everyday clothing, as opposed to the dyed silks (*somemono*) of ceremonial wear. These categories are not those of the textile historian but rather the way kimono are thought of socially. The variety of such weaves and textures was great, and each indicated a particular level of formality. The names defy translation: *ito-ori kinu, tsumugi, futo-ori,* and *omeshi* were by nature informal; *habutae, chirimen, sha-aya,* and *rinzu* could go either way depending on their quality and how they were decorated.

23 The *hakki* was a late Tokugawa simplified version of the uchikake worn by noble ladies. The main difference was in the sleeve: a formal uchikake had a wide unsewn sleeve (*hirosode*), whereas the hakki had a sleeve sewn in the form of a kimono (*tamotosode*).

24 *Osaka mainichi shimbun* (Osaka daily news), January 28, 1908, quoted in *KNF*, 248–50. There is a faint sense of disbelief in this piece, perhaps because it appears in an Osaka newspaper. The rivalry of the two cities is venerable, and the image of Tokyo society women probably confirmed all the worst suspicions of the more conservative Osakans.

25 *Fujin sekai* (Women's world), March 1914, quoted in *KNF*, 353.

FOUR   WOMEN WHO CROSS THEIR LEGS

1 Hibino, *LE KIMONO* (Kyoto), Spring 1985, 4–5.

2 Advertising copy for Keimeisyoji Kimono Company in *Utsukushii kimono* (Beautiful kimono), Autumn 1987, 60. Such sentiments are quite typical of the language used to sell the image of kimono.

3 Philosophically, the cults are known as the Way of Tea, or

the Way of Flowers, drawing on the spiritual meaning of the Japanese words 'way' or 'path,' which stand for the path to enlightenment. Does one wear kimono on this path? The rhetoric of its official proponents would almost make you think so.

4 Aoki Hideo cites an incident that occurred on March 15, 1928, in which a young woman Communist party member was arrested during a demonstration. When police discovered she was wearing drawers, they reviled her as a disgrace to her sex. *Shitagi no rekishi*, 102.

5 The same argument for wearing panties was made after the tragic 1932 fire at the Shirokiya Department Store in which fourteen women lost their lives—because they were too modest to jump to safety nets in their koshimaki and kimono.

6 The *Seikatsu kaizen dōmei* (League for the Betterment of Life) was a coalition of several groups, each with its own ax to grind. Among them were the *Fujin yōfuku dōmei* (Women's Western Clothing League) and the *Fukusō Kairyōkai* (Clothing Reform Association). These groups promoted the wearing of Western-style wedding dresses in place of kimono in the name of economy and published pamphlets teaching women how to sew simple skirts and blouses using the material of old kimono.

7 *Tōkyō Asahi shimbun*, April 10, 1880, quoted in *KNF*, 443.

8 The same thing happened to geisha in the mid- to late 1920s. Where once they had been the women in the vanguard of fad and fashion, faced with the competition of modern dance hall girls, waitresses, and Western-style entertainers they retreated to a conservative mode. Geisha chose to preserve elements of their traditional style as recognizable geisha rather than to evolve into something else. See Dalby, *Geisha*.

9 See Havens, *Valley of Darkness*, especially 15–24, on the spiritual mobilization efforts in 1939.

10 Urban residents were allowed 100 points a year for new clothing purchases. The khaki 'civilian uniform' for men cost 32 points, shirts were 12 points, underwear 4, and socks 1. One overcoat would take fully half a person's allotment of points. Havens, *Valley of Darkness*, 119–20.

11   There are several historical prededents in Japan for the patchwork technique, especially following wars. The *migawari kosode* of the Muromachi period was a kimono with the body of the garment in one pattern, the sleeves in an entirely different one—because they were taken from another garment. And the *dangawari* style seen on Noh robes involves whole sections in different fabric. Each of these modes became fashionable as a dramatic compositions in its own right, but it is likely that they originated in the necessity of coming to terms with fabric shortages.

12   Murakami, *Agura o kaku musumetachi*, 174.

13   Tanaka, *Shin josei no yōsō*, in Murakami, *Agura o kaku musumetachi*.

14   *Utsukushii kimono* (Beautiful kimono), Autumn 1987. The sums here are converted at a rate of $1.00 = ¥133.3. Subsequent drops in the dollar's value have made the kimono look even more expensive than the figures given in the text.

15   The history of repressive clothing for women is recounted in many places. In particular, see Bell, *On Human Finery*.

16   This style of obi is called *chūya* (noon-night), because it was always black satin on one side, a color on the other. I suspect that this style may have originated among geisha (who influenced so many kimono fashions) because, upon rising around noon, they could well have worn such a thing until they changed into elaborate brocades for their evening's work of entertaining. I have never read anything that suggests this origin, but the designs on many of these old chūya obis are often quite chic — just the sort of thing one readily imagines a geisha wearing.

17   For a revealing discussion of how the Nihonjin-ron is illustrated through the medium of language per se, see Miller, *Japan's Modern Myth*.

18   *Umeboshi to Nihon-tō* was a bestseller when it appeared in 1975. Higuchi's discourse upon native clothing appears in the sixth volume, *Yosoi to Nihonjin* (Clothing and the Japanese), of a twelve-volume work on the history of the Japanese.

19   Yamanaka, *Book of Kimono*, 72–87.

1   Segawa, *Kimono*, 1–3.

2   Segawa, *Kimono*, 89.

3   This basic upper-body garment was called by a great variety of terms in different local dialects. I call it a 'kimono-shaped robe' to distinguish it from the modern use of the term kimono.

4   Yanagita Kunio was particularly interested in the *tenugui*. He saw it as an example of how a simple item—an unsewn length of cotton cloth—was used in village life for practical and æsthetic purposes. A tenugui is a hand towel, a curtain, a handkerchief, and a scarf. The regional variations in its manner of tying on the head are legion, and expressive of the variety of folk traditions that Yanagita was so anxious to preserve. See his article "Tenugui enkaku."

5   Segawa, *Kimono*, 204 *ff.*

6   *Jika tabi*, 'field sneakers,' continue to be worn by laborers today. They are one of a small number of hybrid items of dress that combine a traditional concept with a new mode of production. Other examples include the *haramaki* (belly-wrapper), a tubular sweater worn over waist and hips by stevedores, petty mafiosi, and other lowbrow macho types; and modern variations on baby carriers that strap infants or young children to the mother's back in the traditional way, but with plastic buckles and stiffened headrests instead of old-style cloth carriers.

7   Yanagi, *The Unknown Craftsman*.

8   The Japanese title of Tanizaki Jun'ichirō's novel (translated by Edward Seidensticker as *Some Prefer Nettles*), is *Tade kuu mushi* (There are insects who will even eat the indigo plant). Such an insect would have odd tastes indeed.

9   Fukui, *Momen kuden*, 110.

10   Fukui, *Momen kuden*, 140–41.

1   It will be apparent to those familiar with the program of structuralism that I am using the tools of semiotic analysis to probe the kimono system. Yet what I examine differs in an important way from the work of pioneers of the application of structuralist terms to nonlinguistic areas of culture — Claude Lévi-Strauss on myth, for example, or Roland Barthes on French fashion. Most semiological analyses claim to reveal an underlying determinative structure of phenomena that is deeper than, and for the most part inaccessible to, native understanding. In the case of the kimono system, I believe the structuring principles lie relatively close to the surface. On reflection, any Japanese who regularly wears kimono can recognize these principles, at least partially.

2   Since about the 1920s, wearing black for mourning has become standard in Japan. Previously it was the custom in western Japan for a 'bride' (that is, a son's wife in the case of patrilocal residence) to wear white at her mother-in-law's funeral. Again, white signified a change to a new status.

3   The terms *orimono* and *somemono* in reference to clothing types have a specialized meaning that is slightly different from their use as descriptions of textiles. Of course, all textiles are 'woven things,' but orimono in reference to a level of formality means ikat, stripe, or an otherwise loom-designed fabric.

4   Ishikawa, "Iro muji."

5   *Fukuro* means 'pocket,' but it refers here to the fact that this kind of obi is made of two pieces of material. The two sides are now usually sewn together, but they were originally created by a style of weaving (*fukuro ori*) front and back sides that left the middle open, like a pocket.

6   The modern Nagoya obi is not to be confused with early Edo period narrow cords also named Nagoya obi. The written characters are different.

7   Because they are so widely used, the distinction between the two sorts of Nagoya obi is fairly well known. The so-called *fukuro Nagoya obi* (also called an 'eight-inch [*hassun*] Nagoya') is less formal than the nine-inch (*kyōsun*) Nagoya. In addition to being slightly narrower, eight-inchers are sewn without an interface, and doubled back on the tail part. The

more formal nine-incher is wider, has an interface sewn in, and is doubled back on itself at the tail all the way to where the torso-wrapping section begins.

8   Japanese *ochitsuita, hinkaku no takai, yuttari to shita, jōhin na.*

9   In the modern version of this custom, a bride usually performs the ceremony in an elaborately embroidered uchikake over a white furisode. She then immediately changes to a colorful furisode and may at the end change to Western clothes for her honeymoon. The bridal black crested adult formal kimono may be absent from the ceremony, but is usually part of the trousseau. Another popular variation is marrying in a Western-style wedding gown and then changing to furisode.

10   Western-style school uniforms follow the same pattern of the traditional *koromogae.* On the first of June, white summer uniforms come out, and on the first of October, the dark blue or black ones are retrieved from the cleaners.

THE CULTURED NATURE OF HEIAN COLORS

SEVEN

1   Morris, trans., *The Pillow Book of Sei Shōnagon,* 198. Morris uses 'yellow-green' as a gloss for *moegi* (sprout-green).

2   Bowring, *Murasaki Shikibu,* 37.

3   The Omi Lady was a long lost daughter of Genji's friend Tō no Chūjō, fathered during his youth. She is described as pretty but voluble and lacking any sense of subtlety.

4   From the *Masasuke shōzokushō.* I have used a modern transcription of a section of Masasuke's text found in Maeda, *Iro.*

5   Morris, trans., *Pillow Book of Sei Shōnagon,* 252.

6   From the *Masasuke shōzokushō,* a section entitled "Nyōbo no kuruma no kinu o idasu koto" (The displaying of a lady's robes in her carriage), transcribed in Maeda, *Iro.*

7   Morris, *The World of the Shining Prince,* 81.

8   Morris, trans., *The Pillow Book of Sei Shōnagon,* 185.

9   According to the *Goshō nikki*, "The practice of wearing elegant colors dyed in combinations named after and resembling flowering trees and plants, is called *kasane no irome*. It began in the reign of Emperor Tentoku [A.D. 957], although there are antecedents from the Engi period [A.D. 901–922]" (see Yasudani, *Makura sōshi no fujin fukushoku*, 139–40).

10   Such named combinations were sometimes simply called woven colors (*ori-iro*). The restricted *futa-ai*, a lavender produced by a combination of blue and red in warp and weft, is an example of this type of combined color. It is not always possible to know precisely what a color name refers to in a particular instance. For example, the layered color *ume* (plum) was a color overlay in the combination of white layered over maroon, producing a third color, a muted pink. As a set color pair, 'plum' meant white plus pink. In the five-robe combination, *ume* meant colors of plum-pink, scarlet-pink, and maroon in a set order; and as a woven color, it meant material composed of maroon-dyed warp threads and a white-dyed weft.

11   In modern usage, *irome no kasane* means a set pair of colors designated as to top and bottom, or major and minor, called by a particular name and given a specific seasonal reference. The wild cherry (*kabazakura*) combination is maroon over red, a spring duo, and so forth. When executed in clothing, a robe itself is given the major color (*omote*) and its lining will be in the minor (*ura*) of the pair. The lining color shows slightly at the edges. This visible lower edge was not an element of the orchestration of colors in the *Tale of Genji*, although it was the fashion at the time Murasaki was writing (first decade of the eleventh century), and thereafter.

12   Each robe was cut successively smaller so that the layered effect would be a parfait of colors, visible at sleeve openings, hems, and the front overlap. In this usage, individual robes might have an *omote* (front, recto, the robe itself) and an *ura* (back, verso, the lining). Normally we see a set of five robes plus chemise in this type of color layering. If each robe is lined, the theoretical possibilities for different combinations are enormous. In fact, however, certain patterns emerge frequently, some colors are never used together, and the actual number of set pieces, though numerous, was nevertheless finite.

13 The only existing versions of the text are Muromachi-period copies. While there is no absolute proof that Masasuke wrote the *Nyōbō no shōzoku no iro* specifically for Tashi, or that the interlinear remarks in katakana script are hers, it is plausible enough for a convincing reconstruction.

14 Morris, trans., *The Pillow Book of Sei Shōnagon*, 60.

15 *Hitoe* in its general sense means any unlined gown. I use 'chemise' to refer to the undermost one.

16 Research has shown that natural languages throughout history and all over the world all develop a very similar and limited set of basic color terms. These terms also show a regular sequence of development cross-culturally. The earliest color distinctions are always black and white, followed by red. The next stage will see the addition of green and yellow, followed by blue and brown, in that order. Finally the terms for purple, gray, pink, and orange develop. See Berlin and Kay, *Basic Color Terms*.

17 A deep gray called *nibi-iro* was prescribed as official mourning after the death of an emperor, while a somewhat lighter, blued gray *ao-nibi* was appropriate for the death of an empress, or for light mourning.

18 Brazell, trans., *Confessions of Lady Nijō* (Towazugatari), 193–94.

19 Backus, *The Riverside Counselor's Stories*, 123.

20 *Genji monogatari* (The Tale of Genji), 22, "Tamakazura." Waley trans. 462–63, Seidensticker trans. 406–07. The colors of yamabuki go to Tamakatsura; plum-pink to his daughter the Akashi princess; purple to her mother the Akashi lady and the Lady of the Orange Blossoms; the willow colors to the Safflower lady, and plum-pinks and red violets to Murasaki. Utsusemi, the nun, received colors appropriate to her religious station, rather than the seasonably fashionable ones.

21 Maeda, *Nihon kodai no shikisai to some*, 228.

22 Ihara, "Koten no Iro," and Maeda, *Nihon kodai no shikisai to some*, both mention this example.

23 McCullough and McCullough, trans., *A Tale of Flowering Fortunes*, 2:650.

24 Maeda, *Nihon kodai no shikisai to some*, 235.

25 The first June kasane is Sweet flag iris: green, white, and pinks. Then

come two classics: Purple layers on white, and Scarlet-pink layers on white. Mandarin orange (yellow-white-green) and Dianthus (maroon-white) are next. The last, *kakitsubata*, is the only new one, although we recognize its name and colors as belonging to the iris family.

26   See Norma Field's discussion, in *The Splendor of Longing in the Tale of Genji*, of the various male heroes as they visually possess women forbidden to them by 'peeping.'

EIGHT   MORONOBU'S FASHION MAGAZINE

1   See Stern, *Ukiyoe Painting*, for biographical details and their sources on Moronobu's life.

2   A *hinagata-bon* is generally glossed as a 'kimono pattern-booklet,' because that is what most of the genre were used as. *Hina*, however, means baby chick, and by extension something small and precious. Just as the hina dolls of the peach blossom festival are small replicas of the personages of the imperial court, the hina booklets (*kata/-gata*, 'form'; *bon*, 'book') are small versions of actual objects—usually kimono.

3   The woodblock text is in the difficult 'grass writing' style, which a Japanese student of such texts transcribed into legible modern form for me. The translation is mine.

4   Color names had proliferated greatly by Genroku times. Some have the feel of modern color terms used in the language of clothing advertisement—the teals, cranberries, khakis, and forest greens of our mail-order catalogues.

5   The 'palace style' (*goshō-fū*) consisted of a relatively simply coiled middle section. It originated among high-born ladies of the imperial court and in the families of the military lords. By the late seventeenth century it had spread to townswomen of means who desired to appear genteel. See Minami, *Nihon no kamigata*, for reconstructions of historical hairstyles.

6   Women of the licensed quarters were the fashion leaders of their day. Although Katsuyama was a courtesan, the hairstyle named after her

creation had spread into general fashionable currency by the Genroku period (1688–1704). Such a hairstyle on a figure in a print therefore does not necessarily imply that the character is a courtesan, only that she is fashion-conscious.

7   See section on *kanoko* (158–59) in Kanezawa, *Edo fukushokushi*. On the subject of government regulation of dress, see Shively, "Sumptuary Regulation and Status in Early Tokugawa Japan."

8   Morris, trans., *The Life of an Amorous Woman*, 132.

GEISHA AND KIMONO

1   It is easy to tell pre-war kimono because of their red linings. Modern kimono are always lined in white or cream, occasionally tinted at at the edges only. Japanese now feel there is something strange about red linings and would not be caught dead in one. This is an enigma I have yet to get to the bottom of. Yellow linings are also seen in old kimono. Both red and yellow were considered powerful prophylactics against evil influences, so it made sense for people (especially more vulnerable ones such as women and children) to line their clothing in these protective colors. I suspect the current dislike of red linings goes beyond fashion and has something to do with the strong superstitious quality of the color red.

2   Professionals are 'black' (*kurōto*) and amateurs, presumably undyed by experience, 'white' (*shirōto*).

3   By comparison, a Shimbashi geisha's monthly wages averaged about 360 yen at the time. Either she would have gone into debt to finance her taste, or more likely, she would have enlisted the financial support of a patron. See Endō Takeshi, "Geisha no fūzoku," *Fukushoku kindaishi*, 89 *ff*.

NOTES TO THE ILLUSTRATIONS

ONE	KIMONO THEME AND VARIATIONS

Facing 15   Woodblock print from the *Hyakunin jorō shina sadame* (Comparison of one hundred prostitutes) by Nishikawa Suke-nobu, 1750s. From the collection *Nihon fūzoku-zu e*, (Pictures of customs of the Japanese), hereafter abbreviated *NFZE*, 3:138.

TWO	THE NATURAL HISTORY OF KIMONO

Facing 29   Han dynasty funerary ceramic figure of a seated woman. Her robes and the style of wearing them are clearly kimono's ancestors. Private collection.

2.4   This pottery fragment was unearthed in 1983 in Nara Prefecture from the Tsuboi archæological mound. Dating from the mid-Yayoi period (third century A.D.), it depicts a figure wearing a belted poncho-style garment. Takeda Sachiko believes the figure to be male, arguing that it shows that the men's "unsewn width of cloth" mentioned by the Chinese compilers of the *Wa Chronicles* was a poncho. Curiously, she makes no note of the fantastic wing-like appendage sprouting from the figure's left shoulder. From Takeda, *Kodai kokka no keisei to ifukusei*, 124.

2.5   Inokuma Kaneshige reconstructs the poncho of proto-historic Japan according to the sketch in figure 2.6. He also interprets these famous figures from a bronze bell-plaque called a *dōtoku* as wearing ponchos with a seam up the front. From Inokuma, *Kodai no fukushoku*, 22.

2.6   Inokuma argues plausibly that a single width of cloth as produced on a backstrap loom would not have been wide enough to cut a hole for the head. From Inokuma, *Kodai no fukushoku*, 22.

2.7 Female haniwa pottery figure from Gumma Prefecture, male figure from Saitama Prefecture, dating from the sixth or seventh centuries. Line drawings from Inokuma, *Kodai no fukushoku*, 71.

2.8 Haniwa facial adornment representing red colored designs. From Sansom, *Japan: A Short Cultural History*, 5.

2.9 The rendition of this character in the 'small seal' style is clearly derived from the shape of the garment it describes. Picture of the Han-style upper body garment from the *Sancai tuhui* (Illustrations of the three realms), a 106-volume Ming dynasty encyclopedia showing various people, customs, places, and things from the three 'realms' of heaven, earth, and mankind.

2.10 The drawing of the female courtier is a modern sketch of Asuka period courtly attire from Izutsu, *Nihon josei fukushokushi*, 24. The male is sketched from an embroidered figure from the famous *tenjukoku* embroidered banner fragment dating from the early seventh century, now in the Chuguji temple in Nara Prefecture.

2.11 The Chinese lady is reproduced from a photograph of a Dunhuang cave mural in western China. The Japanese lady, who wears the same Tang aristocratic style, is from an incised design on an ivory flute kept in the Japanese imperial storehouse called the Shōsoin.

2.12 Author's drawing of an agekubi robe, based on a garment preserved in the Shōsoin. Kimonoid robe based on a *yi* robe illustrated in the *Sancai tuhui*.

2.13 The high ceremonial style called *mianfu* worn by the emperor during the Tang period in China has a kimono-style cross-over front. The picture to the right is from the famous portrait of Shōtoku Taishi that appears on the Japanese 10,000 yen note.

2.14 Photograph of Emperor Akihito on the occasion of his accession ceremony.

2.15 The man in this drawing wears a round-necked *uenoginu*, while the woman is in layers of kimonoform *uchigi*.

2.16 Sketch of Heian dress from Izutsu, *Nihon josei fukushokushi*, 52.

2.17 Sketch of Heian dress from Izutsu, *Nihon josei fukushokushi*, 44.

2.19 Two court ladies in white kosode and red hakama as depicted in a Muromachi period scroll known as *Oeyama emaki*.

2.20, 2.21 Woodblock prints from *Hyakunin jorō shina sadame* by Nishikawa Sukenobu, 1750s. From *NFZE*, 3:138, 28.

2.22 Woodblock print of serving girl by Hishikawa Moronobu, *Nihon hyakunin bijin* (One hundred beauties of Japan), c. 1695. From *NFZE*, 1:7.

2.23 Woodcut of mid-Edo period kosode from *Tōsei fūzoku tsū* (The modern connoisseur of customs), from Kanezawa, *Edo fukushokushi*, 81.

2.24 Woodblock print of reclining woman by Hishikawa Moronobu, c. 1686. From *NFZE*, 2:142.

2.25 Kosode design from Moronobu's pattern book, *Kosode no sugatami* (The kosode full-length mirror), late seventeenth century.

2.26 The lefthand figures are from Nishikawa Sukenobu, *Hyakunin jorō shina sadame* (Comparison of one hundred prostitutes), 1750s. From *NFZE*, 3:137. In addition to demonstrating the early Edo sleeve shape, these figures show the free variation allowed in obi styles during this era. From *NFZE*, 3:137. The middle figure is also by Sukenobu, from the *Ehon Asakayama* (Picture book of Asaka mountain). From *NFZE*, 3:168. The lady holding an umbrella is from Santō Kyōden's *Shiki kōka* (Passing through the seasons), 1798. From *NFZE*, 11:155.

2.27 Flamboyant character drawn by Hishikawa Moronobu, c. 1686. From *NFZE*, 2:59.

2.28 The fishmonger is another of Santō Kyōden's marvelously busy figures who populate the series of diptychs called *Shiki kōka* (Passing through the seasons), 1798. From *NFZE*, 11:148.

2.29 The seated matron with a simple obi tied in front is by Ishikawa Toyonobu from his series *Ehon Edo murasaki* (Picture book of Edo purple), 1766. From *NFZE*, 9:57. The soignée lady above her with the fashionably wide front-tied obi is by Suzuki Harunobu, from the *Yoshiwara bijin awase* (Comparison of beauties from the Yoshiwara pleasure-quarters), 1772. From *NFZE*, 8:12. The standing woman on the facing page is from Sukenobu's earlier *Hyakunin jōro shina sadame* (Comparison of one hundred prostitutes), 1750s. From *NFZE*, 3:90.

2.30 Illustrations of various ways of tying the obi in the early Edo period from Kanezawa, *Edo fukushokushi*, 106–7.

2.31 *Shigoki obi* style of hitching up a trailing gown, by Nishikawa Sukenobu, *Ehon Asakayama*, 1750s. From *NFZE*, 3:131.

2.32 The upper lefthand figures in summer dress are from a seaside scene by Torii Kiyonaga, 1810. From *NFZE*, 9:183. The early Edo figures below are by Hishikawa Moronobu, 1686. From *NFZE*, 2:137.

2.33 An apprentice courtesan as depicted by Kitagawa Utamaro in the *Ehon Edo suzume* (Picture book of Edo sparrows), 1807. From *NFZE*, 12:162.

2.34 Two-piece *kamishimo* sketch from Kanezawa, *Edo fukushokushi*, 81. Samurai wearing the outfit from Santō Kyōden, *Shiki kōka*, 1798. From *NFZE*, 11:179.

2.35 Figure from a Hokusai sketch, c. 1817. The long-necked lady is also by Hokusai. Private collection.

2.36 A parade of characters drawn from Santō Kyōden, *Shiki kōka*. From *NFZE*, 11:145–87.

THE KIMONO DISCOVERS ITSELF   THREE

Facing 71   A typical Meiji couple. Frontispiece from Fujisawa, ed., *Meiji fūzokushi*.

3.1 Figures from woodcut entitled "The Reappearance of Mizuno Kōtaro," c. 1860. From Endō and Ishiyama, *Zūsetsu Nihon yōsō hyakunenshi*, 48.

3.2 The doll-faced teenaged empress wears layers of wide-sleeved robes over trousers in the updated royal version of Heian dress. She holds a wide fan with multicolored silk tassels, which was the standard period-piece accoutrement for this outfit. Photograph by Uchida Kuichi, 1872.

3.3 Portrait of the twenty-seven-year-old Emperor Meiji.

3.4 Fukuzawa's woodblock printed guide was written primarily for the low-ranking samurai like himself who were keen to educate themselves in the nuances of Western customs. They saw this as their opportunity to rise in the political and social world of the changing order.

3.5   Woodcuts from Inouye, *Home Life in Tokyo*, 143, 146.

3.6   A figure from a group of eclectically dressed individuals in a woodcut entitled *Tenka no jūrai* (Comings and goings under heaven), 1874. From Shimizu, *Meiji mangakan*, 74.

3.7   Woodcut from an illustrated *dodoitsu* songbook, 1871. From Fujisawa, ed., *Meiji fūzokushi*, 759.

3.9   The upper figure appeared in the magazine *Miyako no hana* (Flowers of the capital) in 1899, described as follows: "The now fashion for men is a neckwinder the size of a *furoshiki* (carrying cloth)." The lower figure is from a woodblock called "Famous Places in Tokyo—the Ginza," 1881.

3.10   Women's square white neckwinders from *Miyako no hana*, 1899.

3.11   Shimizu, *Meiji mangakan*, 98.

3.13   This young lady, a student from the Hongo ward, is one of the 'representative types from the wards of Tokyo' (*Tokyo-ku mindai hyōsha*), in the magazine *Kokkeikai* (Funny world), October 1908.

3.14   Ishii, *Meiji jibutsu kigen*, 681.

3.15   Hairstyles from Inouye, *Home Life in Tokyo*, 109 *ff*.

3.17   From Ishii, *Meiji jibutsu kigen*, 680.

3.18   The quarreling creatures are found in Ishii, *Meiji jibutsu kigen*, 678. This theme of a contest between things of East and West provided a rich source of pictorial humor during Meiji. Often figures composed of cultural artifacts perched as heads on human bodies personify the conflicts: shoe-heads battle *geta*-heads, a kerosene lamp bashes an oil lamp, a photograph beats up a woodblock print, a riksha bests a palanquin, and a bale of Chinese rice is shown overpowering one of homegrown rice. In each case the Western item is clothed in yōfuku, the native item in kimono. See also figure 3.42.

3.19   From Inouye, *Home Life in Tokyo*, 132.

3.20   This cartoon sketch by Frenchman Georges Bigot is typical of his Daumierlike way of poking fun at the establishment. His series *Toba-e*

('Toba pictures,' recalling a famous twelfth-century set of ink scrolls depicting birds and animals cavorting as humans) is merciless in observing the earnest but clumsy efforts of the Japanese to create a facade of Westernization. Many illustrations from the *Toba-e* series appear in Shimizu, *Meiji mangakan*.

3.21   *Toba-e* sketch from Shimizu, *Meiji mangakan*, 143.

3.22   The figures on the right are from a scene in the waiting room of a train station in a woodblock by Hiroshige IV, 1873 (private collection). The statesman on the left is a figure from a woodblock print entitled *Kaika konomu danshi* (Men who favor the enlightenment), by Mizuno Toshikata. From Ishii, *Meiji jibutsu kigen*, 52.

3.23   Inouye, *Home Life in Tokyo*, 196.

3.24   Shimizu, *Meiji mangakan*, 163.

3.27   Another representative type from the Tokyo wards—a *kaisha-in* from Kyōbashi. From *Kokkeikai*, October 1908. See also figure 3.13.

3.29   *Kindai Nihon fukusōshi*, 218–19.

3.30   Inouye, *Home Life in Tokyo*, 105.

3.31   Various obi styles from Inouye, *Home Life in Tokyo*, 98 *ff.*

3.32   Author's collection.

3.33   "The botany professor," from *Kokkei shimbun* (Humorous news), October 20, 1908.

3.34   Shimizu, *Meiji mangakan*, 158.

3.35   From *Kindai Nihon fukusōshi*, 183 *ff.*

3.36   Author's collection.

3.37   From *Kindai Nihon fukusōshi*, 16 *ff.*

3.38   From *Kindai Nihon fukusōshi*, 230.

3.39   From *Kindai Nihon fukusōshi*, 157.

3.40   From Inouye, *Home Life in Tokyo*, 103.

3.41   From *Kindai Nihon fukusōshi*, 157.

3.42   From Ishii, *Meiji jibutsu kigen*, 756.

3.44 Edo period lady from Santō Kyōden, *Shiki kōka* (Passing through the seasons), 1798. From *NFZE*, 11:158. Photograph of Meiji girl from author's collection.

3.45 The figure on the right is labeled "a young lady from a good family in Azabu"; on the left is "a lady in western style in Akasaka." From Fujisawa, ed., *Meiji fūzokushi*, 448–49.

3.46 Fashion silhouettes from *Kindai Nihon fukusōshi*, 144.

FOUR   WOMEN WHO CROSS THEIR LEGS

Facing 123   Sketch from *Vogue*, January 1931.

4.1 Advertisement from the fashion quarterly *Utsukushii kimono* (Beautiful kimono), Summer 1981, 187. The models are called *kagayaku musume-tachi*, 'sparkling girls.'

4.2 *Utsukushii kimono*, Autumn 1987, 203.

4.3 Diagrams from *Kimono Salon*, Winter 1982, 164.

4.4 Meiji schoolgirls, sketched by Kajida Hanko, from Endō and Ishiyama, *Zusetsu Nihon yōsō hyakunenshi*, 78.

4.5 The characteristic line of the Taishō kimono was *munedaka na kitsuke*, 'wrapping the obi high on the chest,' which gave a girlish, even coltish, effect because it made the wearer's legs appear longer. Sketch from *Fujin gahō* (Women's pictorial), June 1925.

4.6 From *Fujin sekai* (Women's world), April 1926.

4.7 Two illustrations from *Fujokai* (Women's world), April 1926: *above*, an advertisement for the Miyako-brand *koshimaki* ('hip wrap,' a sort of half-slip); *below*, an advertisement for woolen underwear for women and children, "to keep out the cold."

4.8, 4.10 Underwear to achieve the Taishō line. Advertisement from *Fujokai*, May 1925.

4.9 Summer dress from *Shufu no tomo* (Housewife's companion), June 1925.

4.11 Fashion sketch from *Vogue*, July 1920.

4.12, 4.13 From Endō and Ishiyama, *Zusetsu Nihon yōsō hyakunenshi*, 161.

4.14 From Endō and Ishiyama, *Zusetsu Nihon yōsō hyakunenshi*, 101.

4.15 Advertisement from *Utsukushii kimono*, Autumn 1987, 130.

4.17 Figure from a woodblock print by Nishikawa Sukenobu, c. 1750. From *NFZE*, 1:33.

Endpiece Woman tying an obi by Watanabe Yohei, 1911. From Ishii, *Meiji mangakan*, 186.

THE OTHER KIMONO   FIVE

5.1, 5.2, 5.3, 5.4 From Hayashi, *Japanese Women's Folk Costume*, 18, 26, 31, 62.

5.6 From Inouye, *Home Life in Tokyo*, 47.

5.7 The top left figures are from a woodblock by Nishikawa Sukenobu, c. 1750. From *NFZE*, 3:48. The farmwoman is from Hayashi, *Japanese Women's Folk Costume*, 14.

5.8 Photograph by Linda Butler. Courtesy Linda Butler.

5.12 The houseboy is from Inouye, *Home Life in Tokyo*, 61. The nursing mother is a woodcut by Katsukawa Shunshō, 1792. From *NFZE*, 11:126.

5.13 From *Kindai Nihon fukusōshi*, 82.

5.14 Hayashi, *Japanese Women's Folk Costume*, 42.

THE STRUCTURE OF KIMONO   SIX

6.3 From Inouye, *Home Life in Tokyo*, 120.

6.10, 6.11 Advertisement in *Utsukushii kimono*, Autumn 1987, 88, 279.

6.13 From *Utsukushii kimono*, Summer 1981, 227.

6.20 From *Kimono Bon Chic*, December 1988, 38.

6.21 From *Kimono Salon*, Fall/Winter 1982, 39.

6.22 From *Reisō no shikitari jiten*, 31.

6.24 From Kōbayashi, *Kimono kyōhon*, 146.

BIBLIOGRAPHY

Anawalt, Patricia. *Indian Clothing before Cortes.* Norman: University of Oklahoma Press, 1961.

Aoki Hideo. *Shitagi no rekishi* (The history of underwear). Tokyo: Yūsankaku, 1963.

Asukai Masamichi, ed. *Meiji.* Volume 11 of *Zusetsu Nihon bunka no rekishi* (Pictorial history of Japanese culture). Tokyo: Shōgakkan, 1981.

Barthes, Roland. "The Structural Activity." In *Critical Essays,* trans. Richard Howard. Evanston: Northwestern University Press, 1972

Backus, Robert. *The Riverside Counselor's Stories.* Stanford: Stanford University Press, 1985.

———. *L'Empire des signes.* Geneva: Ed. d'Art Albert Skira, 1970.

———. *Système de la mode.* Paris: Ed. du Seuil, 1967.

———. *Elements of Semiology.* Trans. Annette Lavers and Colin Smith. New York: Hill and Wang, 1967.

Bell, Quentin. *On Human Finery.* New York: Schocken Books, 1967.

Berlin, Brent, and Paul Kay. *Basic Color Terms.* Berkeley: University of California Press, 1969.

Bird, Isabella. *Unbeaten Tracks in Japan.* New York: G.P. Putnam, 1880.

Bock, Felicia. *Engishiki: Procedures of the Engi Era.* Tokyo: Sophia University Press, 1970.

Bolitho, Harold. *Meiji Japan.* Cambridge: Cambridge University Press, 1977.

Bowring, Richard. *Murasaki Shikibu: Her Diary and Poetic Memoirs.* Princeton: Princeton University Press, 1982.

Braisted, William, trans. *Meiroku Zasshi: Journal of the Japanese Enlightenment.* Cambridge: Harvard University Press, 1976.

Brazell, Karen, trans. *The Confessions of Lady Nijō.* Stanford: Stanford University Press, 1973.

Brewster, Jennifer, trans. *The Emperor Horikawa Diary* (Sanuki no Suke Nikki by Fujiwara no Nagako). Honolulu: University of Hawaii Press, 1977.

Dalby, Liza. *Geisha.* Berkeley: University of California Press, 1983.

Descamps, Marc-Alain. *Psychosociologie de la mode.* Paris: Presses Universitaires de France, 1979.

Dower, John. *The Elements of Japanese Design.* Tokyo: Weatherhill, 1971.

Ellwood, Robert S. *The Feast of Kingship: Accession Ceremonies in Ancient Japan.* Tokyo: Sophia University, Monumenta Nipponica, 1973.

Ema Tsutomu. *Kimono: One Hundred Masterpieces of Japanese Costume.* Kyoto: Kōrinsha, 1950.

——. *Nihon yuigami zenshū* (Collection of Japanese hairstyles). Tokyo: Sōgensha, 1965.

Endō Takeshi. *Fukushoku kindaishi* (History of clothing and ornament in the modern era). Tokyo: Yūsankaku, 1970.

Endō Takeshi and Ishiyama Akira. *Zusetsu Nihon yōsō hyakunenshi* (Illustrated history of a century of Japanese dress). Tokyo: Bunka-fukusō Gakuin Shuppan, 1956.

Field, Norma. *The Splendor of Longing in the Tale of Genji.* Princeton: Princeton University Press, 1987.

Fujisawa Morihiko, ed. *Meiji fūzokushi* (A history of Meiji customs). Tokyo: Shunyōdo, 1929.

Fukui Sadako. *Momen kuden* (The cotton tradition). Tokyo: Hosei Daigaku, 1984.

Fukuzawa Yukichi. *Seiyō i shoku jū* (Western clothing, food, and dwellings), 3 vols. Tokyo: Keio University Library, 1867.

Gluck, Carol. *Japan's Modern Myths: Ideology in the Late Meiji Period.* Princeton: Princeton University Press, 1985.

Greimas, A. J. *Semiotique et sciences sociales.* Paris: Ed. du Seuil, 1976.

Hama Tokijirō. *Nihon no kamigata* (Japanese hairstyles). Tokyo: Josei Mōdo-sha, 1965.

Harada Yoshito, ed. *Tōdai no fukushoku* (Chinese dress and personal ornaments during the Tang dynasty). Tokyo: Tōyō Bunko, 1970.

Hasegawa Akihisa. *Fukushoku no rekishi* (History of clothing and ornament). Tokyo: Saera Shobō, 1961.

Hasegawa Shigure. *Zuihitsu kimono* (Essays on kimono). Tokyo: Jitsugyō no Nihonsha, 1939.

Hasegawa Shigure and Sugimoto Sonoko, eds. *Kindai bijinden* (Chronicle of modern beauties). Tokyo: Iwanami Shoten, 1985.

Hayashi Tadashi. *Japanese Women's Folk Costumes.* Tokyo: Ie no Hikari Association, 1960.

Higuchi Kiyoyuki. *Umeboshi to Nihon-tō* (Pickled plums and Japanese swords). Tokyo: Non Book, 1974.

——. *Yosoi to Nihonjin* (Clothing and the Japanese). Tokyo: Kodansha, 1980. Volume 6 of *Nihonjin no rekishi* (History of the Japanese people).

Hishikawa Moronobu. *Kosode no sugatami* (The kosode full-length mirror). Tokyo: Mitsui Bunko, 1929. [Xylograph of late seventeenth-century original.]

Hollander, Anne. *Seeing Through Clothes.* New York: Viking, 1975.

Holtom, D. C. *The Japanese Enthronement Ceremonies.* Tokyo: Sophia University, Monumenta Nipponica, 1972.

Horn, Marilyn. *The Second Skin: An Interdisciplinary Study of Clothing.* Boston: Houghton Mifflin, 1968.

Ienaga Saburō. *Nihonjin no yōfuku no hensen* (Changes in Western clothing worn by the Japanese). Tokyo: Domesu Shuppan, 1976.

Ihara Aki. "Koten no iro" (Colors in ancient days). In Ooka Makoto, ed., *Nihon no iro* (Colors of Japan). Tokyo: Kodansha, 1980.

Inokuma Kaneshige. *Kodai no fukushoku* (Clothing and ornament during ancient times). Tokyo: Shibundō, 1962.

Inouye Jūkichi. *Home Life in Tokyo.* Tokyo: Tokyo Printing, 1910.

Irokawa Daikichi. *The Culture of the Meiji Period.* Trans. and ed. Marius Jansen. Princeton: Princeton University Press, 1985.

Ishii Tamiji. *Meiji jibutsu kigen* (Origins of things of the Meiji period). Tokyo: Shunyōdo, 1926.

Ishikawa Aki. "Iro muji." *Utsukushii kimono* (Beautiful kimono) (Tokyo), special edition no. 3, *Reisō no shikitari jiten* (Dictionary of the rules of formal dress), 1979.

Izutsu Miyakaze. *Nihon josei fukushokushi* (History of the clothing and ornaments worn by Japanese women). Kyoto: Kōrinsha, 1983.

Jameson, Fredric. *The Prison-House of Language.* Princeton: Princeton University Press, 1972.

Jouon des Longrais, Frédéric. *Tashi: le roman de celle qui épousa deux empereurs (Nidai no Kisaki) (1140–1202).* Paris: Institut de recherches d'histoire étranger; Tokyo: Maison Franco-Japonais, 1965.

Kanezawa Yasutaka. *Edo fukushokushi* (History of clothing and ornament during the Edo period). Tokyo: Seiabō, 1962.

Kawakatsu Ken'ichi. *Kimono* (Japanese Dress). Tokyo: JTB Tourist Library no. 3, 1936.

Kimono Bon Chic. Tokyo: Nippon Seihan International. December 1988.

Kimono Salon. Tokyo: Sekai Bunkasha. Fall/Winter 1982.

Kimura Kō. *Kimono no shiki* (Seasons of kimono). Tokyo: Migasa Shobo, 1970.

Kindai Nihon fukusōshi (History of costume in modern Japan). Tokyo: Showa Joshi Daigaku, Hifukugaku Kenkyushitsu, 1971.

Kōbayashi Toyoko. *Kimono kyōhon* (Kimono textbook). Nagoya: Kōbayashi Toyoko Kimono Gakkuen Shuppan, 1975.

Kondō Tomie. *Fukusō kara mita Genji monogatari* (Looking at the Tale of Genji through clothing). Tokyo: Bunka Shuppankyoku, 1982.

——. *Rokumeikan kifujinkō* (Story of the noble ladies of the Rokumeikan era). Tokyo: Kodansha, 1980.

——. *Taishō no kimono* (Kimono of the Taishō era). Tokyo: Minzoku Isshō Bunka Kyōkai, 1980.

———. *Yosoi no onnagokoro* (The feminine heart of dressing). Tokyo: Kodansha, 1985.

Koren, Leonard. *New Fashion Japan*. Tokyo: Kodansha, 1984.

Kuge Tsukasa. *Keshō* (Cosmetics). Volume 4 of *Mono to ningen no bunkashi* (Cultural history of people and things). Tokyo: Hōsei Daigaku Shuppansha, 1970.

Lévi-Strauss, Claude. *Structural Anthropology*. Trans. Claire Jacobson and Brooke Grundfest Schoepf, New York: Basic Books, 1963.

Levy, Ian Hideo, trans. *The Ten Thousand Leaves: A Translation of The Manyōshu, Japan's Premier Anthology of Classical Poetry*, volume 1. Princeton: Princeton University Press, 1981.

Liddell, Jill. *The Story of the Kimono*. New York: E.P. Dutton, 1989.

Lurie, Alison. *The Language of Clothes*. New York: Random House, 1981.

McCullough, Helen Craig. *Okagami—The Great Mirror: Fujiwara Michinaga and His Times*. Princeton: Princeton University Press, 1980.

McCullough, William H. and Helen Craig, trans. *A Tale of flowering Fortunes: Annals of Japanese Aristocratic Life in the Heian Period*. Stanford: Stanford University Press, 1980.

Maeda Ujo. *Iro* (Color). Volume 38 of *Mono to ningen no bunkashi* (Cultural history of people and things). Tokyo: Hosei Daigaku, 1980.

———. *Nihon kodai no shikisai to some* (Ancient Japanese colors and dyeing). Tokyo: Kawade Shobo Shinsha, 1975.

Meech-Pekarik, Julia. *The World of the Meiji Print*. Tokyo and New York: Weatherhill, 1986.

Minami Chie. *Nihon no kamigata* (Hairstyles of Japan). Tokyo: Shikō-sha, 1981.

Miner, Earl, Hiroko Odagiri, and Robert E. Morrell eds. *The Princeton Companion to Classical Japanese Literature*. Princeton: Princeton University Press, 1985.

Minnich, Helen Benton. *Japanese Costume and the Makers of Its Elegant Tradition*. Tokyo: Chas. E. Tuttle, 1963.

Miyamoto Keitarō. *Kaburimono kimono hakimono* (Hats, clothes, shoes). Tokyo: Iwasaki Bijutsusha, 1968.

Morris, Ivan. *The World of the Shining Prince.* Oxford: Oxford University Press, 1964.

Morris, Ivan, trans. *The Life of an Amorous Woman* (Koshoku ichidai onna), by Ihara Saikaku. New York: New Directions, 1969.

———. *The Pillow Book of Sei Shōnagon.* London: Oxford University Press 1967.

Motoi Chikara. *Nihon hifuku bunkashi* (Cultural history of Japanese costume). Tokyo: Yūsankaku, 1969.

Motoyama Keisen. *Fukushoku minzoku gasetsu* (Illustrated folk clothing and ornament). Tokyo: Shubundo, 1937.

Murakami Nobuhiko. *Agura o kaku musumetachi* (Girls who cross their legs). Tokyo: Chuo Kōron, 1963.

Murasaki Shikibu. *The Tale of Genji.* Trans. Edward A. Seidensticker, 2 volumes. New York: Alfred A. Knopf, 1976.

Nagashima Nobuko. *Nihon ifukushi* (History of Japanese clothing). Kyoto: Shunyōdo, 1933.

Nakagawa Ki'ichiro and Henry Rosofsky. "The Case of the Dying Kimono: The Influence of Changing Fashions on the Development of the Japanese Woolen Industry." *Business History Review* 37 (1963).

Nakamura Shin'ichirō. *Iro konomi no kōzō* (Analysis of color and eroticism). Tokyo: Iwanami Shōten, 1985.

Nakano Hisao et al. *Taishō no Nihonjin* (Japanese of the Taishō era). Tokyo: Perikansha, 1981.

Nihon Fūzoku-zu e (Pictures of customs of the Japanese). Twelve-volume series of monochrome woodblock prints by various artists from the seventeenth through nineteenth centuries.

Noma Seiroku. *Japanese Costume and Textile Arts.* Tokyo: Weatherhill, 1974.

Nukada Iwao. *Tsutsumi no bunka* (Culture of wrapping). Tokyo: Tōyō Keizai Shinpōsha, 1985.

Ooka Makoto et al. *Nihon no iro* (Colors of Japan). Tokyo: Kodansha, 1980.

Oshima Tatsuhiko et al., eds. *Nihon o shiru jiten* (Dictionary of Japanese lore). Tokyo: Shakai Shisōsha, 1979.

Pollack, David. *The Fracture of Meaning: Japan's Synthesis of China from the Eighth through the Eighteenth Centuries.* Princeton: Princeton University Press, 1986.

Rosencranz, Mary Lou. *Clothing Concepts.* New York: Macmillan, 1972.

Rudofsky, Bernard. *Are Clothes Modern?* Chicago: Theobald, 1947.

——. *The Kimono Mind.* New York: Doubleday, 1965.

Ryan, Mary Shaw. *Clothing: A Study in Human Behavior.* New York: Holt Rinehart, 1966.

Sahlins, Marshall. *Culture and Practical Reason.* Chicago: University of Chicago Press, 1976.

——. "Colors and Cultures." *Semiotica* 16: 1 (1976), 1–22.

Sakaguchi Shigeki. *Nihon no rihatsu fūzoku* (Customs of hairdressing in Japan). Nihon Fuzokushi Gakkai Henshū, no. 6. Tokyo: Yūsan-kaku, 1972.

Sansom, George. *Japan: A Short Cultural History.* London: Cresset Press, 1931.

Sargent, G.W., trans. *The Japanese Family Storehouse,* by Ihara Saikaku. Cambridge: Cambridge University Press, 1969.

deSaussure, Ferdinand. *Course in General Linguistics* (1915). Trans. Wade Baskin. New York: McGraw Hill, 1966.

Segawa Kiyoko. *Kimono.* Tokyo: Rokuninsha, 1948.

——. *Nihonjin no ishokujū* (Clothing, food, and dwellings of the Japanese). Tokyo: Kawade Shōbō, 1964.

——. *Shikitari no naka no onna* (Women within the rules). Tokyo: Sansaisha, 1961.

Seidensticker, Edward A. *Low City, High City.* New York: Random House, 1983.

Seki Tamejiro et al., eds. *Rekishi fukusō garoku* (Illustrated chronicle of historical costume). Kyoto: Rekishi Fukusō Garoku Hankosha, 1933.

Sekine Shinryū. *Narachō fukushoku no kenkyū* (Clothing and ornament in the Nara capital). Tokyo: Furukawa Bunko, 1974.

Shibusawa Keizō, ed., and Charles S. Terry, trans. *Japanese Life and Culture in the Meiji Era.* Volume 5. Tokyo: Obunsha, 1958.

Shimizu Isao. *Meiji mangakan* (Exhibition of Meiji cartoons). Tokyo: Kodansha, 1979.

Shively, Donald. "The Japanization of the Middle Meiji." In *Tradition and Modernization in Japanese Culture*, ed. Donald Shively, 77–119. Princeton: Princeton University Press, 1971.

——. "Sumptuary Regulation and Status in Early Tokugawa Japan." *Harvard Journal of Asiatic Studies* 25 (1965): 123–65.

Stern, Harold P. *Ukiyoe Painting: Selected Problems*, volume 1. Ph.D. dissertation, University of Michigan, 1960. Ann Arbor: UMI, 1977.

Stinchecum, Amanda M. *Kosode: Sixteenth–Nineteenth Century Textiles from the Nomura Collection*. Tokyo and New York: Japan Society and Kodansha, 1984.

Suzuki Aofusa, ed. *Nihon fūzoku gataisei: Meiji jidai* (Pictorial overview of the costumes of Japan: the Meiji era). Tokyo: Chuo Bijutsusha, 1929.

Suzuki Tsutomu, ed. *Nihonjin no hyakkunen yori: Bakumatsu Meiji no gunshō* (One hundred years of the Japanese people: the military history of the mid- through late nineteenth century). Volume 3 of *Bunmei kaika no jidai* (The age of civilization and enlightenment). Tokyo: Sekai Bunkasha, 1977.

Takeda Sachiko. *Kodai kokka no keisei to ifukusei* (Clothing regulations and the formation of the ancient state). Tokyo: Furukawa Bunko, 1984.

Tanaka Chiyo. *Shin josei no yōsō* (Western attire for the new woman). Privately published, 1935.

Tatsumura Ken. *Nihon no kimono* (The Japanese kimono). Tokyo: Chūo Koron, 1966.

Taylor, Lou. *Mourning Dress: A Costume and Social History*. London: George Allen & Unwin, 1983.

Toby, Ronald. *State and Diplomacy in Early Modern Japan*. Princeton: Princeton University Press, 1984.

Tsunoda Ryūsaku and L.C. Goodrich. *Japan in the Chinese Dynastic Histories*. New York: Perkins Asiatic Monographs no. 2, 1951.

Tsurumi Kazuko, ed. *Yanagita Kunio shū* (Collected works of Yanagita Kunio). Tokyo: Chikuma Shōbō, 1975.

Uemura Rokurō and Yamazaki Katsuhiro. *Nihon shikimei taikan* (Encyclopedia of Japanese color terms). Tokyo: Kocho Shōrin, 1943.

Urano Riichi. *Nihon no kimono* (The Japanese kimono). Tokyo: Bunkafukusō Gakuin Shuppan, 1965.

Utsukushii kimono (Beautiful kimono). Tokyo: Fujingahōsha, 1979. Various issues: *Kimono no shikitari to kikonashi* (The rules of kimono and how to wear it), 1979; special edition no. 3, *Reisō no shikitari jiten* (Dictionary of the rules of formal dress), 1979; Summer 1981; Autumn 1987.

Williamson, Samuel, and Herman Cummins. *Light and Color in Nature and Art.* New York: John Wiley, 1983.

Yamanaka Norio. *The Book of Kimono.* Tokyo: Kodansha. 1982.

Yanagita, Kunio. "Bunka seisaku to iu koto" (On cultural policy) (1941). In *Teihon Yanagita Kunio shū* (Authorized edition of the collected works of Yanagita Kunio), volume 24. Tokyo: Chikuma Shobō, 1967.

——. *Kokushi to minzokugaku* (National history and ethnology). Tokyo: Rokuninsha, 1948.

——. *Kyōdō seikatsu no kenkyū* (Research on communal life). Tokyo: Chikuma Shōbō, 1967.

——. *Meiji Taishō shi* (History of the Meiji and Taishō eras). Tokyo: Heibonsha, 1967.

——. *Momen izen no koto* (Before cotton). Tokyo: Sogensha, 1952.

——. "Tenugui enkaku" (Development of the tenugui cloth). In *Teihon Yanagita Kunio shū* (Authorized edition of the collected works of Yanagita Kunio), volume 14. Tokyo: Chikuma Shōbō, 1943.

Yanagita Kunio, ed. *Japanese Manners and Customs in the Meiji Era.* Trans. and adapted by Charles Terry. Tokyo: Toyo Bunko, 1969.

Yasudani Fujie. *Makura Sōshi no fujin fukushoku* (Women's costume and ornament in [Sei Shōnagon's] *Pillow Book*). Tokyo: Shibankaku, 1974.

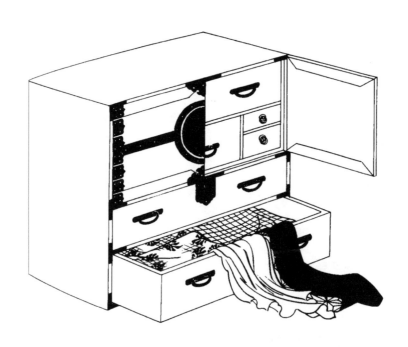

INDEX AND GLOSSARY